# SECRETS TO EFFECTIVE AUTHOR MARKETING

*It's More Than "Buy My Book"*

## MAGGIE LYNCH

# CONTENTS

| | |
|---|---|
| 1. The Truth About Marketing | 1 |
| 2. Marketing for the Shy Author | 27 |
| 3. Defining Your Audience | 44 |

Your Communication Plan — 61

| | |
|---|---|
| 4. Your Brand | 63 |
| 5. Your Website | 72 |
| 6. Your Media Packet / Press Kit | 99 |
| 7. Your Blog | 108 |
| 8. Book Groups and Clubs | 136 |

Engaging With Readers Beyond Basic Communication — 151

| | |
|---|---|
| 9. Social Media Overview | 153 |
| 10. Facebook | 174 |
| 11. Facebook Messenger and Chat Bots | 194 |
| 12. Twitter | 207 |
| 13. Instagram | 216 |
| 14. Pinterest | 228 |
| 15. YouTube | 236 |

Build A Mailing List of True Fans — 251

| | |
|---|---|
| 16. Purpose and Importance of Mailing Lists | 253 |
| 17. Selecting a Mailing List Provider | 260 |
| 18. Setup and Qualify Names | 273 |
| 19. Drip Campaigns | 281 |
| 20. Drive Traffic to Your List | 308 |
| 21. Beyond Onboarding: Broadcast Emails, Launch Emails and Other Sequences | 317 |
| 22. Building and Managing Your Street Team | 325 |

Your Marketing Plan — 337

| | |
|---|---|
| 23. Calendaring PR and Marketing All Year | 339 |
| 24. Launch Checklist | 346 |
| 25. Backlist Rejuvenation | 354 |

| | |
|---|---:|
| Afterword | 361 |
| About the Author | 365 |

Copyright © 2017 by Maggie McVay Lynch

All rights reserved. No part of this publication may be reproduced, distributed or transmitted in any form or by any means, without prior written permission.

Windtree Press

Hillsboro, Oregon

http://windtreepress.com

Cover Design by Christy Keerins

https://coveredbyclkeerins.com/

Secrets To Effective Author Marketing: It's More Than "Buy My Book" / Maggie McVay Lynch. -- 1st ed.

eBook ISBN 978-19449738-3-4

Print ISBN 978-19449738-2-7

United States of America

❦ Created with Vellum

*To all those authors who have mentored me over the past decade through workshops, emails, blogs Facebook postings, face-to-face discussions over lunches or coffee, and even harried self-doubting phone calls.*

*A special shout out to the following authors who have been willing to continuously engage and share their knowledge, not only with me but with thousands of other authors around the world. These authors believe in giving back to the greater community of writers through books, workshops, and often free advice in blogs, short videos, and conference presentations.*

*Dean Wesley Smith*
*Kristine Kathryn Rusch*
*Joanna Penn*
*Mark Dawson*
*M. L. Buchman*
*Kristin Painter*
*April Aasheim*
*Jessa Slade*
*Dianna Love*
*Mary Buckham*
*Roxanne St. Claire*
*Paty Jager*

## Chapter One
# THE TRUTH ABOUT MARKETING

I don't know about you, but it seems that I am constantly in search of the ONE big marketing secret that will make a sudden difference in my fortunes. I am convinced that there is a secret cabal of successful authors who have found "the magic" button to push that makes them millionaires. They are keeping the location of that button secret, and only divulge it to a select few.

Does this sound like you? Always looking for the ONE thing that will work. Unfortunately, with 20 books under my belt—five traditional and the rest indie—and more than a decade of self-publishing and marketing, I know there is no one secret. There is no easy way to just do a few things and be certain that it will catapult you to success. Anyone who tells you differently is lying!

In fact, when you get a bunch of successful authors in one room (I define this as those making over 100K per year), they will share some secrets and other authors in the room will say: "That never worked for me. Or that doesn't work anymore. What works is…" It is darn frustrating!

The truth is that it is a combination of techniques that need to be applied consistently, and that need to be changed based on the changing publishing landscape. For example, what worked in 2011 does not necessarily work today. Even what worked last year in 2016 may not work today. There are a few things, like having a sizable and active mailing list of true fans, that stand the test of time. But everything else? Sadly, not so much.

Even worse, some techniques that work for one genre (e.g., romance) may not work at all for another genre (e.g., science fiction). And what works for fiction has little relationship to what works for nonfiction. When many authors realize these facts, they tend to either throw up their hands and say: "I guess I should never count on making money at writing, then." What follows that statement is the mindset that writing will be their hobby, and soon after they simply stop writing.

For those writers who don't give up, they tend to begrudgingly try to learn what types of marketing will work for them. However, they quickly realize the learning curve is significant and it takes a lot of time. Then they are faced with the dilemma of writing versus marketing, versus paying someone to do all or some of the marketing. That was me in 2011—the begrudging writer who didn't want to spend the time and energy learning this "marketing stuff."

Before you give up on this book, let me say that it IS doable, but it doesn't happen overnight. Also, marketing works best when there is a backlist of books to help spread the costs and assure a better return on investment (ROI) of your time and money. So, if you are just getting out your first or second book, you will want to throttle back on your marketing efforts and concentrate on getting more books out first. Not that you should do no marketing, but don't go all out and spend thousands of dollars on your first book launch (or your second) and lots of time engaging your readers to the point you are not writing the next book.

Of course, if you are independently wealthy and willing to spend money without much return on your investment, then definitely go for it. Experiment. See what works for you and what doesn't.

Money does afford you a quicker start up. However, it does not make up for a lousy book over the long term. You may see a quick return, but once people start reading the book and don't find it interesting or entertaining or helpful (depending on the genre), bad word of mouth will kill any additional success on that book and on others that may follow it.

I will share a lot of ideas on marketing and what has worked for me in this book. I will tell you why it works or doesn't work as best as I can. However, just like that group of very successful authors in one room, not everything that works for me will work for you. Marketing is hard work. It takes testing, analyzing, evaluating, and testing again. It takes a concerted effort to stay on top of what has change or may change in the future and then testing, analyzing, and evaluating to see if the new stuff works for you.

Sorry! No big EASY button to push.

But I will provide you a solid foundation in: the concepts, the technology: the why, how, and when things work; and the means to analyze whatever comes in the future. If you can get that down, you can move forward on your own without many problems.

## THE BIG OVERVIEW

Let's start with an overview of indie marketing—what works and what doesn't. This is the quick and dirty 14-15 pages to give you the scope of the book. Don't worry, I'll get into the details for those things that DO work. So buckle up.

Depending on your pre-conceived notions and what you've read before, you may be ready to fight me on some of these that don't work. Remember, the overriding secret to marketing is *anything* can work given enough effort, time, and money. What I'm sharing with you is what I've found works for me and most people I know. But you aren't me, so you will need to test and see if it works for you—what you might need to do is to tweak a process or an ad to make it work for your specific market.

When I write my books, I am an emotional person. I become best friends with my characters and I tell their stories. The wonderful thing about that approach is that I tend to write emotional books. The awful thing about that approach is that, when it comes to marketing, I don't want to let those characters down by not getting their story out there to thousands of readers. When I finish a book, I truly believe that every person who enjoys the genre I write in *needs* to read this book. Not because all those buyers will make me lots of money (not that I turn down sales), but because I learned something in the process. With every book I learn something about myself, about communication in life, about making tough choices. That makes me believe that a reader might find something beyond a good story that speaks to their life too.

The problem is that marketing cannot be an emotional journey for the author. To be good at marketing, you have to be analytical. You have to be the person who can look at your book and honestly decide if your baby is ugly. If it is ugly—defined as not an easy sell because it doesn't meet the genre criteria—then you have to convince the world that your baby has a special value they can't live without.

Far too many authors think that book marketing is about selling your book. It's not. In fact, the more you try to sell your book, the more you turn off potential readers. Book marketing is about convincing your potential readers of the VALUE of your book. That value is not the story, not the price, not the genre. That value is the EXPERIENCE of reading your book. You need to understand what experience your readers want to have and capitalize on that.

For example, romance readers expect a focus on the romantic relationship. Whether sexy or sweet, whether contemporary or paranormal, the reader wants the EXPERIENCE of falling in love, overcoming obstacles together, and true love winning in the end. To market a romance you need to sell the falling-in-love experience.

In a science fiction novel readers want to EXPERIENCE something new, something that causes them to think of the world in a different way, and if there are some cool gadgets that make sense based on an extrapolation of today's science all the better. Whether social SF or space opera, a part of what you are selling is that sense-of-wonder experience or the learning-something-cool experience.

Every fiction genre has an experience attached to it. This experience is more than the genre tropes. It is a need to feel something: love, fear, hate, admiration, misery, rage, lust, surprise, terror, zeal and many others. If you can make a list of the experiences (emotions) your reader feels when reading your book(s) then you are most of the way to understanding what VALUE you have to sell.

Even nonfiction delivers an experience. Yes, nonfiction tends to be written to teach the reader something. However, great nonfiction also delivers an emotional journey as well. For example, the history of WWII has been written about in hundreds of books. The ones that provide an experience, are the ones that bring the war to the level of its impact on individual lives. When talking about the blitz in Britain one can provide a lot of facts: how many bombs were dropped, how many people died, the years of the war, the politics. But what readers remember are the true examples of a single person or family experience. Sharing the true account of someone who was in a home during the bombing—the sounds, the smells, the fear, the grief—makes the war real and memorable. Or the account of a family who chose to send their children from the city to live with strangers in the country, not knowing how they would fare or if they would see each other again.

If you can sell the *value* of your book as an *experience* then you have set a good foundation for marketing. Once you have that value identified, you need to make sure that, when your readers try your book, that they do get the experience you promised. And the only way to know that is to engage with them. To have your readers tell you what they experienced and if it met their expectations.

## PRIMARY WAYS TO ENGAGE READERS

I could tell you about all the usual stuff—get on as many social media platforms as possible, join book groups, blog a lot, ask questions of your readers, send them lots of FREE stuff. All these tactics are ways to engage with readers, but let's face it everyone is doing it. It's hard to stand out in the crowd. And the readers who engage with you on social media tend to already be your fans, friends, and family. So, the question is how do you get them there in the first place?

The trick is to approach your engagement from the perspective of the reluctant reader—like a teacher might try to engage a student who doesn't want to read. I like this approach because, as an author who will be new to a lot of people, I know those new readers are reluctant to try my books. Here are some interesting ways to take the techniques and use them in your social media and blogging life.

Help the reluctant reader realize that reading books can be a refreshing and rewarding alternative to TV, movies, shopping, or hanging out with friends. Have discussions about the differences between the book and the movie versions of a story. More than 70% of movies are adapted from books. It's a great way to get noticed to talk about a movie and then compare it to a book. Share how a recent shopping trip reminded you of a scene in a book. Connect incidents in real life with stories in your genre. It can be your book or someone else's book in these conversations. In fact, a little of both is good. Remember: You are not "selling." You are engaging. You are being the cool, well-informed reader who happens to also be an author.

Help the potential fan discover, or remember, the pleasures of reading. Talk about where you like to read, when you like to read, why you like to read. Share pictures of great reading nooks. Pinterest has lots of these kinds of pictures. Share your own special place where you read. Libraries have been running a campaign called READ where they have a picture of a celebrity reading a book. Find those and post them from time to time. Whenever you finish a book you've read, talk about it. What did you like? In other words, just be a READER and chat about the joys of reading.

Encourage reading beyond your own books. One of the things that makes potential fans run away from a new author is when the only books you talk about are your own. That is seen as sell, sell, sell. Steer your fans toward good books by other authors. Consider even doing some type of introduction with another author who writes books similar to yours.

One of the things I do with my Launch Team is celebrate their birthday by gifting them a book by their favorite author (and it can't be me). I'm not gifting them MY book, but someone else's book. If it is someone I know and also like, I share what I love about the author's book too. If it is someone I don't know, I ask what it is about that author's books that make them a "go to" author for that person. This not only let's them know it isn't all about me, but it also gives me information about who they are reading and why. I often learn about authors in my own genre who may have books similar to mine—similar themes, similar character traits. After all, I can't possibly know all the books and authors in my genre.

I like finding those new authors, because it opens up my network and often we will find opportunities to help each other in the future. Though I may not see the similarities between my books and a fan's favorite author, the fact my super fans are reading both my books and this other author's books means I should pay attention.

If you enjoy reading aloud, consider putting out videos or podcasts with you reading from your own books and other author's books you like. Always be sure to tag the other author so they know you are giving them free promo with your fans. It will help to build a good reputation for you being someone who is willing to share, not just out for yourself.

The key to engaging readers is to be involved in the same things they are involved in. To go where they go and enter discussions. For example, most bloggers talk as much about movies and TV shows today as they do about books. You need to do the same.

I know some of you may be saying: "I don't have time to read other authors or watch movies or even TV." I certainly feel that way myself. But I also know I need to make time. If I don't make time to read and share my love of reading, then readers won't feel that I have a good sense of what they like in a book. It is work, but it helps me to understand what is important and how I can deliver the experience they are looking for.

## MARKETING VERSUS PUBLIC RELATIONS

When looking at selling a product—a book—many authors get caught up in whether they should be looking at Public Relations (PR) or Marketing. When I started down the marketing path, I thought of PR as fluff, something I couldn't measure for ROI, and that it costs way too much money and takes too much time. Whereas, marketing is direct, measurable, and can get results. The reality is that you need both. AND you need to understand how they work together in order to take advantage of both of them.

My misunderstanding was that my knowledge of PR started and

stopped with newspaper articles, media kits, and pushing events. When, in fact, PR is how one sells an EXPERIENCE vs a product (your book). That experience is critical to sell first. Then the book (product) is marketed as proof that you can deliver that experience as promised.

In short, Public Relations (PR) is the larger picture—the brand as a whole and growing that brand, building a reputation and engagement with that brand. Marketing refers to a specific product within the brand or a set of products. To put this in the perspective of authors, PR is the author brand where as Marketing is about a specific book or series of books.

## PUBLIC RELATIONS

According to the Public Relations Society of America, PR is defined as "a strategic communication process that builds mutually beneficial relationships between organizations and their publics." When you think of a company like Apple, you get a certain feeling about the company. For example, I believe that Apple's brand is one of clean design, good user interfaces, and a nod to being on the leading edge of technology. That's PR. That's what the company has spent years trying to get people to think whenever they think of Apple. It does not refer to a specific product (e.g., the iPhone or the Mac computer or the Apple watch). Instead, it builds an expectation in the public for something good, worthwhile, well-designed, and hip.

As an author, YOU are your company, your brand. Even if you are traditionally published, you do NOT want your brand to be your publisher (e.g., Harper Collins or Penguin Random House) If you let your publisher build your brand and you leave, or they are no longer interested in your books, you have to start over. Much safer for the brand to revolve around YOU.

You want to build an expectation that when someone reads one of your books or comes to your blog or interacts with any content that you produce, that they will have a specific kind of experience. For example, if you think of Stephen King, you most likely think of horror. You most likely think of a particular kind of horror—one that is based on manipulating your mind to think one way so that you are surprised during the story. Stephen King has written more than 100 books. Not all of them are horror. However, I would guess that all of them do depend on manipulating your mind to think against the grain, whether fiction or non-fiction.

What kind of experience does your reader get when she encounters YOUR work? That experience is your brand. You need to communicate that brand all the time, in every piece of content you write, and in everything you do. If you are a single genre writer, and always plan to be, you can associate your brand with a genre. Romance writers tend to create a brand that is about finding love, hanging on to love, relationships, etc. They differentiate themselves by subgenres (contemporary, historical, suspense, paranormal, SF) and then even further by themes —dark or light, sexy or sweet, inspirational or rebel—and other aspects. Most genres have these type of breakdowns to help define your brand within a genre.

On the other hand, there are also a substantial number of authors who write in more than one genre, and also do both fiction and nonfiction. This is where my writing falls. It is more difficult to determine your author brand in that situation but you can still do it.

If you use different pseudonyms for each of your different genre books, some authors still choose to do a genre-based brand and they maintain a different brand for each name. I started off that way—three websites, three Facebook profiles, three Twitter profiles, etc. By about book eight I was pulling my hair out keeping track of all of that. I then combined all of those names and profiles into one website, one Twitter profile, one Facebook profile and looked for a brand that could speak to all those different sides of my writing life.

Most writers have core stories no matter what genre they write in. My core story is one of finding identity/purpose and then following it however difficult that may be. I'm also very interested in the concept of heroes—not the big Batman or Superman type hero, but the everyday hero. What actions/decisions do we make to become a hero and why is it so hard to make those decisions?

Whether I am writing a romance, a suspense novel, SF or Fantasy, all of my characters are engaged in these two things: finding purpose and becoming a hero. Even my nonfiction has those elements. The book you are reading now is designed to help you decide who you are as a writer and how you can make difficult decisions to be more successful.

## WHAT IS YOUR CORE STORY? WHAT IS YOUR BRAND?

Your brand or core story doesn't have to be serious or deeply philosophical. It just has to be true to you and your writing. It might be something as simple as "Love is the answer," or "Be careful where you step" or "Entertainment and Escape."

Once you know this, then it is up to you to capitalize on that through your website look and feel, your social media look and feel, and in all your content. This usually doesn't happen over night. I've been contemplating this question for the past five years as I've branched out to novels in different genres. My website has changed many times from being primarily product marketing toward branding. It is always a work in progress that becomes more defined as I write more books and use my brand to gain better recognition and more readers.

Your brand is a logo, it's a picture, it's content, it's media. It's every way that you communicate with the public at large.

It helps to have a nifty tag line. But don't fret if you can't come up with one right away. At least list what are the values of your brand and begin thinking about how to make sure that message is getting out there consistently.

- PR stimulates awareness of (and hopefully the demand for) your company—you as an author.
- PR strengthens your company's image and how it is perceived. Are you perceived as an inspirational person? A funny person? A serious person? A researcher? A great storyteller? A wallflower? A snarky person? An empathic person? None of these are bad images. The question is how does YOUR image reflect your brand and thus your products.

- PR can even increase search engine visibility and organic searches for your brand by consistently setting up expectations, perceptions, and experiences that deliver on your brand promise.

Despite these benefits, public relations is often not strong enough to stand alone; simply an accurate perception is not enough to measurably and notably increase your income. That is where a marketing strategy becomes your workhorse for income.

## MARKETING

The American Marketing Association (AMA) defines marketing as "the activity, set of institutions, and processes for creating, communicating, delivering and exchanging offerings that have value for customers, clients, partners, and society at large." Marketing is more focused on products and tends to be more measurable in terms of specific tactics that yield measurable results. Most people think of marketing as advertising. That is an important part of it, but certainly not all of it. I think of marketing as a way to provide your best friend with something they really want, even though they may not know it.

Have you ever tried to set someone up on a blind date? If so, you knew the two people as individuals and in that knowledge found a lot of commonalities—perhaps in what they like to do, life philosophy, maybe even fashion sense. That is what marketing does. It defines specific benefits for people who purchase products from your company—your books. It shows them how they will get value out of your books.

Like PR, Marketing wants to build a relationship, to foster it, to watch it grow and flourish. It is truly about adding value. PR says "I have a wonderful home for you to stay in. It matches your personality and the needs for basic comforts in a home." Marketing gets more specific and says: "My home has the most comfortable beds, and there is a swimming pool that looks out to the mountains, and the cook in the kitchen will prepare all the things you like to eat." In other words it defines the value.

PR says you are competent, trustworthy, and will deliver a specific kind of experience and relationship. Marketing specifies what that experience is and how it adds value to the consumer—your reader.

Below is a helpful summary list of five differences between marketing and PR.

1. **Focus**. Marketing focuses on delivering a valuable product, while public relations focuses on relationships with your customers.
2. **Function**. Effective marketing directly contributes to income in a measurable way. In other words, I can say a specific Facebook ad brought in 500 new readers for my mailing list or on another ad I sold 100 books. I can say this because I can track what happened on a per user basis. Public relations indirectly supports goals and objectives. Though valuable, it is very difficult to measure the impact of PR. You may be able to get a sense of PR effectiveness through surveys, but it is not possible (at least for me) to find a one-to-one correlation to sales. PR is your reputation as an author. Without consumers *believing* your book will be a quality experience in a professionally presented package, they won't try it because they don't want to waste their time and money.
3. **Target**. Marketing's target is the customer. Marketers strive to meet specific customer demands in order to move a product (your book) from producer to consumer. PR targets a range of public entities and goals that collectively support your objectives. Examples of these public entities include readers, the media, suppliers or contractors (e.g., your cover designer, your editor, your web designer, your distribution partners), the community, investors (like on Patreon or Kickstarter), reviewers and analysts.
4. **Carryover benefits**. PR contributes to your success by building and maintaining a positive social and business environment. If the public has a favorable perception of you

or your company separate from your products, it can lift your marketing and price promotion strategy.

For example, why can a bestselling author charge more for her books than you can? Because that author's reputation (PR) is that she will consistently deliver a great story that provides a satisfying experience. Only PR generates this feeling. PR is the difference between a reader buying an entire series—investment of both time and money—instead of one book.

Marketing does not create perception of a brand or company. It creates a suggestion of value for a product. Do people go on to purchase other books after finding one they like? Yes, but that is not something you can count on marketing to create. That is why you need both Marketing and PR working seamlessly together to create an environment where you sell consistently.

## PAID, EARNED, AND OWNED MEDIA

*Paid media* – This category is all about advertising, whether that's online, on the radio or television, or even through flyers or signboards at conferences. Paid media plays a major role in the marketer's campaign strategy and consumes the bulk of most marketing budgets. An extreme example is Super Bowl advertisements. According to Bleacher Report in February 2017, the cost of a Super Bowl ad was a record $5 million for a 30-second ad spot.

Marketing tends to cost money on a consistent basis. Though it is unlikely most authors would pay for a Superbowl ad, successful marketers DO consistently set aside a marketing budget that is being spent *every* month.

When I began marketing ten years ago, I was loathe to spend more than $20 in a month. I just didn't see the ROI. Part of that was because I didn't have a good backlist then. Also, part of it was that $20 isn't enough to make a big enough impact to be able to measure ROI. Sure, when I'm only selling 10 books a month and, after an ad, I sell 15 books the next month I might believe the ad worked. However, a difference of five books in such a small sample size is not really easy to correlate to that marketing effort—especially over 30 days. Far too many intervening variables come into play over a 30-day period.

On the other hand if I ran Facebook ads for an entire month and spend $150 ($5 per day), and my mailing list goes from where it has been for a year at 400 subscribers to 3,000 during that month, chances are I CAN make a direct correlation to my marketing. Both the mailing list size to start is a larger number and stable, and the percentage of change in a short period is extreme.

In 2016 I started using a good budget for marketing efforts. I learned two things. 1) Getting people on my mailing list increased sales of my backlist. 2) If I stopped my ads for a month or two it created a *very* noticeable decrease in sales. Paid advertising needs to be a consistent part of the career author's budget. The question is to make sure you are making more money (after deducting ad costs) than you were without advertising.

**Owned media** – Examples include websites, blogs, Facebook and Twitter profiles. Most authors think of these platforms as places for marketing instead of PR. I would suggest that social media should be 80% PR and 20% marketing. Social media's nature is to build relationships and interaction with readers (PR). Though there are selling opportunities on social media via ads and boosted posts (marketing), those should be targeted at bringing in *new* readers not selling to readers who already follow you and are more likely to buy. Those who already follow you are looking to engage. They have already drunk your author Kool-aid and they want to buy your products. If you use social media to primarily sell, then even your best fans will no longer pay any attention to you and they will stop engaging.

This doesn't mean you never tell them about a new release or encourage them to buy your book. You do that through email and one mention on your Facebook page (that you then boost for new reader engagement). Then you spend your marketing budget adding more people to your email list, moving them through the process to becoming superfans, and thus getting more consistent sales.

**Earned media** – Earned or "free" media is part of the PR professional's playbook. Earned media is published through third parties such as bloggers, journalists and other influencers. It also includes word-of-mouth recommendations via social media. Earned media is perceived as more credible than paid media because of third party-endorsements. How do you get earned media? In exactly the way it suggests. You EARN it. That means you have become an expert on something, or you have consistently delivered on your promised experience with your fans.

For example, I frequently do talks with author groups to share my knowledge of indie publishing. If they like my workshops, they share that information with other author groups. Over many years, I've built a reputation as a reliable/knowledgeable person on topics relating to technology and author businesses. When a newspaper or magazine needs an expert, they contact me for quotes. When an author organization or group needs an article or wants to do an interview, I accept. The fact they asked is an endorsement of my worth.

Not everyone wants to be an expert, or do workshops, or stand in front of people and talk about their experience and opinions. However, anyone can be an expert if they put their mind to it. If you write mystery fiction, you can become the go to person on recommending other mystery authors. Or you could become an expert on the variety of ways authors kill characters.

Do you have a day job that provides background for your books? You can become an expert on that. Do you do research for your books? If you write Historical Romance, perhaps your research provides you expertise on period dress, or Regency dancing, or specific politics and wars at the time of your book. Did you spend significant time looking into poisons and different ways to kill off a character? This is something interesting to share with other authors or a reader group. It is a way to be known for something other than trying to sell your book. The key is to offer it freely and become known as "the person who knows".

## WHAT EXACT TECHNIQUES WORK BEST FOR AUTHOR PR AND MARKETING?

The answer is "it all depends." I know that is frustrating to hear, but it is true. It depends on the experience you're promising your readers. What works for a humorous writer of contemporary dating romances is different than what works for a writer of dark, paranormal novels where it is never certain the hero will win the day. Everything from voice to graphics to emphasis on mood and themes depends on the experience you are promising the reader.

It also depends on YOU. What kind of personality do you have? How do you represent yourself in person and online? Are you serious? Funny? Shy? Outgoing? Do you like being the center of a party or a participant? Or are you the one—like me—who would prefer to find a nice little corner and spend the entire evening getting to know one or two people who have interesting things to say?

I ask these questions because every technique requires follow-though, and that follow-through requires a certain kind of personality. The way an introvert approaches a marketing plan is **very** different from the outgoing person who gets their energy by interacting with readers all the time. If you can't follow-through, then you might as well not do it at all.

No matter your personality you CAN build a marketing plan that works for you. The key is being true to yourself. Don't try to be the person you *think* you must be to market. If you aren't true to yourself, you will be miserable and you will give up on it or rarely engage.

## BRAND BUILDING EXAMPLE

I'll use myself as an example. Here is my tagline: "*Stories of making heroic choices one messy moment at a time.*" Probably just in reading that line you have already formed some opinions about my books, and maybe about me too. The question is: Do your perceptions of me match what I intended with that tag line? Here's what I intended it to say:

- I'm serious.
- I'm interested in every day heroes.
- My characters aren't going to have it easy. Those "messy moments" mean conflict and being unsure whether they will win the day.
- Every step of their journey will require them to make some hard decisions—heroic choices.
- The ending will be satisfying. Heroes always win in the end.

So, from the PR side here are some of the things I thought about for my branding.

- Quotes about overcoming hardship
- Links to articles about making the hard choices (top 5 things you can do to overcome ...)
- Adding a little humor now and then so people don't think I'm so serious that I'm boring.
- Sharing emotional things, inspirational content—things that make most people cry or go "Ahhhhh"—as well as practical things to get through the hard times. There are plenty of videos and memes out there to share on these topics. You don't have to make them all up yourself.

I do Facebook posts and Tweet all of the above regularly. It isn't hard to do this because it reflects ME. I'm not trying to be someone else. Why do I share pictures of my cats? Because they are heroic in their own right. They are rescues and were able to make it until they were found. One of them not only nursed her own four kittens but adopted an abandoned stray kitten and raised it as her own—a great metaphor for characters in my stories that show how we choose to make families. Cats show love and caring, and curiosity, and play in ways that I can't often capture in pictures of people.

Of course, all of my posts aren't about my cats, but the point is it is fine to use things from your personal life that reflect your brand. In fact, most readers LOVE learning about author's personal lives. Being an author is one of those mysteries to many people. How can someone spend so much time alone in her imagination and turn out book after book? What makes that kind of person tick?

My Pinterest page reflects my personal interests—living tiny, traveling to interesting places, all about my home state—Oregon, reading nooks and crannies, and lots of quotes that are uplifting. All of these things let readers know that I am human and have many of the same experiences they have. But it also still reflects my brand—*making heroic choices one messy moment a time.* Once readers believe I am a good person and I am reflected in my books, they will approach my books with the belief that my characters will seem true to life—that they can also share experiences with them. In other words, I am already creating the same EXPERIENCE with my posts that I deliver in my books. At least that is what I'm trying to do. Without ever saying: "buy my book," I am still driving readers to my products.

On the Marketing side—the analytical side—I need to define the VALUE of my books to deliver that experience. That value is executed, first, by writing a good story that delivers on my promise. No amount of marketing, PR, price discounting, or reviews will overcome a story that doesn't deliver. Always focus on writing and finishing a good story before putting any marketing effort into selling it.

Assuming the story is good and that it does in fact deliver the experience I'm promising, marketing becomes a discoverability engine. It provides a way to let people know the book exists and to trust it will deliver the experience I've promised.

You can write the most amazing book that delivers on the promise of your brand, and never sell past your immediate family and friends. It happens all the time to good writers. In a world where over one million new titles are being put up every year, it is significantly more difficult for someone to find you and your book. That is where marketing is critical. Unless you are a celebrity, or someone with a huge platform and thousands of followers, just putting up your book will not get you more than the barest trickle of sales. You must drive traffic to that product constantly.

What does my marketing entail? First, it is done through email and social media campaigns to my fans. These are not only BUY MY BOOK campaigns. Instead they are campaigns to explicitly proclaim the value of my book by talking about the characters, doing excerpts, providing social proof (reviews), and getting good word-of-mouth from books that preceded the new one.

Techniques for this vary, but the #1 way that works for me is engaging directly with my fans and then asking them to share what they like with all their friends; and finding ways to reward them for that sharing. For example, when someone joins my list, they enter into a sequence of emails they will receive over the next two to three months. The first two or three emails do not sell anything except me. I strive to show them I care about them (e.g., never spamming, how often I'll contact them, etc.) I share information about the book I gave away for free and what it means to me. I talk about my excitement in writing that book and what I learned in the process.

It isn't until at least a month, and sometimes more, has passed that I tell them about a product (next book in series or a boxed set) they might value because they liked the free book. No hard sell, just an expression of value.

It's not that I never talk about a book release, or never have a link to buy my book. I DO! When I do a launch for a new release, I do send out an email about it's availability and let them know they can now get this experience again. I also do a Facebook post and a Tweet and Instagram about the availability of that book. But I do NOT do that three times a day for several weeks. I do NOT obsess over the fact my selling numbers are down one day and increase the "buy my book" fever on the next day. I trust that my relationship with my fans will win out. I concentrate my direct marketing on potential new fans.

In reality, I am marketing all the time, but 90% of marketing is about proving the value of the book so that the reader will WANT TO buy it—will be dying to buy it when it releases. This marketing takes place over a long period of time. It does not take place the two weeks before and after release and then I move on. Also marketing is continuous. It is not something that only happens for a launch or a new release. If readers ONLY hear from you to exhort them to buy something, they will stop listening. Some will run to get off your email list and they will stop going to your social media sites.

The marketing begins three to six months BEFORE the book will be released. It starts with sharing my excitement about the writing. I focus on the experience I'm having during the writing. This experience has a corollary to the experience my readers will have when the book is available. I share excerpts along the way. I share my cover that is so perfect because it matches the theme, or character, or overall experience of the book. I am building the expectation that my readers will love the book as much as I do.

EVEN IF YOU HATE YOUR COVER BECAUSE YOUR PUBLISHER DIDN'T DO WHAT YOU WANT, you are still going to share it and explain how/why it does help to provide the experience the reader wants. If you complain to your readers about what is wrong with the cover or the story, or the characters not cooperating by making your writing easier, then your readers will approach the finished product with the expectation that it is not good because YOU are not happy with the way it turned out. That makes them reluctant consumers and unlikely to buy the book. Even if you offer it at a big discount or free, they may not download it OR they may download it but not read it. Who wants to read a book that even the author didn't enjoy writing or producing?

You can also give your fans opportunities to see related books as you are ramping up—perhaps share a famous author who writes in your genre and would have readers similar to yours. Give away that author's book in a contest. It shows your book can be positively associated with that popular author's book. Perhaps your character wears a certain kind of bracelet, or necklace, or shoes. Post pictures of it. Give something away related to that picture.

This doesn't mean you have to do giveaways every week leading up to a launch. This is just one technique. It does mean you need to build anticipation for an amazing experience. Think about your dream vacation. You finally get a chance to go, but it is three months away. What are you doing during that three months? Chances are you are looking at pictures of the destination, reading articles about what to do, asking people who have been there what they most loved about that location. It is the same way with building anticipation for a book.

The idea is that by the time that three to six month period is up, your readers should have been engaging with you, talking about the book, getting excited so that when you launch the reader feels she absolutely **must have** your book. There is never a question of you having to beg them to buy it. The only question is how quick can they click your link.

## BUT IT'S NOT SO SIMPLE!

I've tried to simplify the process. The theory IS simple. The execution is not. It's easy to be caught up in the PR and marketing—and obsess over whether it is working or not—and never write another book. That would be a mistake. You can also spend a lot of money and get nowhere, either because you only have one or two books or because you've chosen the wrong things to spend your time and money on. Or because you don't know who your readers are. Most books fit in a narrow band of readers. Even in the big genres like romance and mystery and thrillers, your book won't be a good fit for all of those readers. You need to find that group of readers who are most likely to love what YOU write—your voice, your themes, your way of crafting a story in a sub-genre, or your way of sharing the experience through a nonfiction book.

Most of the things I've mentioned above take time and energy over a long period of time. And then you start all over again. The more books you write, the more time you need to spend on PR and the more you need to be analyzing what is working for you. The fewer books you have available, the more time you need to spend on writing the next book and getting your backlist developed.

## QUICK SOCIAL MEDIA MANAGEMENT TRICK

Again, you have to know yourself. I know that I can't do Facebook and Twitter and Google+ and Pinterest and…and…and…every day. So I choose to use a piece of software, Buffer (buffer.com), that allows me to plan them all at once and post to any number of them at the same time. If I'm really on top of things, I can plan these posts out months in advance and schedule them. When I'm not on top of things, I try to set aside a couple hours each week to at least schedule my posts for that week.

In the process of fitting PR and Marketing into your writing life, you will learn some things about yourself and how to balance writing and marketing. Here are some truths I've found for myself:

1. **I must write every day before I look at email, before I look at how my books are doing, before I do posts anywhere.** If I don't do that, it is extremely easy for the day to slip by without me writing a single word on a new

book. Your schedule may be different. It may be that your best writing time is after dinner when everyone in the family is off doing their own thing (TV, listening to music, even sleeping). Find a time and consistently write during that time.

2. **Spending money or a lot of time on marketing before I had three books in my inventory was throwing money into a dark hole without return.** Spending time writing the next book, with the occasional branding and sharing of the process, is much more successful.

3. **Building a mailing list is the easiest and most consistent marketing effort I can directly correlate to sales.** 30-35% of my true fans on my mailing list WILL buy my book on release. Another 10-20% will buy it within the first couple of months. No other marketing I've done is as easy as sending my release out to my list.

4. **Approximately, 10% of those who download a free book will actually read it.** But once they are on my list, approximately 30% will engage and buy my next release. This really makes a substantial income difference when your mailing list is in the thousands. Thirty percent of 500 people on your list is only 150 books. Thirty percent of my current list of 12,000 is 3,600 books. That can make a significant income difference, a ranking difference, a number of reviews difference. Work on building a good mailing list.

5. **The more popular I become, the more marketing works for me.** I used to look at bestselling authors and think: "Geesh, that person doesn't need to market, she's going to get thousands of fans buying her book anyway." But I now know she's there because she survived those lean years. To stay at that bestselling level she needs to keep doing what has worked. She still needs to keep investing in marketing, spending money on ads, keeping engaged with readers, delivering on the promise of her brand.

Here are things that might be fun but have NOT sold very many books for me:

- **Book Signings.** I average 7-15 book sales no matter the venue or the number of people who attend. I give up anywhere from 3 hours to an entire day—after adding in driving time, set up and take down—to attend and participate in one of these book signings. That is an entire day I am not writing. Not worth it to me for marketing or PR. I do still do them once or twice a year. But I do them not for sales. I do them as a way to support a bookseller who I love, one that supports local authors and/or indie authors. But I never do it hoping to make sales in the hundreds of books.
- **Facebook Parties.** The most I've ever sold from an FB party was 20 books in 2014, and that was an anomaly. It's never happened again. Most FB parties consist of the author, along with other authors, giving away books with the hope the readers will fall in love with the story and buy more down the line. It's nearly impossible to know if they buy unless they come to my direct sales site. For the most part, giving away a free book does nothing for me unless I get them on my mailing list.
- **Blog tours.** In 2011-2013, a good blog tour for a new release used to bring me 40-50 book sales. Not any more. I stopped doing them in 2014 when I could not attribute more than two or three book sales to blog tours. Blog tours are great for book bloggers who get affiliate money from people clicking to look at the book. It no longer gets me anything and, because they are static Q&A or just a cover and blurb, they also don't get me good engagement with readers. Even on the big tours where the potential for 30K or more impressions is there, I find that those who are engaging are the same 5-15 people at every stop with only a couple unique to that stop.
- **Ads in book-specific venues.** I've put ads on sites that a

get million hits and in magazines that have 100,000+ readers. I've spent $10 for a month of ads and $300 for a ¼ page placement in a national magazine. No matter the venue, the average number sold because of an ad in those venues averages 10 books. Not worth the money for me.

**NOTE:** *This does NOT include Facebook Ads, Bookbub Ads, or AMS Ads. Those ads exist in an entirely different eco system that is advanced, costly, and is a book in itself. Those Ads DO consistently work for me. However, you need a minimum of three books in series to make them work best, and a budget of at least $150-$300 per month. THIS book is focusing on marketing that most any other can accomplish for under $100.*

- **Blog interviews.** I have never seen a single sale from any blog interview or article I've contributed to as a guest blogger. That's not to say I should never do it. But it is not a marketing technique that provides measurable return on my investment of time. The reason I continue to do guest blogs is because it builds my brand. I see it as PR and I actually enjoy writing the posts.

All of the things above that don't work for me, in terms of marketing, can work as PR. If you are counting them as PR, then don't approach them with a specific product to sell. Instead approach them with the idea of engagement and of getting your brand known to new people. Over years of doing this consistently, it does add to the discoverability quotient and your branding efforts.

The question you need to ask yourself is if it is worth your time and effort at this point in your career. If you are giving up writing the next book because you've scheduled 12 blog interviews, 4 Facebook parties, and three in-person signing events, then you are giving up on the most important part of moving your career forward—having more books to sell.

**Bottomline:** The #1 technique to enhance sales is to build your mailing list. The #2 technique is to consistently engage with your readers in whatever platform they favor. The #3 technique is to understand Ad creation and execution in specific reader markets.

All PR requires time and energy (and can cost money). Marketing requires time and money. On the PR side, do only those things you enjoy doing and save your time and energy for writing. On the marketing side, do only those things were you can measure ROI. If it doesn't work for you, don't do them.

## HOW TO APPROACH THIS BOOK

The remaining major sections of this book will expand on each of the techniques that work. Specifically, on the PR side I will talk more in depth about building a brand and developing a consistent communication plan. This includes your website, blog, social media, and other things you do to engage with your audience.

There is a lot to cover on the PR and marketing side. In fact each of the three big items: 1) consistent communication plan; 2) mailing list; and 3) using ads to drive traffic, could be a book in themselves. This book focuses on the "free" or inexpensive ways to do marketing, on the organic growth process. The paid marketing side is not something every author is ready for or can afford.

Therefore, an indepth look at using paid advertising like Facebook Ads, Bookbub Ads, AMS ads and others, are covered in the *Advanced Marketing through Paid Ads* book. Understanding the paid ads world, the concepts of auctions and bids, as well as split-testing and scaling are all complex concepts and too much to fit in this book which is already well over 100,000 words. However, I will give you resources for connecting with that type of marketing if you want to move more quickly.

In this book I share my experience with the techniques for organic and small money spends to grow a reader base and to consistently market both front list and back list books. Again, not everything can be covered as markets and software changes regularly. In those areas, where change is rapid, I will also link to other books, courses, blogs or resources that can provide more depth quickly for those few things you really want to pursue when you are ready to move on them.

On the marketing side, I will go in depth on using your social media platforms to engage readers, grow your reader base and sell to them in a way that will make them WANT to buy your books. This includes how to build a mailing list of true fans, including a team of super fans (often called a Street Team, Launch Team, or ARC Team). How to use Facebook Messenger as a complimentary platform to your mailing list for those who primarily engage online and do not regularly read their emails. I will also show you how to leverage your organic and social media reach with other marketing tools that do not cost over $100. This is a budget-friendly take on marketing that is particularly appropriate for those just starting out with one to three books and for those whose current financial situation simply doesn't allow for spending thousands of dollars to promote their books.

The final section is on planning and budgeting your time for this type of marketing. Ideally, marketing is not something you do whenever you feel like it or when you happen to have a few extra dollars available. If you do it that way, you won't get good data on what works and what doesn't and you won't be able to maintain any kind of consistency of sell through or income. It is only through consistent PR and marketing that you can learn where to invest and when to invest based on your audience, your books, and how you publish.

I'll pull it all together at the end by providing you with some downloadable planning sheets that you can use for enhancing brand awareness, book pre-launch build up, book launch, and post launch maintenance.

Let's get started!

## Chapter Two
## MARKETING FOR THE SHY AUTHOR

*"Writing used to be a solitary profession. How did it become so interminably social?"* – Meghan Tifft in The Atlantic

Let me share a scenario with you that describes my true feelings about interacting in a world where being social seems to be the requirement for making any money at all on my books. I suspect it will resonate with anyone reading this who is shy or identifies as an introvert.

In 2007, I attended my first RWA (Romance Writer's of America) National meeting. This meeting had been built up to me as being the place I had to go to make my mark. For those who are not familiar with this conference, it is the place where the Rita is awarded (the romance writer's Oscar) with much celebration and ceremony, and people dressing up like they are at the Oscars. It is also the one place where famous and successful romance authors will appear together with those who are aspiring, or only have a few books out. These authors meet to network, celebrate the genre, and to offer workshops and wisdom for those still working their way up the ranks. In other words, it was something I REALLY wanted to attend and felt was important to my own success.

As wonderful and amazing a conference as it is, the environment is made for extroverts not introverts. In fact, it is an introvert's worst nightmare made manifest in three to four intense, compacted days. Furthermore, there seemed to be a lot of advice stated as rules. Here are just a few:

- **Dress professionally**. At that time it seemed to mean wear clothes you would wear on a job interview for a management position. And somehow also wear comfortable shoes because you will be walking for miles. Personally, I've never learned how a dress and my comfy tennis shoes are fashion forward.
- **Always wear a smile**, act confident, and look happy to be there. No one likes a shy, retiring person. This is a great rule. The problem is I wasn't confident. I was terrified to be there, constantly afraid I would say or do the wrong thing. And it's hard to be someone I'm not.
- **Greet people with verve** and just the right amount of fawning without being obvious. This applies to happenstance greetings while standing next to another writer, as well as pre-workshop greetings while waiting for the speaker to get started. There were many examples given to me about how to approach a famous author, editor, agent in the elevator and make conversation in 30 seconds because it may be the only time I actually see that person. Needless to say, I never tried an elevator conversation. I feared if I opened the door they might actually ask me a question and learn what a stumble-tongue I had.
- **Write and rewrite your pitch** to editors/agents prior to attending. Then wait patiently for at least an hour for your turn to get five minutes with someone who can make or break your career. Okay, in hindsight this was absolutely ridiculous. There are many people who have great careers that never meet their editor/agent until well after contracting a book. And now, many authors have chosen to

be indie and don't care about editors and agents. But at the time I was a huge believer.
- **Always plan to eat with a group of people** (preferably not people you already know) in order to be constantly networking. The corollary to this is don't hang out with your friends. You get to see them all the time and already know how they think. Use your few days to meet and get to know as many people as possible—preferably successful writers, editors, and agents. So now, in addition to doing the thing that is not at all natural—engage with a stranger—I must also eat in front of them, not spill food on my white blouse (which always happens), while carrying on witty conversation.
- **Most important, hang out at the bar in the evening.** That is where writers imbibe and share their deepest secrets —the ones that can make you into a star. While there, of course, you need to mingle and network and somehow inconspicuously work your way into groups with the successful writers. Be sure not to fan girl and to act like you know what they are talking about, because the minute they spot you are a fake you will be ignored completely. Hmmm... not sure if being ignored is a bad thing or a good thing.

To make matters worse, you are already spending a fortune for the conference fee and the flight to the venue and the hotel room. Most people save on the hotel room by sharing with one to three other people. Another introvert's nightmare where you have no place to escape with complete quiet.

You may think I'm exaggerating, but for me at that first convention this was my reality. People were nice. Romance writers are some of the most supportive people I've ever met. They founded the organization on the belief that women needed to support each other to get ahead. I don't share this to dissuade you, but to prepare you.

For an introvert, attending a convention like this appears to be a recipe for disaster. It can be so daunting that many writers just don't go. For someone who is truly shy and fearful, attending a conference with all these rules and expectations is certainly a great opportunity to enter therapy for months afterward. In fact, I might suggest that therapists needing an extra buck set up shop in a well-advertised suite at the hotel.

Not having a therapist at my elbow, I spent far too much money getting a massage on the second day. Massage therapists provide a nice, meditative place where I could be quiet and have someone work out the stress kinks in my back and shoulders while having no requirement to speak.

I did make it through that first conference and many others. Though I had done a good deal of conference attending and even given presentations in my non-writing career, this was completely different. The rules were different, my objectives were different, and most importantly I felt I had very little control over any outcomes. And, when I finally got home, I realized it did not meet my expectations. My career was not changed. I didn't get a contract—though everyone asked for a manuscript to review. And, not one of my new found "friends" remained in contact.

Not all of it was awful. I DID learn things at the workshops. I did leave feeling that my craft and my business planning could be improved. However, I could have accomplished that in the quiet of my own home by reading books about it and not have spent a couple thousand dollars to feel extremely uncomfortable for four days.

## BUT NOT ALL IS LOST FOR THE INTROVERT

If this account resonates with you, I hope you keep reading. There is a way to use face-to-face events like conferences, workshops, and opportunities to read an excerpt at a book signing to our advantage by setting appropriate expectations and learning a few techniques for making it less stressful.

For me, my romanticized writer persona was a great fit for my introverted way of living in the world. I am married to an introvert, so we are both very comfortable with not speaking to each other for hours at a time and for taking time away from each other to recharge. Many movies and biographies of writers portray them working alone, creating masterpieces, and somehow finding those few people who were close friends and celebrating with them. In fact, it was the celebration of solitude and the work itself that seemed to be the secret to success.

In reality, the introvert is not held up as the epitome of success. In our world of constant connectedness and sharing, it is easy to believe there is something wrong with those of us who prefer this type of solitude. Publishers and marketers tout "platform" and "persona." There seems to be this requirement to be in constant contact with readers, other authors, and the variety of people that help to make our books publishable.

It is okay not to get energy from constant self-narration in public. I find it exhausting to always be talking and sharing—whether that is in front of people at the podium or online through Facebook and Twitter. It seems that I cannot look at my phone or open my laptop without being inundated with hundreds of requests for me to "connect" or "like" or be a "friend."

This doesn't mean I'm uninterested in networking or uninterested in my readers. In fact, I am deeply interested. But I am interested in REAL connection, in real understanding—not in the daily bits of gossip or distraction that seem to permeate the experience.

If you became an adult before the mid 1990s—when the Internet became mainstream and social media began to bloom—you probably grew up without an expectation of constant sociability and had a small (under 100 people) network of friends and contacts. I became an adult in the 1970's before personal computers, the Internet, social media or any of this connectedness. I could count on one hand (and still do) the number of close friends I had. My biggest mailing list was my Christmas card list of approximately 120 close friends and assorted relatives. When I began building my email list of readers in 2007 I was proud of the 200 people I had on it.

Now we are solidly in 2017, the expectations of authors seem to be better embraced by extroverts—those who get energy from interacting with people on a regular basis. I would never have conceived of having 12,000 people on an email list, or 10,000 people following me on Twitter. Even the more than 1,500 people on my Facebook Author page boggles my mind. I have techniques for growing all of those, but am I expected to now "engage" with them on a daily basis? And what does that mean?

Whenever I do a face-to-face marketing workshop with authors, a number of people come up at the end and comment on how hard marketing is because they are shy. Some of them may truly be "shy." I would suggest that being "shy" is often a manifestation of being an introvert. There is a difference between feeling uncomfortable, or drained, being around a lot of people (introversion) vs being fearful of being around people (shy). The key is determining what your limits are and learning techniques to simultaneously engage at the "social" level while still reserving significant time to be alone and recharge.

Because I do face-to-face training, as well as video training, and writing books about marketing most people don't think of me as shy or introverted. In fact, in spite of decades of attending conferences and doing face-to-face meetings, as well as online sharing, I'm the epitome of introversion.

If you are familiar with the Myers-Briggs personality types, I am INTJ. In a nutshell, I get my energy from solitude rather than talking to people in person, in forums or blog posts. At least in the social media space, I have an opportunity to take time to compose my posts and think about my response, and correct my word choices. In person, I am forced to perform with all of my weaknesses on public display: a forgetful mind for people's names—even those I've known for years—places, and everyday things; a complete lack of personal ability to be fashionable in anything (in spite of being a regular viewer of Project Runway); and the ability to regularly demonstrate a full stop mind pause while searching for a common word that I spoke only moments ago.

All that being said, as authors we do need to find a way to put ourselves out there both virtually and in-person. The key is being selective in how and when you do that and making sure you have lots of opportunity to recharge alone. Don't let others perception of what you MUST do to create an environment where you are miserable at all times. I'll share some of my tricks and how I get by. These may or may not work for you. You won't know until you try.

Start with those tricks that are the least fearful and do them several times. Then move to the next one and the next. Do NOT try to do them all at once. It will be enough to scare the most stalwart person into becoming a permanent hermit.

***Lesson 1: When attending a networking event, a party, or a book signing, treat every person as if you are having a one-to-one conversation.***

Forget the rest of the people around you. Focus on one person at a time. It will take away the overwhelming feeling of how many others are in line to see you or hanging on your every spoken word. Remember, there are many readers or colleagues who are just as afraid of meeting you and talking to you as you are of them.

***Lesson 2: Ask questions to get people to talk about themselves.***

Most people want to talk about themselves, so give them an opening by asking a question. What kinds of books do you like to read? Who is your favorite author? What book have you read in the last five years that really left an impression with you? Or, if you are talking to other authors formulate questions in advance. What books do you like to read (yes authors are readers too)? Is there a particular author you've always wanted to emulate? Who do you consider your mentor? How do you decide what book to do next?

Doing this one thing will make life so much easier. For outgoing people, they will talk on and on and leave the encounter feeling like you are the most interesting person they've talked to that day. The shy people you interact with will appreciate that you asked a question and they didn't have to think about asking you one. I would even go as far as to admit you are an introvert or shy, or to admit this is a scary situation. People naturally want to help, and it makes them feel more comfortable that they don't have to be perfect either.

**Remember:** Many readers are shy too. I was surprised to learn that many readers are terrified to approach a "real author" and talk to them. It doesn't matter whether you are well-known or small potatoes.

The fact you are an "author" with a published book is enough to cause a real fan girl moment. So, asking them a question makes them feel comfortable AND will then help them to ask you a question, which will make you feel more comfortable.

***Lesson Three: Roleplay conversations in advance.***

If you are the kind of person whose tongue becomes paralyzed when you meet someone new, then you need to do lots of practice runs with a friend. Roleplay likely scenarios you will encounter. Make sure who you practice with is someone who cares about you. Give him/her a list of every fear you have, every question you know you will be at a loss for words to answer, and practice, practice, practice.

Because I rely so much on the mind-to-fingers connection in my computer for processing words, it really is NOT unusual for me to be talking to someone--even someone I know well and not be able to remember a characters name in my book, or the setting, or even what the title of the book was (depending on how long ago I wrote it). The reality is sometimes I even forget names of people I've known for a long time, when put into a stressful social situation with strangers. This is because I am so present focused that anything not immediately at hand goes into some mind storage without the key available to unlock the vault.

If we ever meet at a conference, ask me to tell the story of what happened when I first introduced my husband (then fiancée) to my family. Believe me it was horribly embarrassing! But he married me anyway. And I digress.

Before I attend an event, I sit down with another author friend who has done a lot of these conferences and have her ask me lots of questions about my books. In other words, I practice remembering and responding. It isn't only one time either. If it is a big event, like a national convention where I'll be facing thousands of people, I'll practice this 10-15 times in the week before.

***Lesson Four: If things go wrong admit it and move forward with a smile.***

Things WILL go wrong. Prepare for it and practice your reaction. Something unplanned *always* happens to me. I have two choices when that happens: 1) Go into panic mode and hope no one noticed—which diverts my mind and makes me forget even more; or 2) Admit it to the world and move on. Though admitting it seems counter-intuitive, it actually removes the pressure because I don't have to try to hide it or "look cool." It has the added benefit of giving me a good story to share in the future—a story that proves I am just as human as the next person.

Here are two examples of things that commonly go wrong for me and how I've learned to handle it without falling apart.

**Equipment is Not Available.** My presentation is based on my PowerPoint slides. I love PowerPoint because if words go out of my head, I have at leaset a few of them on the slide. However, more than once there was no projector in the room assigned to me, despite being requested months in advance, and no additional ones are available. I don't bring paper copies of slides as handouts because I find they get thrown away. It's a waste of good paper and money.

I've watched this happen to other people and sometimes the speaker simply cancels the workshop because she sees no way to continue. When this happens to me, I tear a blank page out of my notebook and pass it around as a signup sheet for emails, and I promise to send the slides that evening to anyone who wants them. I then take a few minutes to write the primary topic of each slide on the board, to give the attendees something to follow for note-taking. I then use my computer slides as my personal talking points drawing on the board (if available) as needed to clarify complex structures.

**No Memory for Names.** I am often faced with situations where I've been introduced to someone and then a few minutes later, or an hour later, I run into them again and cannot remember their name. This has happened so often that I've learned to just be up front about it. I say something like: "Hi I'm Maggie. I'm sorry, I've forgotten your name even though we have been introduced. I wish that everyone had to wear big name tags all the time so I'd never need to be embarrassed." I've never had someone react with anger—even a big name author or editor. In fact, most of the time the person says: "You know that happens to me all the time, and I didn't remember your name either. Don't worry about it."

I could share pages of examples of things that go wrong while at face-to-face events. The point is, we are all human. Unplanned things happen. If we can just admit it and move on, it will make the incident forgettable instead of becoming a *cause celebre* to be repeated in apocryphal convention tales because of my reaction to it. The best news is that admitting it will make most people relax as they realize they don't have to be perfect either.

**Lesson Five: Schedule alone time to recharge.**

When the face-to-face event has passed (e.g., the book signing, the meet and greet session, or even a particularly charged meeting), I need, and always take, alone time. I walk like a woman who has an important place to be—at a fast pace—to a place where I can be recharge. It may be my hotel room, my car, even the bathroom on a different floor from the convention. I give myself permission to skip the next session if needed, or to arrive late, so I can have some recharge time. These days I actually schedule regular alone breaks instead of trying to go to every workshop or conference event. It is more important for me to recharge and have good energy for the next event than to try to push myself beyond my limits and not be effective.

I rarely go to any of the social events, and I definitely don't go to parties or drink with crowds in the bar. These are not my thing and only drain me to the point I can't sleep and ruins my concentration for the next day of events/workshops. If you don't like to drink and party then don't. No one will think lesser of you. If you do get enjoyment from that environment then go. Do what's right for you.

I know I need time to recharge, to not have to talk or look at anybody. It allows me to regroup and to regenerate. Most people don't question it or notice it. On occasion a well-meaning person might jokingly say: "Oh don't be a party-pooper." Or, if the person believes this is a career-changer, she might say: "This is really a great chance to make friends with successful people."

Just be honest if someone pushes, and assume they are trying to be helpful. I say: "I'm drained from taking in all the new learning today. I need to rest and recharge in order to be at my best tomorrow." That's it. No apologies for being me. Just stating fact. Most people don't push after that and I'm on my way.

What about sharing a room? It is costly for authors to attend conventions and the room cost is often the biggest expense. If I can afford it, I get my own room because it guarantees I won't have to make conversation when I'm trying to recharge. However, I can't always afford to do that. If I am sharing a room, I make sure the group I am sharing with understands who I am and what I need, and has no problem with me being alone in the room while they are off dancing the night away.

I'm fortunate in that I have found two friends to share a room with on a regular basis. One is a definite extrovert and a beautiful social butterfly. The other is an introvert by nature but feels more comfortable in social situations than I do and actually enjoys attending a number of the parties. Sharing a room works for us because we all accept each other for who we are. They never try to lure me to a party. They know if I'm in the room I am there to recharge. They know if I don't join in the conversation when they come in the room and dissect an event, it is not me rejecting them or their experience. They give me space and if they are overly stimulated and I need more quiet, I know I can leave and go somewhere else for a while too (e.g., the business center at the hotel, or take a walk outside).

Finally, for in-person events, be judicious in what you choose. At this point in my career, I choose only one convention type experience a year. And that one tends to be one that is primarily formatted around small group discussions rather than parties. They are less expensive and meet my needs for learning and sharing, rather than socializing.

I schedule no more than four events per year where I am asked to speak or do a workshop. I find that to be a nice compromise for me. I DO like helping authors and sharing my knowledge. However, I am also cognizant that I don't travel as well as I used to and I don't sleep and recharge as quickly as I have in the past.

## VIRTUAL MARKETING FOR THE SHY AUTHOR

So, how do you translate this same approach to online? Even though people don't necessarily see me physically, except through Skype or Google Hangout, I do still have a sense of not wanting to disappoint people, and I try to make sure I present myself professionally. It is that fear of doing something "wrong" or being a pain in the butt to fans that can really get in the way of good marketing.

Similar to marketing in a group face-to-face, I tend to focus on individuals instead of worring about the amorphous big group of fans or questions that are asked while participating online. That means I am focusing on individuals and not the group. I listen to their question or comment and try to respond to their specific needs. I can do that because I really do care about helping. In that way, it doesn't feel like I'm pushing anything on my fans.

You can do the same thing in social media. Post things that YOU find interesting. Share things that relate to your books, characters, life that you would want to hear from another author. Stick with your brand, but also make sure it matches who you are personally. In other words, your primary purpose is not to sell your book. Your primary purpose is to get to know your readers and to help them evaluate how your book fits their needs. I find that just being myself works really well. I don't have to remember how to be something different.

Create a persona as an author. This doesn't mean being fake. What it means is choose what part of yourself you want to be public. We all have multiple facets of ourselves. We have moments of great fear. Moments when we say, at least to ourselves: "Hey that was pretty good!" Moments where we stood up and talked and actually interacted like a pro. Find those parts of yourself that you can mine for your persona.

For example, my author persona is the positive, helpful side of my real personality. It matches the theme of my books: *Stories of people making heroic choices one messy moment at a time*. I write those stories because I believe that IS how to get through life. I like stories where people persevere and come out on top, no matter the challenges they face.

Does that mean in "real" life I am always upbeat and heroic and wonderful? Of course not. I have times of being down or feeling overwhelmed just like everyone else. While writing this book, I am in the midst of packing my house and getting ready to move. Believe me, I am not in a good mood every day. In fact, I am tired and feeling stressed that this book is late to publication and will be even later because of the moving I have to do over the next two weeks. However, I don't need to present that bad mood to my readers. Even other writers, who will buy this book, don't need to hear that from me. They have their own challenges and day-to-day struggles. What they want to hear is how to move forward, how to overcome set backs, just like my heroes and heroines do in my fiction.

I can always find something positive to share in spite of what is happening to me right at this moment. I can always turn adversity into lessons with positive outcomes. That is my brand and that is who I am most of the time.

That isn't to say that my choice is right for every author. I know authors who post the daily ups and downs of their lives for all to see. Every challenge, from small to large, and every perceived hurt is discussed at length. Whether it is lack of sales, a snub by a friend or lover, or a real tragedy (like death or divorce) some authors feel comfortable sharing all of that. It turns out there is an audience for this type of relationship as well—as evidenced by the vast numbers of people who tune into reality TV to watch people implode or survive. So, if it works for you go for it. It's just not me.

## BUT WHAT ABOUT THE SELLING PART? I HATE SELLING ANYTHING.

I hate selling too! In fact, for more than ten years I vowed to my family and friends that I would never ask them to "buy my book." I didn't want any of them to think that my friendship was predicated on them buying my books.

Unfortunately, what happened then is that same attitude began to permeate my relationships with readers. They became like friends as they wrote to me, shared personal stories, talked about my books.

Some shared economic woes. Soon I wondered if I could ever ask anyone to buy my books.

I credit something I learned from a post on CopyBlogger in 2011 https://www.copyblogger.com/online-sales-techniques/ when I first switched from traditional contracts to self-publishing. In the article, Jonathan Morrow proposes six ways to sell without selling your soul. The first one is the most important. It is "forget about making the sell and focus on helping people."

This recalled my time in the software industry. I was not a software salesperson, but I worked with them all the time. My job was to identify which of the many products we sold (I was with a very large company) would best solve the problems a particular company was having. I would never be able to sell a product I didn't personally believe in or couldn't recommend to my best friend. However, I could recommend a product I really believed would work for that person.

So, I apply that same philosophy to selling my books. I don't try to convince anyone to buy my book—even when I'm running a huge campaign in the hopes people will buy my books and I can get some income. Instead, I offer a specific kind of reading experience and let readers decide if that is the experience they want. In fact, because I'm still searching for more readers who like my kind of books, I continue to offer a free book for them to try and make the decision themselves.

When I talk about a book I'm working on or one about to launch, I talk about all the things I love about the book. I'm not making stuff up or pretending I love the book. The reality is I do love the book. I love the characters. I love their journey. I love the way they are able to resolve things in the end. I am simply sharing my own love and excitement about the story.

Then I make the book available for purchase. Note: I don't "sell" the book. I don't ask my readers to "buy" the book. I make it available to them and I know that those who opened my emails and liked me sharing my own excitement, were also building anticipation about the book. That group—and it is never all of my readers—will buy the book when it launches.

In fact, when I set out to write a new book I am thinking about my readers and about myself as a reader. I ask questions about what would

I like to read? What kind of problems would I like to see presented and resolved in a story? And that is the book I write. It seems natural then, that readers who have followed me will want to read that book too.

As I've discussed, I write in multiple genres. One might think that each of those groups want something different and so I need to change my "sales" tactics for each group. It turns out that MY readers are all looking for the same story—a story of people making heroic choices one messy moment at a time. In other words, people who face challenges we can all relate to and are up to the task in spite of how frightening it might be. The only difference is the way each group prefers to see those challenges rendered. Some people prefer to see those stories rendered with futuristic settings and imagined future worlds (science fiction). Others prefer to see them portrayed with magical or paranormal elements (fantasy). Yet others want a romantic story to be an important part of the theme—one where the heroic moments are interwoven with someone else's story that eventually becomes a permanent partnership (romance/women's fiction).

Even my nonfiction readers want this similar experience. It is likely you are reading this book because you want to make a better income from your writing (a challenge you haven't been able to overcome). Perhaps you've tried many other touted techniques in the past, and you are now ready to make some difficult (heroic) choices and commit to them even if they cost more money or take more time, or are more frightening to implement. My nonfiction books, like my fiction books, never portray this process as easy. It is messy and there is no one right or wrong answer. And it requires taking them and trying them one at a time.

I challenge you to identify what common themes are running through your writing. What is the experience you are offering your readers? How does providing that experience HELP your readers to feel good—to feel a value worth paying for—in your books. Can you create a campaign that gives readers the opportunity to buy your book without forcing it down their throats?

Your themes do not have to be the same as mine, and they don't need to be something that makes you a Pulitzer prize writer. It may be the way you HELP your readers is to provide an escape from every day life instead of a mirror of the present. It may be that you help them by providing a quick read that can be completed in just an hour or two because people are busy and need those brief flights of fantasy. It may be that all of your books offer a life of inspiration, an uplift from the daily drudgery; or a way to get the readers adrenaline going with an intense experience. No one way is the right way. Just find YOUR way.

## SUMMARY

Let's face it, we all want to make more money on our books. In fact, that's why you bought this book. Right? Most of us—and especially introverts or shy people—have a hard time doing the things that seem to be recommended to make this a reality. No one I know wants to be that sleazy salesperson who backs people into a corner until they click on the BUY NOW button.

To get to the point where you can make sales and feel good about it, you must believe your book has an audience. You must believe your book(s) are something that your audience not only wants to read but is aching to experience.

Readers buy books because they want an experience--escape, emotional validation, a good laugh or cry, to find answers, to live a fantasy vicariously through your story, or just to have a fun time for a couple of hours. If you have targeted your audience effectively, you ARE delivering what they want. It would be really sad if they never had a chance to buy your book and have that experience because they didn't know your book existed.

The way you HELP is to let them know your books exists. A big part of that discussion with your readers is describing what type of experience they will have—escape, a fun romp, pathos, finding family, dark secrets. If they like your description they will buy the book and, if it delivers that experience, they will buy the next one and everything you write in that series. And many of them will take the time to write you personally and thank you for writing it!

If you are a true introvert and find all of this challenging, I highly recommend this book: *Quiet: The Power of Introverts in a World That*

*Can't Stop Talking* by Susan Cain. Alternatively, if you can't wait to read it, because you are aching for an answer and more validation, check out this TED Talk with author Susan Cain. If you are like me, after watching the video you will still want to have the book too. https://www.ted.com/talks/susan_cain_the_power_of_introverts?language=en

## Chapter Three
# DEFINING YOUR AUDIENCE

In the past, many marketers encouraged writers to think wide in terms of their audience. Authors were encouraged to consider cross-over possibilities and encouraged to try to write a book that meets the needs of the widest possible audience. In other words, write a bestseller. Even in the old days, when the traditional publishing gatekeepers dictated genre and story structure, and tried to set guidelines for getting that bestseller out of potential authors, they could not predict what would make a story hit the zeitgeist. Today that problem remains and the competition is more robust.

There are a few things publishers look for in predicting a bestseller. Most of them are completely out of your control. 1) Celebrity; 2) Topical—a book that matches up with whatever the trending topics are today; and 3) A book that is that combination of different and the same in a hot genre. Outside of being a celebrity, the next two are lucky chances. The book you wrote four years ago about a woman president can suddenly become a hot commodity the year a woman president is actually elected. A book that seems to follow the basic tropes of vampire lore, but with a twist where a particular group of vampires do not want to drink your blood, is just enough of a difference at the right time to capture the zeitgeist.

It todays publishing market, with millions of books available at the click of the mouse or a swipe of the tablet or e-reader, spending all your time trying to write a bestseller and hit a wide swath in the market is not productive. Nor is it likely to happen.

Instead of thinking wide, becoming a successful indie author requires you to write a book that can be found (discovered) among the millions that are available. Instead of wide, you need to think NARROW to compete. Thinking your book is for everyone is a common mistake authors make. Finding and marketing to your niche audience is a much more powerful way to reach the right book buyer and grow your audience from your family and friends to people you've never met but love your books.

Across the board and within genres — romance, mystery, science-fiction, fantasy, thriller, self-help, personal finance or business — today's book buyers are more sophisticated than ever and have many more tools for finding a new book. They no longer have to walk into a brick and mortar store and choose from the 10-15 genres that store offers on the shelf. They no longer have to wade through index cards in the library catalog to find the right genre or topic and select a book. Online databases, keywords, subject categorization, and recommendation engines are the tools that savvy readers use today to find their next book.

With the advent of Google and large vendors, like Amazon, Apple, Kobo, who have sophisticated search engines, book buyers can actually NARROW the field to find what they want and need. Instead of coming through the romance section of a store or library, a buyer can find a Victorian romance with a ghost (paranormal element) as a major part of the plot, and a time-traveler heroine from the 21$^{st}$ century. It only requires some keyword searches.

To cater to readers' specific wants and present them with the perfect book, vendors maintain a lot of data on how readers do searches and make selections. They have growing lists of subject categories, keywords, and metadata combinations that have a high percentage of delivering at least an acceptable book for every search. For YOUR book to show up in that search, you must take advantage of those categorization schemes. It is no longer enough to say your book is a mystery or a romance or a self-help manual. The sub-genre categorizations used for searches has skyrocketed in order to deliver a potential fit not only quickly but accurately.

## HOW VENDORS DEFINE AUDIENCES

As of August 2017, there are over 5.5 million books in the Amazon Kindle store alone. Out of those 5 million books, 1.4 million are categorized as a romance—the largest fiction genre in their database. No one is interested in looking through all those pages of potential books (or even 10% of those pages) to find something that is interesting to read. After entering search criteria, the average consumer looks through two, maybe three pages of potential matches. That is only 36 books a consumer reviews. For most authors, even those making 5 or 10 book sales every day, their book will not show up in those first three pages in larger categories. So, how do you get discovered?

Fortunately, most buyers narrow their searches via one or more subcategories. For example, romance has 26 subcategories ranging from sweet and Christian to werewolves with shifters. The buyer knows that she must put in a few more keywords to get the story she wants to read. That means, it pays for the author to also narrow her book's audience to find the best reader for what she writes.

For example, my books tend to cross between contemporary romance and women's fiction. They are what I call "issue" books. In other words, the protagonist's psychological wound relates to a contemporary problem many women understand (e.g., alcoholic parent, divorce, rape, men who stray, single parenting, etc.). For me to find the best audience for those books, I would not want to categorize my books only in the broad category of romance and compete against 1.4 million other diverse titles. I also would prefer to narrow it beyond "contemporary romance", where I would be competing with 237,923 books. But there is no category under "Romance" called "Women's Fiction." There is also no category anywhere called "Women's Issues."

However, if I start with the "Women's Fiction" category, and then select the subcategory "Contemporary Romance" I am now competing against only 80,655 books. Almost one-third of the previous competition. That is still a lot of books, but my chances of ranking higher in that category—and sometimes even making it in the Top 100 after a promotion—are a lot better than the previous categorization scheme.

Sometimes I can do even better than that, by narrowing further. For my book where the protagonist deals with the effects of divorce, I can narrow it even more to only 584 books. *Literature & Fiction > Women's Fiction> Divorce* Now that is a nice narrow category (target audience) and one where my chances of showing up in the top 100 are very good.

Though romance is the most deliniated genre in terms of sub-categories, many large categories on a vendor site have a breakdown of the genre to some extent. For example, the larger category of Mystery, Suspense, Thriller only has three immediate subcategories —mystery, suspense, and thriller. However, within each of those designations is a plethora of sub-categories ranging from mystery action & adventure to crime to amateur sleuths and international intrigue.

The same holds true for other genres as well. You can do this yourself on Amazon by typing in a broad category, and then clicking on each of the subcategories listed below it. Let's take a look at the numbers of books available by the Science Fiction category and then the subcategories. If you write Science Fiction, review the list below. Is there a good subcategory that fits your story and is significantly less competition than 254,594 books?

Science Fiction (254,594)
Alien Invasion Science Fiction (14,567)
Science Fiction Adventure (68,903)
Science Fiction (254,594)
Hard Science Fiction (14,108)
Dystopian (15,524)
Exploration Science Fiction (4,597)
Post-Apocolyptic Science Fiction (20,931)
Space Fleet Science Fiction (5,354)
First Contact Science Fiction (12,883)
Cyberpunk Science Fiction (6,044)

If you are writing what used to be called "space opera," is it possible you are writing "space fleet science fiction"? You are if it is along similar story lines presented in Star Trek or Star Wars or Halo, Space Fleet SF tends to be stories where government organizations or private contractors provide pilots and crews to work in space. There is a structure and rules, a mission, defined leadership. What about "first contact" science fiction? Do your stories veer toward seeking out or running into new aliens or civilizations? Perhaps your book fits into both Space Fleet and First Contact SF, like Star Trek. Good news is that vendors realize there is some cross-over in subcategories and it is okay if your book fits in both.

Each subcategory offers a much better chance of finding an audience who matches very closely to your book and, therefore, developing additional readers that will also love your books.

Too often new writers get caught up in the specifics of their story when thinking about subjects. Here is a typical conversation I'e engaged in many times with a new author.

***Author:*** It is set in space and it has a military crew protecting their part of the galaxy, but it doesn't fit the category exactly.
***Me:*** Why not? It sounds like Space Fleet Science Fiction to me.
***Author:*** Because it doesn't account for my captain being human from the 18$^{th}$ century, who has put in cryo-sleep by aliens and awakes in the 25$^{th}$ century and has to fight those same aliens.
***Me:*** Those are interesting details, but the core of your story is still military crews protecting their corner of the galaxy. You need to look at where your story fits and choose that. Don't focus on where it doesn't fit or the uniqueness within the genre. There are many books within a category with something different about their character or story arc.

**Bottomline:** It is a very rare situation where you cannot find a nice narrow category that fits your book. Also remember that you get to choose more than one category at each vendor. If you need the step-by-step specifics about selecting categories and keywords, please refer to my book *Secrets to Pricing and Distribution: Ebooks, Print and Direct Sales.* http://maggielynch.com/book/secrets-to-pricing-and-distribution-ebooks-print-and-direct-sales/

## FINDING, CHOOSING THE RIGHT GENRE CATEGORIES

At this point I know someone reading this book is saying: "Wait! I write mystery books with paranormal elements and a romance. I need three different categories to define my audience."

Yes, you may be able to fit into more than one category. However, that doesn't mean you are able to market and grow readers in those three categories. You will have to choose where to start. The basis of that is which genre category is the most important to the story or the most prevalent. When you started writing the book, what was the core story?

Do get a great breakdown of genre definitions visit this Writer's Digest page and see if it helps you with defining your book. http://resources.writersonlineworkshops.com/resources/definitions-of-fiction-categories-and-genres/

Let me give you an example from my book Expendable http://maggielynch.com/book/expendable/ and how I decided on romantic suspense as the defining genre.

When I first conceived of Expendable, I thought of it as a medical thriller along the lines of Robin Cook or Michael Crighton. I wanted to explore the idea of using biogenetics in humans to grow organs for those who can afford it. As I started writing and my characters became more real to me. I realized the book was about PTSD and how people deal with trauma—whether that is through war, injury, or abuse. That meant it fit into a more literary fiction slot. However, as I wrote there was plenty of jeopardy and thriller elements too. Then, to really confuse me, my two lead characters started to fall in love and their relationship mirrored their healing and their relationship also put everything in jeopardy.

So, was I writing a thriller, a romance, or a literary novel? The answer is yes. But those audiences are very different and marketing to all three of those audiences at once would be time consuming and costly, and would likely leave a lot of the readers unsatisfied. I had to choose. When I did a closer analysis, and stopped fighting my desire to be a unique and special snowflake of an author, I realized when I finished the book that the core story was about relationships, love helping to overcome trauma, set against the background of a thriller. Then I was able to put it squarely into romantic suspense which has both thriller and romance elements, but the love story (relationship story) is the core driver.

If I had less relationship building, or the love story was a minor part of the book, I could have fit it into thriller without a problem. The bottomline is what is the overriding genre in your book? What part of the it really drives the story.

What about Outlander? That isn't pigeonholded into genre. It is Mainstream fiction. Yes, that is how New York published it. Certainly, you can publish your unique book as mainstream fiction. However, to build your audience around a category of "mainstream" fiction you will need a lot of time and money. That category is as diverse as all the genres. Mainstream fiction includes books like Outlander (Historical, Thriller, Romance, Time-travel) as well as books like The Kite Runner (Literary). And many things in between. Mainstream fiction is also any genre book that broke rules AND became extremely popular. It may have been written eto genre but then became a huge success. Examples like this are Girl on A Train (Mystery, Thriller) or The Time Traveler's Wife (SF & Romance) and Twilight (Paranormal & Romance with vampires and werewolves).

Though the books do cross genres, let's look at what is the most popular selling category for each one. That will give insight into the largest audience.

**Outlander** – Romance > Historical > Scottish

**Kite Runner** – Literature & Fiction > Asian American

**The Girl on the Train** – Literature & Fiction > Literary

**The Time Traveler's Wife** – Science Fiction & Fantasy > Time Travel

**Twilight** – Teens > Science Fiction & Fantasy > Fantasy > Paranormal & Urban > Vampires

When you look at the above list, are you surprised at what is the most popular category (as measured by actual sales and how the reader found the book)? Two of them surprise me. I would have pegged The Time Traveler's Wife as more romance than science fiction. I would have pegged The Girl on the Train as more mystery.

When looking at your core story, consider what that means for your audience. You need to start narrow and then build as the book becomes more popular. If you are having a hard time deciding where your book fits, look at books that have similar themes as yours. Check those themes in the different genres you believe match yours and see what books are at the top of the list in those genres. Ask yourself if your book easily fits among those. If not, don't start there. If it does, you have a beginning.

## IF I NARROW MY AUDIENCE WON'T I MISS OUT ON THE BIGGER AUDIENCE?

No, you won't. That is the beauty of database categorization. Every larger category works like a tree, where all the subcategories are branches, and the sub-sub categories are leaves. Even if you choose a leaf, the tree is still there and linked to everything else. In other words, if a consumer selects Space Fleet Science Fiction, which exists in the following tree: *Science Fiction & Fantasy > Science Fiction > Space Fleet Science Fiction* your book will also show up in a listing in each one of those categories in the tree. If someone only types in Science Fiction, it will still show up in the listings. However, because of the number of books in that broader category (the competition) your book may not be near the top of the listings. Instead it will be buried many pages down.

By competing in a narrow category, you are really serving your core audience. The more you sell to that group of people, the higher your ranking is and that means your book is shown more often to new people who don't know you. As you build your sales in a small category, you are also moving your book up in the rankings of the next larger category up the tree. If you end up at number one in your category of 5,000 titles, then chances are you will have also made the Top 100 in other categories further up the subject tree.

It may seem counter-intuitive; but narrowing your audience really is the key to finding success in the long term. It is much more difficult to consistently meet the needs of a large and diverse audience than it is a more homogenous one. This also translates to branding for that smaller audience, delivering on the core story expectations of that audience (Reader Cookies), and being able to engage your fans in a way that makes them become super fans.

Super fans are those readers who love your core story and will read anything you write in that core story. Often, even if you slightly change genres, these super fans will follow you if your core story stays the same. And that is how you are able to eventually cross genres and diversify your audience to larger and larger numbers.

For example, I began building my list based on my Sweetwater Canyon series of novels. I see these as both Contemporary Romance and Women's Fiction. They weren't quite Contemporary Romance in that they are "issue" novels as much as romance novels. Some Contemporary Romance readers don't like their romance to be tainted with weighty issues. On the other hand, many Women's Fiction books don't have romance at the core of the story. They might be more about relationships in a family or between friends. I narrowed my audience to those romance and women's fiction readers who want both a core romance, as well as family/friend relationships to be equal in order to find that sweet spot. That is also when I found my core story that crosses all genres—"stories of making heroic choices one messy moment at a time." Those heroic choices could be very personal, like overcoming rape, or more traditional heroes like saving a child from harm, or saving a world from disappearing.

Slowly, my romance/women's fiction readers hesitantly tried my fantasy novels. Some of them really liked them because they found the core story was still the same. It was still about making choices. It was still about finding out what you are meant to do. It was still about relationships and overcoming obstacles. It was just set in a fantasy world. Have they all crossed over, no. At the moment my list of about 12,000 readers is fairly evenly split between romance/women's fiction and fantasy with a slight lead to the romance side (5,800 vs. 6,200). Of those 12,000 approximately 1,000 are on both lists. I see that as a good start.

By narrowing my audience, I actually defined and found my kind of readers. I had tried to sell to the broader audiences for about four years with very little success. Once I narrowed and focused on marketing to that more narrow audience, I grew my readership significantly.

## LET'S GET STARTED WITH YOUR AUDIENCE DEFINITION

Nonfiction writers tend to have no problem defining their audience. That's because they have a specific expertise and have most likely been hanging out with people who want to read and learn about that, or have been teaching people who want to learn about it. However, fiction writers don't have it so easy. If you write straight down the center of a genre (e.g., cozy mystery, humorous contemporary romance, literary fiction) it is definitely easier to define your audience. You can learn about competing books and market directly to those books and authors. On the other hand, if you write like most of us do, a novel that has elements of more than one genre it is more difficult.

**Here are questions that may assist you in narrowing your audience.**

**What books have you read that are most like the book(s) you write?** If you haven't read a book with any similarities to yours, you need to start reading more or be a little more analytical about finding matches. For example, if your book takes place in France in 1940, you will certainly want to think about what was going on historically—Germany's invasion of France. That will give you a clue that fiction books about that period of time might be where your audience is found. If your story has romantic elements during that period, search for historical romance set in WWII. Now that you found those books, scroll down and look at the categories associated with them. Those may be the same categories to associate with YOUR books. Do this exercise more than once and then follow-up on the books and authors you found. Make notes on how those author's describe their readers, what their website features about their books and readers, what their social media pages do to attract readers.

Here is an example of a book I found that takes place in the period and location above. It is Kristin Hannah's book *The Nightingale*.

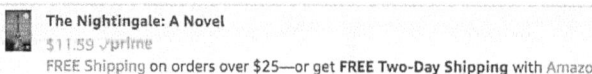

## Product details

**Paperback:** 608 pages
**Publisher:** St. Martin's Griffin; Reprint edition (April 25, 2017)
**Language:** English
**ISBN-10:** 1250080401
**ISBN-13:** 978-1250080400
**Product Dimensions:** 5.6 x 1.6 x 8.3 inches
**Shipping Weight:** 1.1 pounds (View shipping rates and policies)
**Average Customer Review:** ☆☆☆☆☆ • 35,452 customer reviews
**Amazon Best Sellers Rank:** #240 in Books (See Top 100 in Books)

Categories
#3 in Books > Literature & Fiction > Women's Fiction > **Sisters**
#104 in Books > Literature & Fiction > Genre Fiction > **Historical**
#142 in Books > Literature & Fiction > **United States**

Note that this book is first classified as Women's Fiction. That is because the core story is the story of two sisters and their very different experiences during WWII. Note the difference in sales ranking between that first category and the second category, which is Historical Fiction. All of Kristen's rankings are amazing, but there is a defined difference in audience.

**Narrow the categories you found to further differentiate your book from others.** Now that you found a category—let's say Historical Romance set in WWII—you need to think about what is different about YOUR book compared to all the books you identified above. For example, is your story focus equally the saga of an entire family in that historical time? Or is it more focused on the romantic relationship? It is likely that the books you found are diverse. Now narrow it to those books that match even more closely to your book in terms of themes, time period, location. Don't worry about genres at this point. As you narrow and look at the categories, you will probably begin to see one or two genres coming up more and more often.

Look those books up on various vendors. (I find Amazon to be the most easy to use for this kind of research). Again, check the categories and make note of that.

**Check out the "Also Boughts" associated with each author's books.** This represents what other books a reader viewed or purchased after buying this book. This will help you broaden your reader profile by showing other categories that are also attractive to the reader.

***NOTE***: This is only accurate for books that have a good following. You will often first see books by the same authors or in the same series. Keep clicking on the right arrow to see other books beyond that author. If you look at a book with only a few followers, looking at "also boughts" can be deceiving. They are more likely a reflection of rejecting the book of that author and moving to a known author they like.

Again, here are the also boughts for Kristin Hannah's book *The Nightingale*. If you are not familiar with the "also bought" book, look it up and see what are the similarities and differences between the books and how they best match yours. For example, two of these "also bought" books do NOT take place in France. One is in the U.S. and the other is in Italy and Germany. However, they all take place during the historical period of WWII. What is similar? Three of them focus on family, particularly sibling relationships. The Lila Girls focuses on three best friends—a kind of created family. Each one explores the feelings and experiences of being uprooted, of trying to find a way in a world that is nothing like the characters knew before, and of feeling helpless or powerless to be with each other at a most horrific time. Each one is a coming-of-age story tied up in a particular historical period. Each one is written in a literary style that is lush, descriptive, and emotional.

How does this help you define your audience? You now have themes and styles to compare to your book. Perhaps your book matches the historical period and the sibling relationship, but it is written with more humor. Then none of these books is the best fit for you. You need to add "humor" to your search with the other elements being the same. That might lead you to *The Guernsey Literary and Potato Peel Pie Society* by Mary Anne Shaffer and Annie Barrows.

1. **Look at the broader demographics**. Now that you've successfully narrowed not only the category for your book but something more granular about the types of experiences your reader desires, it is time to look into demographics like age, location, interests. Why care about that? Because when you get to the actual marketing, you will want to know these in order to spend your time and money wisely.
2. If this is the first book you are publishing and you have a small or no reader list, then begin with a profile of you and your likes. Try to be as specific as possible. Here is my profile specifics:
3. Gender: *Female*
4. Age: *63*
5. Profession: *Author, retired from academia*

6. Favorite Reads: *Women's fiction and science fiction*
7. Blog or Social Media Follows: *Authors, New Technology, Political Action, How to lead a meaningful life.*
8. Posts on my page: *cats, grandchildren, positivity memes*
9. If my personal likes can be generalized to my readership, I can now take this information and try looking for people who are similar to this profile. Though I will broaden it a little to include: women who are age 55+, tend to be educated, read women's fiction, romance, science fiction and are looking for an experience that speaks to leading a meaningful life. Notice this is not exact, and a number of people will fit this profile. However, it is definitely more narrow than all women age 18+ who read romance or women's fiction.
10. **Analyze social media followers for the author's you found.** Bypass anyone on the page who is also an author, unless you are writing books for authors. You want to zone in on readers. This is surprisingly easy to do on Facebook or Twitter by moving your mouse to the person's name. A window will popup with a summary of the reader and often a picture. It will show their name, perhaps a location, colleges or universities in their profile, and any friends you might have in common. Not everyone will have this, as not everyone completes profile information or allows it to be made public. But many will. You can get a good sense of demographics and guess general age groups and likes/dislikes from doing this kind of research. You can also click on the person's page and see what they've posted publicly.
11. I wouldn't spend days doing this. Some author pages have thousands of followers. However, you might put a couple hours into it until you get a sense of the readers for this author who might be the readers for your work too.

For a more extensive checklist of questions to answer to narrow your audience further, check out PR woman extraordinare, Joan Stewart's, helpful post at https://publicityhound.com/blog/how-to-find-readers-for-fiction

## CONNECT WITH THE READER TYPES YOU HAVE IDENTIFIED

Now that you have an idea of who your reader's might be, you need to find them and connect with them. This requires both active research and actual engagement on your part. Don't expect to make this happen over night. It takes time. You need to discover what your common interests are and find ways to learn more.

Whatever you do, do NOT treat this exercise as if everyone is a meal ticket. You are contacting them only to have an opportunity to sell your books to them. They will spot you and kick you out faster than a "deletrius" spell.

One of the things my readers always tell me is, "I love the way you treat your readers. You aren't always trying to sell us stuff. You think of us as real people, as individuals." The direct, hard sell technique does not work with readers. It's just noise to them—and especially noise they all know how to ignore and turn off.

Readers are looking for community—among other readers and with the authors they love. So instead of thinking of a new reader as a way to get money, think of them as someone interesting you've just met and you want to get to know more. Ask questions. Comment on their posts and statements. Add value by sharing what you are doing and why. Discuss common interests. Share relevant links. In short, be your authentic self.

Choose the social media platforms that cater to readers. Places like Goodreads, some book bloggers, book groups, reader groups within Facebook. When you go to these platforms, you go as a reader too. Share what you like about books, other than yours. Find common interests. After you've established yourself and readers feel comfortable with you, you can bring in information about being an author or a book you've written that applies to the conversation at hand. Be very careful about this, and always check before joining, if there are rules for the group about "no authors" or "no selling."

Some readers are also influencers. This mean they have a platform that makes recommendations of books and authors on a regular basis. These may be reviewers, book bloggers, or even an author who loves talking about a variety of books. Just as with the readers above, you want to give first before asking for permission to talk about your work. Share their posts and links, as they apply to your work. Work to increase their profile. Be sure to always use their handles on social media so they know you are promoting their expertise. Leave comments and/or ask questions that point to their expertise and help them grow.

Karma works wonders in these situations. Usually, when you have selflessly expended energy helping someone else grow, they will reciprocate and help you when the time is right. If you have a great idea for a cross-promotion opportunity that will help both of you, you can approach them after you've spent lots of time recognizing their worth to the community.

On occasion, the person you helped so much never does reciprocate. If you were being authentic from the beginning—in other words truly interested in their content and their site—then your time was not wasted. If you were not authentic, then you should not have been there in the first place. It was a waste of both yours and the influencer's time.

I've found that investing in the book community and in other author's careers always gives back to me ten fold in the end. I only participate in communities where I also have an interest as a reader and an author. For me, one of the reasons I write is to connect with people in a meaningful way. I am as interested in getting to know them and what we might have in common as I am in selling them my books.

I'll be sharing more about using social media to engage with readers in the chapter about that under *Your Communication Plan*.

# YOUR COMMUNICATION PLAN

Your Brand
Your Website
Your Media Packet / Press Kit
Your Blog
Book Groups and Clubs

## Chapter Four
# YOUR BRAND

Branding is one of those things everyone tells you to do, but no one tells you how to do it or why it is important. This is part of the PR component I discussed in the first chapter. This is the thing you do to let people know what the EXPERIENCE of reading your books will be. And that "experience" will always point back to YOU, and your company brand. That experience will also help you define your target audience so you can actually find people who will love YOUR books. Let's begin by looking at how you build a brand.

When it comes to building a compelling author brand, there are two main areas that require your focus: brand identity and brand awareness. These become key to everything you do in marketing. Once you have nailed down your brand identity, and use it consistently, a lot of the marketing parts will fall into place more naturally. You won't have to be constantly rethinking your promotional look and feel for each campaign.

**NOTE:** There is a difference between brand and genre. Be careful not to over-invest in the styling or look of a particular genre as part of your brand, unless you're certain that it "fits" with your brand strategy and story longer term. Also ask yourself if this is the only genre you will be writing for the rest of your career.

I write in multiple genres. This means my brand has to work for all of them. Though I can create images and looks for my products (books) in each genre, I still need to adhere to the broader look and feel of my brand.

## FIRST ESTABLISH A BRAND IDENTITY AND PURPOSE

This is where you pull together the visual, written and in-person brand elements that support your brand—the experience you are promising your readers. It's not just what you say, but *how* you communicate your message to your audience through both words and images.

### *Elements that Help Form Your Brand Identity*

**Main logo** – It may be graphic or font based. In the early part of this century, graphic logos tied to genre tropes were all the rage for authors. However, as authors embraced their brand as being about them as a person and writer, more font-based logos took shape. The vast majority of best selling authors have a font-based logo that is their name. Some also have a tagline below that defines the type of story they write.

Take a look at these bestselling author pages to see font-based branding. These name fonts are not only on their website but on marketing and often match the name on their books as well.

Nora Roberts - http://www.noraroberts.com/ name font, no tagline
Mark Dawson - https://markjdawson.com/ name font, no tagline
Collette Cameron - https://collettecameron.com/ name font and tagline
Cathryn Cade - http://cathryncade.com/ name font, no tagline

Take a look at these four author pages to see branding that is clearly author-based. It contains a picture of the author, the name, and a tagline. No other graphics.

Karin Slaughter - http://www.karinslaughter.com/
J.D. Robb - http://www.jdrobb.com/ Though this is a pen name of Nora Roberts, note that she chose to use a different brand for this, focusing on both her image and name.
Jayne Ann Krentz - http://jayneannkrentz.com/
Gina Fluharty - http://www.ginafluharty.com/

A number of authors, particularly those in the romance genre and those who write across multiple genres, including romance, seem to want to include a primary image as their banner—some images represents the genre(s) in which they write, while others represent the themes that permeate their stories. Some include a tagline and some do not. Here is a selection of websites across many sub-genres in romance.

Christy Carlyle - http://christycarlyle.com/ Obvious historical romance relationship
Paty Jager - http://www.patyjager.net/ Though she writes in multiple genres from mystery to historical and contemporary romance, they are all westerns and reflect a western culture.
Maggie Lynch – http://maggielynch.com Multiple diverse genres. Used a theme-based image rather than a genre-specific image
Courtney Pierce - http://courtney-pierce.com/ Leans toward literary novels but with a baby boomer sensibility
Jenna Bayley-Burke - http://www.jennabayleyburke.com/ Contemporary romances on the steamy side
Rosalie Redd - http://www.rosalieredd.com/ Paranormal

There is no ONE right way to demonstrate your brand. Some of the branding techniques include: using specific fonts, building a logo—whether that is a traditional logo or a specific image that is associated with your brand, or some combination. The key is to define it and stick with it in all marketing efforts. Images become memory triggers, and those triggers create awareness over repeated use.

Some authors avoid branding because they are afraid they will change their mind. That's okay. Nothing is in stone. It took me five tries before I settled on my current brand graphic and tagline. If it is too much to come up with a graphic, then I suggest you go with a font-based brand. You can choose a font you like or pay someone to create a font that is unique to you. The ones at the top of the page with the four font-based author examples all have a font created specific to that author and his/her brand.

My logo is primarily graphic, but has nothing to do with a specific genre. It is a woman rock climbing an underneath edge of the rock while dangling over the water. It fits my tagline about *making heroic choices one messy moment at a time*. Because I write across diverse genres with a small percentage of cross-over readers, I felt this graphic was a good metaphor for the theme and tagline I use as my brand. I believe it embraces the combination of strong women, difficult and even dangerous choices, and heroism all in one image.

All of these elements are part of the experience promise I make to my readers in every book, no matter the genre. The font used for my name is also replicated on my book covers using the Maggie Lynch name. My genre-specific pen names (Maggie Jaimeson and Maggie Faire) each use different fonts for the book covers in those genres. Perhaps, in the future, I'll have a unique font created for me. For now, I am happy with how my brand is represented.

This same logo is used everywhere I have a presence on the web and where they allow a logo to be loaded: my website, Facebook, Twitter, Google Plus, Linked In, YouTube. It is also used on my business card, bookmarks, flyers, my email template, and other types of paper and online communication products. In other words, it is the primary representation of my author brand.

**Brand tagline** – This is a highly concise mission statement. This mission statement is not like the typical mission statement of how you are running your business. It is a statement of the "experience" your reader will have with your products, and that extends to your communications about your business. Your tagline is worth spending some time on developing. If you are having trouble with it, ask people who know you and your work for ideas. Often a friend or another author can encapsulate your brand better than you can yourself.

Also, don't worry if it's not perfect. It CAN be changed. I went through five taglines over a decade before I settled on the one I have today. It took me that long to really have a good sense of what my multi-genre brand could be. The benefit of doing this work is it helps you when planning all your PR and marketing as a guide to direction.

If you can't come up with a tagline that's fine too. As with the examples above, many authors chose not to have a tagline. If you make that choice then the brand is even more reliant on your name and what that represents.

**Brand colors** – choose two to three main colors (get the hex codes so you can use your exact brand colors when designing your own graphics). This does not mean that every book cover or product needs to use these colors. However, when you are pushing your brand visually (particularly online) using the colors can be a way to instantly identify you.

A great example of really using a brand color is Historical Romance Author Collette Cameron. Her company identity is Blue Rose Romance. You see blue in every post she makes. In fact, many of her brand postings share blue roses, blue dresses, blue jewelry, blue desserts. It isn't the only thing posted, but it is frequent and when people think of her they definitely think blue—a highly saturated blue.

Though my logo definitely contains some colors—brown, blue, and peach—it hasn't found its way into a lot of my other marketing imagery. For some people specific colors are VERY important. To others it is not. Your choice.

**Brand style elements** – patterns, icons, graphics, fonts or other style elements. Again this can be used with everything. Including your products (e.g., your name font is the same on every book) or it can be used only as it relates to your brand graphics. Authors who have invested in having a name font unique to them, do use it on ALL their covers and in all communication. This makes particular sense if your brand is your name and there is no other logo or image consistently a part of your brand.

## BRAND AWARENESS

Once you have your brand story and other brand elements defined, the next step is developing a plan to promote and solidify your brand in the eyes of readers.

- How will you demonstrate the feelings, values and unique qualities that you want attributed to you and your writing?
- How will you grab your reader's attention or pique their interest?
- Who needs to know about your books? Which types of people would be most interested in your writing? (And where can they be found?)
- What are other authors doing in your genre or niche? What are their competencies and how can you position yourself and your work differently?

There are three aspects to creating more awareness for your author brand:

### Goals and Objectives

Identify your goals and objectives. Everything you write or create should be moving you closer to these goals. You need to know where you are trying to take your readers (the buyers journey), and create goals and objectives for your content that will move people to action.

*Note:* These are not typical goals like "I will write three books this year," or "I want to make $25,000 this year." These are goals for how you are going to shepherd new readers to engage with you and to love you and your books, with a certain percentage becoming superfans.

## Promotion

*Content strategy* – Your publishing plan of action for your books, blog, social media, audio, video and email list will all require lots of content delivered on a variety of platforms. Capitalize on each platform's strengths to share different aspects of your brand story. Each platform has it's own strengths and weaknesses. Some are image heavy whereas others are text heavy. I will talk more about this in the chapter on social media. Though you may use the same foundational content across all your communications, it is presented differently for each platform.

*Brand style guide* – Create a brand style guide that includes your brand specific fonts, colors, brand elements, patterns and imagery, so that all your marketing materials are consistent and at your finger tips. We live in a visual world, and readers make connections based on visual consistency with brand.

I am not a visual person at all. Thus my ability to suddenly notice a building that has been in my neighborhood for years. What this means for my brand style, is that I am not good at differentiating colors that are very similar, or fonts beyond whether they are serif or sans serif. In fact, I often don't remember images I may have chosen for a post one week and accidentally repeat them the next.

Consequently, I've learned to make lots of notes so I wouldn't forget what I'd chosen: exact font name and sizes for different markets; color hex codes for online content and pantone names for printed content; and I create different sized images for online and for print and save them all in a file. Without these notes I would likely have 5 similar but different name fonts for my covers, 15 different red tones for buttons, and slightly different colors in my logo every time I used it.

This helps tremendously when/if you hire others who need to adhere to your brand—cover designers, ad creators, or a PR company.

***Audience definition*** – The more you know your audience, the easier it is to establish a framework and a way to focus your efforts for reaching and connecting with your type of readers – those who'll find the most value in what you write. This is really hard for authors starting out or those who have published one book without a good sales history.

One of the ways to start building this profile is to poll your readers anonymously. Explain that you are trying to understand who likes to read your type of books, and invite them to take an anonymous survey. You will want to determine things like age, gender, genres they read, names of books they like, names of other authors they like, etc.). This information will not only help you with your branding, but it will make a huge difference when you start advertising.

When I first started doing ads on Facebook for my romance series, I thought my readers were primarily females, age 25-40, who liked sexy books. In the beginning I targeted broadly (e.g., all adults over 18). Based on who actually clicked and joined my list and then engaged with me, I learned that the majority of my readers were actually age 45-60+ (65% of them) and only 15% were in that 25-40 age range. Also, though they enjoyed my books, at least half of them prefer sweet and clean books (no sex), even though they did make an exception for me.

Knowing your audience may take time. But learn as much as you can in the beginning and then give yourself some leeway to develop a more comprehensive knowledge as you get to know them better and can narrow your campaigns to meet those specific needs.

***Digital media kit*** – This is a marketing package for your book(s) that makes it quick and easy for the media and others to feature you and your work. It usually includes a bio, very brief descriptions of your work (think of it as a tweet), and any images attached to your brand including a headshot and logo (if you have one).

***Street team*** – The audience for your street time (also called a Launch Team or VIP reader group) is a subset of your larger audience. These are your superfans. This group of readers loves your work so much they likely buy everything you write—sometimes even when it is out of the genre they normally read. Word-of-mouth is the best form of promotion there is, and these superfans are the most likely to tell everyone they know how wonderful you are. If you nurture your super-fans with extra perks and benefits (always within your brand story), they will want to support you even more. Some authors have even had fans who identified so well with the brand that they begged for thing like branded t-shirts, bags, mugs, and other things to have the author close to them.

**Collaboration** – Once you know your brand and audience, you can seek out other authors and companies who have similar brand styles and audiences. This might include authors outside your primary genre if their brand matches up with yours. It might include profit or nonprofit organizations that share an audience interest like yours. By building your network, you can find many opportunities to join forces to benefit both of you.

## BRAND GROWTH

As your brand evolves, you'll need to gauge your audience's interest and ask for their input and feedback along the way. Continue to build brand equity by continuously re-evaluating, refining and growing your brand reputation.

What elements of daily life are part of maintaining the brand?

- Website
- Social Media Posts
- Blog Posts, Guest Posts, and Articles
- Emails to your fans
- In person events—signings, talks
- Anything else you enjoy doing that relates to your writing

I'll cover each of these in subsequent chapters.

## Chapter Five
# YOUR WEBSITE

Building a website is a huge decision for an author to undertake. It is your #1 static marketing site. Even if you don't sell books direct, any time someone encounters you for the first time they are likely to go look at your website. Your website is considered the official place to learn about you, your books, your plans, and to get a good sense of how or if your work hangs together. Do you write in series? In what order should the books be read? Do you write in more than one genre? What is your background? Do you have any awards? These are all things readers, other authors, and industry professionals want to see on your website.

Because of using Google Analytics, I see that the visitors to my website come from referrals from retailers as much as they come from referrals from Facebook where I primarily drive traffic to my website. That means my website needs to meet the needs of whoever is coming to learn more about me or my books.

Your website is your public face to your readers, as well as to other industry people you may be wishing to attract (booksellers, bloggers, journalists, TV news departments). To put your best foot forward, it must look professional. That doesn't mean it needs to be super fancy with special icons and fly-in email list builders. It doesn't have to have special quizzes so readers can decide which of your characters match them. Though all these are fun, they are not necessary—especially if you are just starting out. The most important aspect of your website is to make sure the domain reflects who you are, it is easy to find your books, and that the buy links are apparent. Even if you don't sell direct, you want to be sure the buylinks reflect where someone can purchase your book (e.g., Amazon, Kobo, Apple, GooglePlay, etc.)

Typically when an author asks me to look at their website and critique it, I am continuously surprised by the number of authors—sometimes with three or more books—where their website is only a blog, or they have no domain that reflects themselves or any brand, or that the picture of the author is something taken in their kitchen with bad lighting and it appears they have a hangover. I do understand people don't want to put out money for a website, but even on a free blogging platform you have options to look professional and to assign your own domain to the platform.

Below is a quick checklist of the parts you need for an author website.

**Domain Name** –You need to purchase your domain. Yes, this is going to cost you anywhere from $15 to $25 per year. Let's be reasonable, if you can't invest $15 per year for a domain, then you will have many problems as you pursue this career.

Your domain should be YOUR name. That means the earlier you buy it the more likely you are able to find your name available. When I began writing novels in 2004, I had decided my penname would be Maggie James. My husband's name is James and I liked the shortness and ease of that name, while honoring his support of my writing. The first thing I did was search for the domain maggiejames.com. I immediately found out it was not available, nor was maggiejames.net. There was another author who had that name and she wrote in a genre very different from me. Then I tried maggiejamesfiction.com Again there was another author, this one in the U.K. I ended up changing my pen name to Maggie Jaimeson (there were a lot of Jameson and Jamison authors, so I spelled it the old Irish way for girls name Jaime a female version of James).

You may try a lot of variations to get the name you want. Using a hyphen, using the word "book" or "author" after your name. There are also now many more domain options available with .com, .net, .biz, .co and others.

***Tip:*** If you are using a pen name instead of your own name, choose carefully. If possible, make it something that is fairly easy to remember and easy to spell. The mistake I made with Jaimeson is that no one knows how to spell it. Even seven years later! In 2017 I made the decision to bring all my pen names under one moniker, Maggie Lynch. I will admit, it is a relief not to worry about the different spellings of Jaimeson anymore.

I recommend you *do not* get a domain name with your series name as the primary domain to represent you as an author. A career author is likely to write more than one series and you don't want to be stuck with that as your primary website name. Nor should you get a domain name with your book name. You can get these as subsidiary domains on your website, if you wish, or simply have pages/sections on your website that relate to these series or books. You don't want your brand to be based on the first book or series you wrote.

**Home page** - Do you have a home page (one that doesn't show your blog latest posts)? Does it convey your brand? It should minimally include the cover of your most recent book and a call to action such as how to join a mailing list or how to buy your book.

In the past, home pages on author websites typically had some type of welcome message. e.g., "Welcome to Maggie's world" or "This is the combined site of writer Maggie Lynch, Maggie Jaimeson, and Maggie Faire." This welcome was often followed by a brief bio or some friendly information about the author. This welcome message on the home page is **no longer recommended**. You can leave that to your author page or other informational pages. If you have a strong brand, anyone coming to your page should recognize who you are (your name is on there) and what you write.

The reason for the change is that most Internet users spend very little time on any one page unless they are immediately intrigued or looking for something specific. Stats vary from staying on a particular page from 5 seconds to 15 seconds. This means you need to make it easy for the visitor to get to exactly what the need within about 5 seconds.

*Menu* – Do you have a menu bar that visitors can use to help navigate? Is it easy to understand, and well organized? Using that 5 second rule, the menu is critical for the user to quickly get where she wants to go. You can't put everything in the top level, so you need to group them by categories that will be obvious to the visitor. That top level should answer the first question a reader or industry person wants answered.

- What books have you written? (**Books**)
- Who are you? (**About**)
- How do I contact you? (**Contact**)
- Are you going to be coming to my state? Town? Bookstore? (**Events**)
- Are you any social media that I follow? (**social media buttons in header**). Often social media links are also provided on the Contact page.
- How can I join your mailing list? (**Mailing List** menu item or something else that is obvious for joining)

Minimally, you must have the first three menu items. Books, About, and Contact. Depending on how far down the road in your career, you may benefit from the other items as well. Let's look at each of the menu items in more depth, their content, and how they might be structured.

**Books** - Have you set up a listing page for each of your books, including blurb and cover image? Do you have a directory page for your books? What about a series summary?

When you are just starting off and have one, two, or three books, they may be all contained and maintained on one page fairly easily. However, if you are reading this book on marketing, I'm guessing you are planning a career and that you will have many more books as your career continues. My advice would be to set up a structure for your books that allows you to display them in a variety of ways and combinations without you or a webmaster needing to constantly make changes in all those places.

For example, I have 20+ books available in 5 genres. I also have 4 ongoing series that will continue to have books added to them. I need to accommodate a website visitor who only wants all the information about a single book, as well as someone who wants to know about an entire series, or someone who is interested in all the books I've written.

This type of structure is best done with a website builder that uses a database (also called a content management system (CMS)) that allows you to load each book and all it's information and then include it in a variety of displays. For example, if someone clicks to look at my latest release in the Sweetwater Canyon series. She will get my book page with all the information on that book. At the bottom of that page she will also see all the books in that series and can click on any one of them to see all the information on that book.

This one capability is what requires the author to choose an actual CMS such as WordPress, Joomla, Drupal, or SquareSpace instead of a blogging platform (Blogger, Wordpress.com, and others). There are "designer" platforms like Wix and Weebly that appear to operate like a CMS, but are not a true CMS. These website building platforms work differently than a Content Management System. They do have components and applications that function as part of a CMS, but you have no control over that portion of the management system.

Though you can make blogging platforms look like a beautiful website, they are not set up as a content management system for product sales. Though you can make beautiful websites on "designer" platforms, you do not have control of the content management side and how it works.

Each website building platform handles how to do this in a different way. In WordPress, the one I know best, this is accomplished using the Portfolio Tool, which is free. There are a number of plugins that use the Portfolio Tool through a template to make it easier for you to setup and modify. You can change the way things are displayed, the number of displays, the sizes and many other parameters—including what your portfolio is called—to make it fit your needs.

If you get frustrated with configurations and having to setup new Portfolio items in the native tool, I highly recommend you use a plugin such as Novelist or My Book Table. Both of these plugins are designed for WordPress and are specific to the needs of authors needing to display their books and information associated with their books. Both plugins have a free version, so it doesn't hurt to try it out and see how you like it.

**The Novelist.** https://novelistplugin.com/

Of the two plugins, I tend to favor the Novelist plugin because of its ease of use for the non-technical user. Yet it has extensibility for those who aren't afraid to do a small amount of coding. For the nontechnical user, it provides a drag and drop template and fill-in-the form capability for each book, which allows tracking series information as well. The basic plugin is *free* and includes single book pages, series pages, an archive (All Books) page, and a way to show selected reviews or pull quotes. Along with this is lots of functionality for changing how and where things display. All for free!

One downside to the Novelist plugin is that the buy links default to a text link (e.g., Amazon, Kobo, Apple). If you prefer to use images you must download the vendor buy logo from each vendor site to your media library and then select it instead of the text link. This is not a difficult process, and the documentation provides you the link to the vendor and exactly how to do this with step-by-step screen shots. However, it would be nice if they already had them available for you.

The Novelist plugin does not have a PRO version, everything you need to get books on your website is in the FREE version. However, the developer has created four paid modules you can add for additional functionality. Those modules include: 1) ARC team management; 2) an Event Calendar; 3) the ability to integrate Goodreads data on your book pages with things like star ratings and reviews; and 4) the ability to automatically generate 3D covers of your book from a 2D cover. The cost of each of these additional modules varies from $10-$35 depending on the selected module and its complexity. If you choose to purchase all four of the additional paid modules there is a 30% discount making the entire upgrade package of four only $68, instead of $97.

**My Book Table.** http://www.authormedia.com/all-products/mybooktable/

My Book Table is a popular WordPress plugin that has been around for eight years. It was the first plugin geared toward authors and their books. It does similar things to Novelist. To me, it has an older and more formal look and feel than Novelist does. Also you can't easily change the way things are displayed on the page. My Book Table has a free version that provides the basic template for each book and short-codes for putting more than one book into a list. However, to get the added grid view to show a series or related books you must upgrade to the Pro version. In my opinion, you would not be happy with the Basic Free package. So, if you decide the way My Book Table works is preferable to you, go ahead and pay for the PRO version before you put a lot of effort into getting frustrated with what it doesn't do.

Another big downside, for me, is it does not automatically track series information to provide a grid view. You must select each book you wish to include in the grid.

One thing Book Table provides that Novelist does not is a set of native icons for approximately 20 vendor sites. In addition, it allows you to add affiliate codes so that each click will enable that affiliate code to be applied. The native icons are not the logos from each site, they are an attractive rectangle with the text name (e.g., Amazon) inside the box. The cost to upgrade to Pro is only $49.

## INCORPORATING SUBMENUS IN YOUR BOOK MENU ITEM

The other consideration for your books menu structure is how to provide a quick way to find the books of most interest to the visitor. Should you break it down by genre? By series? By themes? If you write under more than one name, you might want to have submenus with your different author names. You definitely want a link to ALL of your books in some form. It might be pictures of all the covers that then links to each book; or a simple text-based list of your books and how each book may or may not relate to a series. Some authors simply provide a link to a PDF, while others put this directly on a website page.

**Remember:** You want to make those first 5 seconds really easy for the visitor to find what they want. Because I write across multiple genres and have multiple types of products for my books, I decided to have three menu items related to my books: 1) Types of book products in the menu titled Bookshelf; 2) Books by series titles; and 3) Books by genre. Each one has a submenu to help in the navigation. In the case of the books by genre a third menu tier was needed for nonfiction and romance to further designate sub-genres. In the romance submenu, the arrow points to a third submenu where the reader may select contemporary romance, romantic suspense, or SF romance. In the nonfiction genre, the arrow points to selecting author guides or teaching and learning books. Using a third tier is actually quicker navigation than listing subgenres in one long list that may get lost.

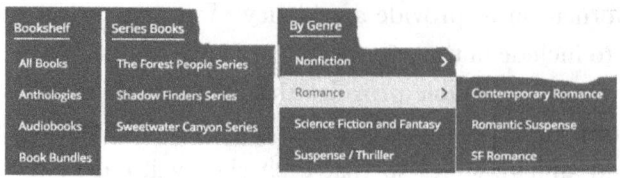

My rule of thumb is to try to keep all drop down menus under eight items. I actually prefer six items or less. In order to this, you might have to consider that third tier depending on how many books you have and how much you want to provide instant navigations for the variety of readers you attract. When submenus go beyond eight items, customers can get lost or, even worse, never see the additional items because they need to scroll beyond what is on the screen. This is especially true for people who use mobile devices like tablets and phones to look at websites.

You may not have a need for such a complex menu structure right now. However, as you continue to write and produce more books it is nice to have the availability of that kind of structure within your website that will make it easy to add when the time comes.

**About Page** – The primary purpose of the About page is to provide a brief, professional bio on your site. It should include a photo of you that you feel comfortable with other people using to represent you and your brand. This "official" bio is the same one you will want to use any time you are a guest on another site, doing face-to-face events, or having the media write about you and your work. I would recommend it not exceed 200 words, with something between 100 and 150 words being ideal.

Often the About page will also include, or link to, a media packet or press kit. The media packet is a set of downloadable images and documents that any media entity (newspapers, magazines, TV news or entertainment, etc.) might want to use as background information to create an article or introduction about you and/or your books. However, it is not just for typical media like journalists or magazine editors. It may also be requested by retailers, book bloggers, event planners, conference heads, anthology editors and other industry professionals. Anyone who is interested in promoting you and your work can benefit from this information. I will go into what's included in the press kit in detail in the next chapter.

In addition to the "official" author bio on the About page, some authors include other information about themselves, their lives, or fun facts about their past. The key is to remember that whatever you include, it should be a part of your brand story. For example, if your brand is someone who is inspirational and uplifting, then you don't want that bio or additional information to be depressing or confrontational. On the other hand, if your brand is as an advocate of a cause or an iconoclast who is proud of being an outlier, then confrontation may be your first name. Also remember "voice" when writing for this page. If your brand is writing stories or nonfiction with humor and a little snark, then that additional content should reflect that same voice.

**Mailing List Opt-In** - Do you have a sign up form for your mailing list? Do you offer a freebie incentive to anyone who signs up? How do you make it easy for someone to sign up for your mailing list or download the incentive offer?

At a minimum you want some type of form where people can provide their email address and opt-in to receive emails from you. Preferably, this form is directly connected to an email platform that you will use to automatically send these messages confirming their signup. The automation saves you having to spend your day responding to every request. (e.g., MailChimp, MailerLite, ConvertKit, Constant Contact, Aweber, Infusion Soft, etc.)

Some authors make the mailing list sign up form a menu item. This definitely makes it easy for people to find quickly. Others, use some type of website overlay or popup that appears after a specified period of time. I personally dislike popups and choose not to use them. However, there is a lot of data that shows they are effective.

Authors who are offering a free book as an incentive to provide an email may use the same techniques discussed above. An alternative to that is to have the incentive and email signup offer be the first thing that appears on the website. It might be in the header, or the first section below the header. Let's look at a couple of examples of these techniques.

*Sidebar Signup Form* – Terri Reed http://terrireed.com , Inspirational Romantic Suspense author. The advantage to this approach is that the sidebar remains on every page of this blog/author page. The disadvantage is that the form takes up little space in comparison to the primary content. It is also on a light grey background, which when contrasted with the colorful covers may be missed.

*Sign up incentive remains in header for every page* – Joanna Penn, http://thecreativepenn.com multi-genre author in fiction and nonfiction.

The big advantage to Joanna's approach is that the offer remains in the header at the top of every page on the website, reminding readers to signup yet not is not considered as obtrusive as a popup that covers important content. The one disadvantage is that if a reader already has that book or doesn't want it, she has no way to sign up for the email list and get other information she may want from the author.

On my page, http://maggielynch.com multi-genre author in fiction and nonfiction, I chose to have multiple signup incentives linked to segmented lists. I offer three books for free that I believe appeal to three different audiences. This is the first content displayed on the home page.

In this example, the potential reader is given the option of choosing to download a free book in a genre she likes. Or, if she doesn't want any of those books, she may simply sign up via a general email form link below the incentive. This is also an example of how a multi-genre author may capture a variety of readers in one spot and offer something of value to each reader.

The primary disadvantage of having everything on the home page is that the offer *only* appears on the home page. The reader is not reminded to sign up on any other page.

There is no one right way to get sign ups to your email list. The most important thing is to have a way for people to sign up and for you to capture their email for future contact.

Later in this book is an entire section, with several chapters, detailing how to setup and build a mailing list, as well as how to drive traffic to it to build your list faster.

**SEO** – SEO stands for Search Engine Optimization. Techniques for maximizing your SEO is an entire book in itself. You don't build a special menu item or a page that is titled SEO. This runs behind the scene on every page to help search engines (Google, Bing, Yahoo) find your pages more quickly.

In short, it is the ability to put in special coding, called meta tags, that tell search engines how to index that page. Without these tags, search engines index the page by reading everything and making every word equal. With meta tags, the search engines prioritize certain words—like keywords, headers, small descriptors—to be indexed first. This means when a reader puts in a one or two word search item that matches those prioritized items it is more likely your page will display close to the top.

The good news is that, depending on the website building platform you choose, some of that background tagging is already built in (e.g., page headers and the beginning of a description are put into the meta tags automatically). Some website building platforms also have special plugins or added functionality you can use to help you maximize SEO without any coding. This functionality is provided through prompts and form-fill options. Typical examples of things you can put in a form are keywords associated with the page, a specific 120 character descriptor of the page instead of it automatically taking whatever the first 120 characters that appear on your page, and to designate content as "cornerstone." The software then takes the information you provided on the form and does the coding for you on the backend so that search engines will recognize it and use it effectively.

I personally love Yoast SEO, https://yoast.com/ which provides a free plugin available to self-hosted Wordpress sites (not Wordpress.com). It provides fields to enter things like keywords and the short description. It coaches you on things to look for when completing the form, from reading level to how much your keywords match up with what is already in the text of the page. There is also functionality built in for those pages you don't want indexed in search engines like a Thank You page for taking part in a survey, or a private page you set up for a workshop but don't want the entire public to see or have access.

Of course, Yoast SEO is not the only option. There are other plugins or themes that include their own version of SEO assistance. Bottomline, if you have an option for adding a plugin you like or using some type of a checklist to enhance your SEO, I advise you take advantage of it.

If you want to have a better understanding of metadata and it's importance in search engines, be sure to read my book, **_SECRETS to Pricing and Distribution: Ebook, Print, and Direct Sales_**. (http://maggielynch.com/book/secrets-to-pricing-and-distribution-ebooks-print-and-direct-sales/) I spend a lot of time talking about book descriptions, categorization, short and long descriptions and other parts of metadata that are critical to discoverability. These same rules apply on your website.

**Contact** – A contact page usually includes a form that asks for a return email, the person's name, and then a description of what they want to discuss. This is used in lieu of providing a link to your email address. With the dominance of email scrapers and scammers on the Internet, it is not advised for you to provide your personal email on your website. It only invites spammers to start bothering you and soon you'll be wondering if you need a new email to get them to stop.

Other things authors may include on the contact page are links to various social media accounts, as well as places readers can follow you such as Goodreads, Bookbub, or Amazon. If someone else manages your intellectual property rights for you, you may wish to list them as well (e.g., your attorney or an agent). Consider making available a physical address or phone number for your business or your publisher's business. If the physical address for your business is your home, I advise getting a post office box instead. The last thing you need is sales people calling your home or sending leaflets and flyers to purchase all kinds of products.

As an independent publisher who operates completely out of my home, I use the basic contact form and my social media links. I do not provide my personal address or a P.O. Box. Depending on how your business is set up, you might wish to provide more information, or you might choose to use the contact form as a filter and then forward the information to any one else who needs to know.

**Social Media** – If you want to build engagement with your readers, you want to be sure they can quickly contact you via social media. Most websites provide links to social media through icons in the top right of the header or somewhere in the footer. I personally prefer the header because not everyone will scroll down to see the footer.

In the last two to three years, I have found that my readers and my industry contacts are much more likely to contact me via Facebook Messenger than through email these days. And people who want to know what's going on in my career tend to follow me on Facebook or Twitter. So having at least those links easily accessible is key.

**Events** – There are a variety of ways to keep visitors informed of the professional events you attend or participate in. Some people rely on posting it in social media or on their blog. Though I think this is definitely something you want to do, it is important to also have it on your website. Remember, your website is the "official" keeper of all your author happenings. Someone may have seen your twitter post about doing a book signing in their area, but two days later they have seen hundreds of other posts and forgotten where and how to find it. Your website can be the keeper of these through a calendar or some type of event functionality.

If you use something like Google Calendar on a regular basis, you can easily set up a subset of your calendar listings that you want to show on your website. Google will provide some code that you can copy and paste on an Event page you have set up. I prefer to use a plugin on my website. It allows me to enter specific information that can be display in a variety of ways (e.g., month, week, day) and as a calendar or a list.

There are hundreds of plugins available to Wordpress. I've tried four or five over the years. The one I prefer at the moment, and have been using for three years now, is called the *All-in-One Event Calendar* by Time.ly Network. https://wordpress.org/plugins/all-in-one-event-calendar/ It provides a lot of functionality with a easy user interface, while at the same time allowing for a variety of ways to display it. As with most plugins, the base calendar is free. If you want some extensibility you pay a small fee for an upgrade. Most people don't need more than the base calendar.

## Overwhelmed?

You don't need to check off all the items on this list. You definitely do not need to implement every one of them immediately. If you are just starting out, get the critical ones done first: Home, Books, and Contact. You can start with a free site and then work your way up to a paid site if you are willing to rebuild.

I prefer to use Wordpress as my platform because it has so much flexibility with thousands of plugin options. The core program, several templates, and hundreds of plugins are all free. You may also purchase more complex templates and plugins if you like. (NOTE: This is the self-hosted version of WordPress, not the wordpress.com free site) Some authors are overwhelmed by so many options and prefer a website builder that only requires a few decisions and not a lot of research into choosing among hundreds of themes and options. This is where "designer" programs like Wix and Weebly appeal to authors. It is important to take your time with this decision.

When making your selection remember to consider more than where you are at this moment. Think about where you will be in two years. Also evaluate your willingness to learn and to change. If you do not want to learn more than once, be more discerning in your choice so you make the best choice that will last you a long time. If you don't mind experimenting, giving up and rebuilding, then take a chance on whatever sounds good now and know you will likely make a different decision in a year or two.

The article below looks at Wix, Weebly, Squarespace, Go Daddy Website Builder, Jimdo, and Wordpress.

https://themegrill.com/blog/wix-vs-weebly-squarespace-godaddy-website-builder-vs-jimdo-vs-wordpress/

## USING SOMEONE TO BUILD YOUR WEBSITE FOR YOU

Because I have a technical background, I currently prefer to build my own websites and have complete control over them. However, even though I've done that for years, I have to admit I am considering handing it over to a professional in the future. I just can't afford the time to keep up with all the new technology; and websites do need to be refreshed every couple of years.

The next best thing for a control freak, whether you have technical skills or not is to hire a company or an individual web developer to do it for you. When looking at web developers consider whether you want them to design and build it, but then YOU want to maintain it. OR, if you want them to design and build it, AND keep it updated for you.

The majority of professional web developers have options for both. You pay a single fee for getting the website designed and built – ranging $400-$600 for a very basic site to several thousands of dollars for a complex site. Most authors in the middle of the career end up in the $1,500 to $2,500 range for their website.

Website maintenance rates tend to be a monthly cost ranging from $25-$50/month on the low end to $150/month at places that also include monthly promotional efforts along with general management and updates. On the high end it can be $1,000/month or more if you are running a large business site with multiple income streams and direct sales.

## WHEN YOU NEED TO HAVE A WEBSITE READY TO GO

You should have a website by the time your first book is released. You should have a mailing list set up and be gathering names from the time you announce to the world that you are writing a book. Beyond that, any other marketing, other than having a regular brand presence on social media, is not worth your time. I mean you should have an FB biz page and a Twitter account, but I would just schedule general branding posts.

**Coming Soon Books.** If you KNOW you can deliver on books in a regular timeframe, I strongly suggest you also put up your COMING

SOON books--particularly if you are writing in series. This is especially important when you are starting out and only have one book out.

Readers are very reluctant to pick up a new author with only one book. They are even more reluctant to pick up that book when they know it is the first in a series and you don't have any other books available. You can gain a SLIGHT edge by posting your next book cover(s) and giving them a blurb with a timeline for release. It doesn't have to be exact dates (I tend to use seasonal release timelines if it is more than three to four months out, like Fall 2018). Doing this helps the reader to believe you are professional and that it will happen. Some readers will go ahead and buy that first book knowing the next book release is not far away. Better yet, if you REALLY have an exact schedule, put that book on pre-order with a link. You can do that with most vendors up to 90 days out. Pre-order definitely telegraphs to the reader that the next book is real and ready to go.

***Tip*:** Do NOT do this if you really don't know that you can make that deadline. If you do have it on pre-order, some vendors (like Amazon) will take away your ability to pre-order if you don't deliver on time. Even if you don't have it on pre-order, your reader may forgive a couple months delay. However, if you said Fall 2017 and the book doesn't come out until Fall 2018 they will have forgotten you or decided they can't trust you.

## HOW TO DECIDE WHICH WEBSITE DEVELOPER OR COMPANY TO CHOOSE

The best thing to do is to ask other authors whose sites you like. Some authors put their website developer's name and link in the bottom of the page. Many do not. If an author is happy with her website, she will usually be happy to share who did it for her.

If you are paying for someone, you want to get a Content Management System (CMS). I would not hire someone to develop a WIX or Weebly site for example, nor a straight HTML site. If you are paying out money you want to invest in a CMS.

If you are non-technical, it may seem overwhelming to choose someone to do something you don't understand yourself. I've known many authors—a few of them well-known bestselling authors—who have been bamboozled by someone who talks the jargon but doesn't really know what he/she is doing. Some of them paid out thousands of dollars before they realized something wasn't working right. Price is NOT directly correlated to expertise. I've seen some beautiful, well-designed websites for $600-$800 and some absolutely horribly designed websites for $2,500 and vice versa.

It pays to do your research. Web designers are good at putting up pretty pictures of their designs. But you want to be able to go from that picture to the actual website and test it out yourself. Make sure the menu is easy to navigate and that every page goes somewhere. Make sure you aren't getting lost or thrown out of the system. Make sure the websites that developer creates have the look and feel that you want.

If you go to a website (e.g., maggielynch.com) and find that the design on the site is different from the design on the portfolio page of the web designer, it is then time to contact that author. Ask if they hired someone different or went back to the same person for an update. Ask some pointed questions about what they liked or didn't like about working with that person. Often, when an author changes designers it's because they learn that it could have been better—that the skills of the first designer were not as good as they thought.

Do NOT hire any web designer to be paid by the hour. Always get a finished bid that details what is included in the design and the timeline. Here are important elements typically included in a web design contract:

**Domain** –Who supplies the domain and where is it registered. This is the actual name of your site (e.g., maggielynch.com) Some authors smartly register a domain as soon as they have their name(s) available. Others ask their website design company to do this for them. Be sure that YOU are the owner of the domain. If you aren't, you are tied to that designer forever. Sometimes that can make it very difficult to move hosts, designers, or take control back for whatever reason.

**Authorization** to undertake the work. Some contracts call this a "Statement of Work" where they summarize what will be done and in what timeframe.

**Included elements** – most developers have certain standard packages and related pricing. Some create every package individually based on the client's needs. Minimums to look for are:

- *Consultation time.* This is the number of hours dedicated to talking to you in advance of the design and during the design. Typically, this ranges from one to two hours in most contracts.
- *Number of pages included in design.* Most base packages begin with a five-page design—home, about, books, news, and contact. If you want more than those five pages, be sure they are articulated in the contract.
- *Menu structure.* How many menu items are included and is there submenu navigation as well. Typically the number of menu items reflects the number of pages included. However, you also want to know exactly how this menu will look. Are there drop-down submenus? What about tertiary menus?
- *Words or text content.* How many words per page are expected and who supplies them? Typically, you are the one responsible for deciding what goes on each page. A good designer will give you some guidelines on how many words is the norm. Some web designers, for higher priced packages, will include an editor or marketer who writes or reviews your text and makes recommendations on the best way to attract readers.
- *Links to external pages.* These are links to pages outside your website. For example linking to: your publisher's page if you are traditionally published; buy pages (Amazon, Nook, Kobo, Google, etc); an external multi-author blog you might participate in; courses or workshops you teach through another company; and anything else that exists outside your website.
- *Custom graphics package.* Some website designers have very basic templates and you choose the template you want to use. The masthead is your name or perhaps a small logo.

Other designers offer a personally built graphic look. This might include only a personalized masthead graphic or it might include a larger graphic that serves as the background.

- The graphics package should detail on which pages the graphics will appear and exactly what the graphic or several graphics are included. My personal page (maggielynch.com) has a masthead graphic. That graphic appears on every page of my website. Here is an example of an author with a personalized graphic look and feel beyond the masthead. http://www.jenniferniven.com/ Notice that the menu items are unique—not just words—and that the fonts and display are unique to the quirky, vintage woman look of her site.
- *Number of photos and other images.* Many web designers detail how many photos or images they will include in the package. Typically this is one per page. So, for a five page package you are allowed five photos. If you plan to use a lot more images be sure that number is covered in your package price. Otherwise, paying $10 or $25 for every photo on a page can add up really quickly.
- *Search engine listings.* Most designers guarantee to list your website with the major search engines. This involves providing a "site map" and the location of your site to be indexed. Be sure the specific search engines are designated. Though Google is the biggest, they are not the only ones.
- *Email response link.* You want to have a link to your email list. Is the web designer going to set this up for you or is that your responsibility? Be sure it is clearl in the contract.

**Installation of the website**. Most designers prefer to install your website for you. However, this means giving them credentials to do this. Make sure it is clear where the content for your website resides. Is it on a server where YOU are paying to host it and have control over moving it or cutting access to your designer? These are big hosting companies like HostGator, BlueHost, DreamHost, GoDaddy and hundreds of others. Or is your website hosted on your designers server? This means your designer has full control over it and if you decide to go elsewhere you need to move it from that person's control. If your designer IS hosting it on his/her server, what is the monthly charge to you for that service?

**E-commerce installation** (if needed). If you are going to handle sales from your website and need to process the payments and deliver the books, you need some type of e-commerce installation. Most authors don't do this at the beginning of their career, and many never do it. However, some authors do go this route after they have a decent fan following and see the economic benefits of driving traffic to their own site.

E-commerce installation is an advanced skill. If you want this capability you want to be sure your designer has not only done this for many other businesses, but specifically done it for authors. Unlike setting up e-commerce for a clothing store where it is a product that is shipped to a physical address, authors need to deliver their product electronically AND support that delivery with a download that goes smoothly every time. If the reader needs assistance getting that download to his/her device, who is going to provide that assistance? Preferably not you.

**Site Maintenance.** Most designers charge a monthly or annual fee to do the maintenance for you. This includes all backend maintenance like upgrades to core programs, plugins, and security. It also should include how many changes per month are included in the charge. How many pages, text, new books can be made before an hourly rate kicks in.

**Completion Date.** When will the website go live? Be sure you have a date detailed. Do not leave it at something ambiguous like "about 3 months." Think of this like building a house. You would never let a builder work on it without a date you can move in. It is the same for your website.

**Approval Process.** Once the designer has completed the website what is the approval process? Is it all or nothing or are so many changes allowed without paying extra? How much time are you allowed to request changes. How much time does the designer have to complete the changes once the request has been made?

**Fee Payment structure.** Most designers require some percentage of the design costs up front, just to get started. Then the remainder due on completion. For more complex sites, there may be interim payment schedules based on percent of completion.

**Copyrights.** Who owns the design, the images, the text? You or the developer? You should own all of the above. You are paying the developer to create it with your content, your images, your text. Even if you didn't generate it, you will have paid them as a contractor—work for hire—to create it for you. Do not sign a contract where the designer owns any of the copyright on YOUR site.

**Termination of the relationship.** Should you decide to leave for any reason, what is the process to terminate the relationship? So many days notice? In addition, what if the designer decides to terminate the relationship, how much notice will you get? Designers go out of business all the time or decide they want to use their skills as a paid employee instead of a freelancer. You need to be sure the termination clause is understood on both sides.

Included in this clause should also be information about **Passwords, Access, and Transfer protocols.** Be sure that you get all administrative passwords and website access information, including any backend access and information about related site access (e.g., domain registration, hosting outside the designer's company) that you may need to manage the site should you decide to no longer use this company. In fact, you should request this up front and always make sure it is updated in your personal file you keep at home. **Be sure there is some agreement language about *cooperative* transfers** (or at least not blocking a transfer), so that you do not have to rebuild from scratch should you decide to take your website elsewhere.

Outside of the contract itself, you also want to get a feel for the person who will be your primary contact. Do you feel comfortable talking to that person? Does he/she take time to answer your questions in a way you can understand? Are they willing to share references and contacts. Just like you would an employee, ask what they perceive as their own strengths and weaknesses. Don't accept that they have no weaknesses. Everyone does, and you want to be sure you are aware of them.

If you feel "dumb" whenever you get off the phone, or out of a meeting with this person or company, it is not a good fit for you. Even if you are the least technical person on the planet, the job of your contractor is to make sure you have enough understanding of what is going on to make sure the website you receive really meets your needs. Someone who uses language like, "It's too technical for you to understand, but trust me I'll make it right." is someone you don't want to use.

If you are evaluating several designers or companies, consider the following questions to ask the developer or design team. Remember, YOU are the boss and they are your contractor for whatever period of time you decide to use them. The last thing you need is someone who can't communicate, may not have the skills to do the job, doesn't deliver on time, or is always adding more costs to a job after you had a fixed price contract. These questions may give you some insight into their expertise and if it matches your needs.

**Ask: "Which CMS (Content Management System) do you use to develop?"** – As stated previously, there are many systems in play from Wordpress to Joomla that are open source, as well as proprietary platforms such as Expression Engine. Some larger firms may develop in multiple platforms. Most companies that are run by an individual or a two to three-person firm, tend to focus on one particular CMS (e.g., Wordpress). Make sure that whatever is their specialty is the platform you want. If it is something not familiar to you, take the time to research it and see how many other developers use it. You do NOT want a proprietary platform that is difficult to be moved to another company should things not work out or this team go out of business.

**How many websites have you developed with your chosen CMS?**—Prices tend to be lower with newer people or companies because they are building their portfolio. However, you don't want to be the first person they use to figure out their process. Even new computer science graduates have developed at least four or five basic sites as class projects.

**How many websites have you developed for authors?**— Though any good developer can create a website for an author, they don't know our industry and what are the norms in terms of display, SEO, or the look and feel of pages. If you feel confident in what you want and that YOU know the industry, then go ahead and hire someone who has never developed an author page knowing that you will be educating them. If you do not feel comfortable with your own knowledge, and are hoping the web developer will help educate you, then it is best to choose a developer who has developed a variety of websites specifically for authors.

**Are you good at customizing templates and at what cost?**—All developers use templates for their sites—whether a standard few they've designed from scratch or purchased templates from a template vendor. The reason for this is because it saves a lot of time in development and helps them to cut costs and be competitive in the market. However, you probably don't want to look exactly like everyone else. Though anyone, even a design novice, can customize a template by trial and error. There are technical trade offs (like slowing down the system or opening a security hole) if they don't know what they are doing. There is also a risk of losing all changes when the base template is updated if the customization exited outside of the template. A good, professional developer will know how to do the customization to avoid those problems.

**What is your knowledge of server hosting and/or management?** –Servers are the platform on which websites reside. If you are considering having a web developer host your site on their own servers, you want to be sure those sites are secure, can serve pages quickly, and that they know how to take care of common problems—particularly server updates. If you are going to pay separately for hosting your pages (e.g., on GoDaddy, DreamHost, HostGator and many others), your web developer will still need access to the hosting company and its servers to test and install your website effectively. Ask if they are familiar with that particular webhost.

**How well do you know CSS?**—CSS is a scripting language that developers use to put consistent rules around the design of your site. For example, you want your font type, color, and size to be consistent from page to page. You don't want Times New Roman for content on one page and then Lucida Handwriting on another. Additional common items, like buttons, should also be presented consistently in size, color and font. The color(s) of your header and footer background, which pages get different headers, or even whether certain content is contained inside a framed box or not are all parts of CSS. Even the consistent placement of images on a page can all be defined or changed through CSS.

Though most CMS platforms provide some of this out of the box, you may want to make some changes that fit your brand. For example, you may want a color scheme of light to dark browns with a pop of sage green for certain instances. Another author may prefer a color scheme of reds and oranges even though she uses a similar design. You want to be sure your web designer has a good handle on this. All of that is done through CSS to be consistent and to serve the pages faster. Anyone web designer should be able to do this. But some people who develop primarily from templates, may not have this capability well in hand.

**How does your design handle the diversity of ways consumers look at sites from desktops to laptops to tablets and phones in your design?**—With the ubiquitous nature of mobile devices in use these days, it is critical that your web developer knows how to make your site look good no matter the device. In addition, search engines (particularly Google) will push down site ranks for any site that is not mobile ready. Most designs call this "responsive"—meaning that a single site will automatically resize and present different menu options for the different display environments. Some designers—particularly for really large sites—may decide to use a separate website just for all mobile needs. This means they build an internal query whenever someone logs on and then sends them to the website that fits their device. If the designer is taking the latter approach be sure to get the reasoning for that approach. It will definitely be more costly than the all-in-one approach with a responsive design.

**What other skills do you and your team bring to the table?** —Answers may be varied, but some additional skills that I would consider important are:

- Graphic design, unless you just want a basic name header and no other graphics on the site
- SEO as it relates to authors
- Javascript—which is the language most often used for special routines that need to be integrated with third party applications (e.g., for YouTube videos to display, or your opt-in form from your mail provider, or a quick poll)
- Marketing expertise—to understand techniques for building a website that draws readers in and makes them want to stay and purchase

The list can be endless. Part of what you are looking for here is how you might be able to grow with this company. Because investing in a good website is costly, you might hope to stay with this company as your career grows. What you need/want from a website design when you have two or three books is very different from what you need/want when you have twenty books or more.

## Chapter Six
# YOUR MEDIA PACKET / PRESS KIT

As I indicated earlier, your media packet or press kit is something you will use over and over again. Even if you never get an interview for a newspaper or magazine, taking the time to build this is invaluable. You will use it on guest posts, blog bios, in every media that asks for you to do an author profile.

Also, remember this is NOT set in stone. This is a living, breathing document that you will review regularly, add to (particularly book pages), and rewrite as your career grows. For example, when you are just starting out with your first book, your bio is going to reflect your pre-author life as much as your author life. I remember my first bio talked about the career I had while writing my first few books. It focused on my non-fiction publications, even though I was writing mostly fiction.

Now my bio is able to provide numbers of books published to show I'm not a one or two book author. Sometimes, I also include a wonderful pull quote or short review that fits my brand and is very positive about my writing. Later in your career you may also have specific awards or bestseller status you can tout. Though my books have received awards, they are not national ones or ones that are recognizable to the general reading public so I don't mention them. And I'm still waiting to hit a bestseller list outside of Amazon.

Let's take a look at the variety of elements that should be in your press kit.

## CONTACT INFORMATION AND BIO

Your contact information should include:

- Full name
- E-mail address
- Phone number
- Website
- Links to your social media accounts (Twitter, Facebook, Instagram, etc.)
- If you have an agent, manager, or publicist, their information should go here as well.

You should also include a high-resolution, professional headshot in a downloadable image folder. A good size would be around 1500 x 2100 pixels at 300 DPI. Don't forget the 300 DPI as that is print quality.

**Author Bio**

This is actually a series of four bios, written in different lengths to **make the media's job easy**. If you provide only one long bio, journalists and others who need just a short paragraph about you must wade through your bio, find what they need, and write it to the word count they need. This slows them down. And there's **no guarantee** that what they write will be accurate or that the sections they choose are the part of your bio you want to emphasize.

Include an "Author Bio" sheet with bios, all written in the **third person**, in these four sizes:

- **Two-line bio.** This should be 140 characters which, coincidentally, is the maximum size of a Tweet. Why so

short? Because if someone wants to tweet a description about you, you've already written it. Also, a two-line bio might be all you're allowed in the author resource box if you write an article for a magazine.
- **Short Bio** (50 words). This is ideal for longer author resource boxes. Concentrate on your expertise or sales (if large) or awards.
- **Medium bio** (100 words). Include everything in the short bio. Include your most noteworthy accomplishments.
- **Long bio** (400 to 600 words). Write an overview of your life and writing career. Include everything in the medium bio. You can use this to tell a story.
- **Speaker introduction.** This is very helpful for meeting planners and others who invite you to speak. **Never let them write your introduction.** Insist that they read the one you provide. Write up to 300 words.
- **5 Fun Facts You didn't Know About Me.** These can include trivia from your personal or business life, unusual hobbies or travels, or anything that will give readers a glimpse into your personality. You can write more than five, if you wish.

## PRODUCT DESCRIPTION (BOOK)

If you are pitching a specific book that is launching, you need to have a complete one-sheet for that book. This sheet includes your book cover. (Note: High definition book cover images should also be included in the image folder I mentioned above) Below your cover add the following information:

- Title
- Author
- Publication date
- Available at (*list retailers both online and in print*)
- ISBN (*include both your e-book and paperback*)
- Retail price (*include both your e-book and paperback*)

- Page count
- Genre/subgenre (*This should match the categorization you provided when you uploaded the book to a distributor. e.g. contemporary romance, spy thriller, urban fantasy*)

Write a blurb for the book in four different lengths. These should be in the third person. Lengths are a two-line summary (think in terms of a tweet), a short summary (no more than 100 words, a long summary (no more than 400 words). Consider what the book has to offer, the most compelling parts of the story, or the niche the book serves. Write short and pointed sentences that are appropriate for a general audience, and pitch your book in as few words as needed.

**Series One-Sheets:** If you are just starting out, you can do this for each book. If you are already well into multiple books and series, you might consider doing a Series one-sheet instead. That would display all the books in a series with a link to the full book description on your website. Instead of writing summaries of each book you would write a summary of the series in the four lengths described above and include reviews or pull quotes that relate to the entire series.

## PROMOTIONAL INFORMATION

This section can be any number of things. But it's essentially everything you have that can be used as promotional material. If you have sales copy from email campaigns, print campaigns, and social media campaigns you can include copies of those here in PDF form. These typically include taglines, headers to grab the reader's attention. You can format the PDF with a sample image from a Facebook post, a tweet, etc. And then a brief one line description of what kind of campaign that was used in. If you've done successful ads, you may already have something like this to use.

Book Awards and Honors should also be included in the Promotions section. If your book earned a starred review from a reputable source like Publisher's Weekly, Kirkus Reviews, BookLife, Midwest Book Reviews, Library reviews and others like genre-specific recognized sources such as Ellery Queen and Romantic Times can also be included here.

If you don't have these kind of reviews, don't worry. Use some great pull quotes from the reviews you do have.

## PRESS RELEASE

This is a one-page pitch of everything in your press kit. It should be target-specific (this means geared toward the entity you are targeting: newspaper, magazine, organization) and include all of the relevant information that both readers and book buyers need. Include contact information, a headline and subhead.

Start with the **most interesting aspect** regarding you or the book. For example if you are sending a press release to your local paper, you may want to start with the words "Local author releases..." Local papers like pointing out local people. Think of how you can tie your expertise or your book to something that people in the community can recognize. Sometimes that might be a question followed by your connection. "Can you imagine that dragons live under the Hawthorne bridge? Local author, Maggie Lynch, does just that in her latest release, *There Be Dragons*." This YA novel is the first in a series of ..." In this example we have a local author connection, the book takes place in a city the paper covers. If you are involved in your community through volunteer or professional work, be sure to mention that as well. Local newspapers and magazines depend on local advertisers, and any time they can mention those networks they are happy to point it out.

Remember, you are writing all of this in third person, as if you are the reporter on the story. Include a quote from the author (you). It can include why you wrote the book, what you hope readers will experience, or some other tidbit that conveys your excitement and your brand. If you are writing non-fiction your quote might include what readers will learn or the types of advice included in the book and why you are the expert to provide it. Include a **call to action** with a link to a website where readers can buy the book.

## INTERVIEW QUESTIONS

Most journalists, broadcasters and bloggers who want to interview you **will not have time to read your book.** That's why they will welcome a list of interview questions. They won't necessarily limit the interview to those questions, but the list will provide a handy springboard that will help them start the conversation. Be sure to include a combination of questions about you as a person, as well as about your book.

The reality is the vast majority of interviewers will NOT read your book. To help them sound as if they did read your book, prepare your questions to sound like they did. In other words, give a hint as to an interesting answer is expected. Below are a couple of examples on how to rewrite a question so that it makes the interviewer look informed.

*Very basic question:*
"What inspired you to write this particular book."
*Better question:*
"Your book deals with some challenging topics including PTSD and the use of biogenetics and human trials, what was your inspiration for that?"
*Very basic question:*
"Why did you choose to use a child in this book?"
*Better question:*
"The child in this is book is both hidden from the world and the central plot device for much of the action. Were you ever concerned about potential pushback from readers by having a child in harms way in this book?"

Both the basic and better questions get at the same responses. However, the better question provides the interviewer with something that shows deeper knowledge and suggests something really interesting will be in the response. It also helps you to prepare and focus on the most interesting answers (even to a basic question) that you want to give—ones that highlight important themes, challenges, complications that will make the reader/listener pay attention and more likely go look for your book.

## BOOK REVIEW EXCERPTS

You should be asking for book reviews **before you launch the book.** When you get them, choose excerpts from the best ones and compile them in a sheet along with basic information about the book. These excerpts might sway a journalist to write about you. Or they might prompt someone to buy your book and maybe even write a review.

## ADDITIONAL PHOTOS AND MEDIA LINKS

In items above I talked about setting up an image folder where you would include high-resolution images for download. Though you will also have the images included in the one-sheets, it is important to also provide them in this folder so that they can be included and resized as needed for anything printed or put on the web.

In addition to your headshot, it is good to provide a few environmental shots that show you in a variety of settings. For example, a cookbook might include photos of you in the kitchen, whipping up a favorite dish, or shopping at a local farmer's market. If your books tend to be dark and suspenseful, you might consider a picture of you in that type of setting (look at the two different pictures of Nora Roberts for her romances vs her darker J.D. Robb books). Small newspapers, newsletters and bloggers will welcome these photos that are different than the usual headshot. Both print and online media are tending to move away from headshots to photos that show the author's personality, making the reader feel the person is more accessible.

Include links to any other media that might be interesting to the press, (e.g., book trailers, video interviews, you reading an excerpt). Newspapers, reviewers, interviewers are all looking for good media to share with their audience on social media too. Just remember that whatever you include should match your persona/branding and present you in the way you want your readers to see you.

## TITLE PAGE

Once you've completed all the sections in your press kit, you need to create a title page and an index to the sections to make it easy for someone to navigate. On the Title Page put your name and contact information. If you have a tagline or some pithy descriptions to encapsulate who you are as an author, include those on the title page as well. That might be something like USA Today Bestselling Author, or some other bestseller moniker if you have that. Or some type of major, recognizable award winner. If you are like most of us, without bestseller status or awards, include two or three review quotes that highlight you as much as your book.

After the title page, create a table of contents for each section.

Finally, once everything is compiled put it on your website with links to the sections AND create a PDF with the entire media kit and the table of contents to make it easy to download, study, and share.

**Remember, your media kit doesn't have to be perfect!**

Your press kit doesn't have to be complicated or fancy. The people who are requesting it are looking for easy to read information to help them put together a story. Keep the format and font simple. No need to add fancy graphics, sidebars, or other elements. You are marketing yourself and your brand, so think of it as marketing copy—short, quotable points and potential headline leads that can be copy and pasted into articles.

If you're putting one together for the first time, you probably already have some of the materials needed like your bio and book blurbs. Start with the items you already have and see if you can hone the writing to be brief, clear, and yet interesting. Always think in terms of quotes you would like to see about you and your work. Then work on adding the other materials mentioned above as you have time to create them. You do not want to be in the position of having to create a press kit at the last minute for the editor, reviewer, or librarian who requests one.

Set up a schedule for reviewing your press kit at least annually. If you are prolific, writing three or more books per year, you might want to do reviews every quarter to make sure new material has been included. If you are just starting out, definitely set up a quarterly review and work on adding one more section of information that perhaps you didn't have before.

Having a media kit is helpful to you in many aspects of your career. Not only do you now have the materials ready to go when booksellers, librarians, journalists, interviewers request it, but you have honed descriptions of yourself and your books that you will use everywhere in your career. Landing pages, your personal website, guest blogs will all need one or more parts of this kit. You've now compiled all of your pertinent marketing materials in one simple document for easy access as you build your own advertising campaigns in the future.

## Chapter Seven
# YOUR BLOG

Blogging has been around for at least twenty years. It started in the mid 1990's when people could create a "homepage" and post their thoughts. It was all done in HTML until some type of editor was created. Around 1997-1998 the first "weblog" was created—Live Journal. It was shortened to the term "blog." In 1999 the precursor to Blogger appeared, and soon after other platforms sprung to life. Blogger is credited with bringing the blog to mainstream by providing a better experience for non-technical writers. By 2001, Moveable Type and WordPress were emerging.

To say that blogging has become a juggernaut is an understatement. In 1999, according to a list compiled by Jesse James Garrett, there were 23 blogs on the Internet. The most popular ones were either technical, futuristic or political. Just seven years later, by mid 2006, there were over 50 million blogs. It is now a decade later and the estimate is there are over 480 million blogs on the major platforms—WordPress, Blogger, Squarespace. This doesn't even include micro-blogging platforms like Tumblr with its 330 million alone.

We do know that content is being consumed online more widely, more quickly, and more voraciously than ever before. As of this writing, WordPress stats alone indicate that 91.8 million posts are published on WordPress blogs every month, and more than 409 million people view 22.3 billion blog pages each month. https://wordpress.com/activity/ There are many other platforms in addition to WordPress.

It easy to look at those stats and say a swear word while wondering how you can possibly compete with this gazillions of words every month. That is a good question, actually. The key is to remember that no one reaches these billions of readers with one blog. It is your job to find that slice of those blog readers that will be interested in what you have to say. This means your blog needs to be focused, consistent, and as professional as possible. That doesn't mean formal or boring. It does means your blog needs to be consistent, well-written, and delivering interesting articles.

In the past couple of years there has been a lot of discussion around the efficacy of blogging for authors. It takes a lot of time to do it well, and the question is if that time would be better spent writing the next book. Does anyone actually sell books because they have a good blog following? The answer is most do not get sales from blog followers. However, some people do.

There are lots of opinions on the efficacy of blogs for books. People tend to fall into two camps.

**Camp 1:** Whether you like it or not you must blog for reasons of platform building, providing critical additional SEO for search engines, and to provide a place where your fans, who like to read longer articles, can be in touch with you.

**Camp 2:** The blog is dead. Enough said.

**Maggie's Camp:** Hogwash on both of them. I don't believe that any one platform is a MUST for any author. The only must for an author is you must write and publish books. Everything else is up for grabs depending on the career you want, the time you have, and what you actually enjoy doing. If you see that writing blog articles is taking up precious time you need to finish a book, then don't do it! If you love it, or see it is a break from your book but still fitting your brand, then go for it.

The idea the blog is dead is ludicrous. Every time new technology comes along, an entire group of articles appear saying whatever was before is now dead. When television started growing, the headlines read that Radio is dead. Well, it's been more than 70 years and radio is still around. In the last decade there has been a lot of proclamations that print books are dead because of ebooks. To the contrary, people keep buying those darn print books. In fact, for books they really want they will even purchase hardback versions.

Those who say: "The blog is dead" are the same group who quickly abandon a media platform for the most recent social media fad. This group of pundits believe the blog died when Facebook became popular. Facebook died when Twitter came on the scene. Both Twitter and Facebook will soon be dead because of YouTube. YouTube will be dead because of ... you name the latest fad. It is true that online technology ebbs and flows about as fast as the waves crash at the ocean. But it takes decades for something to die. More often, a particular platform will give way to something similar that has added new features or better meets the needs of users. Remember MySpace? MySpace as a way to communicate didn't really die. It gave way to a similar platform, Facebook. Video blogging (vlogs), Instagram, Snapchat, Vine Videos, Tumblr. All these platforms address a specific need that isn't addressed by the others (e.g., shorter, faster, less or more summarized information). On the other extreme, I wouldn't be surprised to see a new magazine creator that takes blogs, based on tags, and automatically collates it into a magazine that you can then name, catalog, and archive or sell.

## BLOGS ARE NOT ONLY FOR NONFICTION AUTHORS

For nonfiction authors, blogging can be critical to building their platform. Nonfiction relies more on platform and expertise than fiction. If you are writing a book about the impact of the environment on health, you are going to be picked up much more easily if you are a physician or an environmental researcher, or had a substantial career in dealing with environmental issues. If your background fits none of these, you need to prove to the wider public why you should be trusted as an expert on this subject. One of the ways to do that is through blogging.

Even if you are a physician or environmental researcher, if you are not a well-known expert or a celebrity, you may still wish to do regular blogging. To prove expertise, a blogger tends to write small articles around the topic of their book and build up a good following. If you do this *before* the book is released, you can build up credibility and a good following so that when the book releases you have a built-in audience. Even better, if you start blogging well before you write your book, you can use all the work you put into those articles as a great start for writing a book on the topic.

A number of successful nonfiction authors have actually begun their careers as a blogger, and then realized they have generated so much content it could make a book. It some ways, blogging seems more natural for the nonfiction author. Most nonfiction writers have been churning out articles for years. Research summaries, position papers, discussions on new ideas. It isn't that hard for a nonfiction writer to turn out one more article—this one geared toward the general public instead of another scientist or expert.

Almost every author, both fiction and nonfiction, is told that blogging is good for them. That it is critical for building a platform. Unfortunately, the vast majority of authors fail miserably at this task because the use their blog like any other social media. That is they post disconnected memes, images, cat pictures, kid pictures, or comments on the holidays with none of it relating to their writing. The other thing authors often do is post about their writing journey. Again, maybe interesting to them and a few writer friends, but meaningless to their brand UNLESS they are writing nonfiction about the writer's journey.

I've been this person in my blogs. One who follows edicts shared with me from other authors who picked it up from other authors or a web search somewhere. I had a blog called "Maggie's Meanderings" for a number of years that was really me talking about whatever I felt like discussing. It ranged from my journey, to cool technology, to the occasional my next book is coming out, and even to some sharing of what was going on in my personal life. My blog title was fitting. I really was meandering. Even with a mailing list of hundreds, only about ten people tuned in regularly. Not even my mother read it. In fact, no one other than those people who already knew and liked me cared one wit about what I was sharing.

## WHY DO PEOPLE BELIEVE THEY MUST HAVE A BLOG?

It is in the mistaken belief that the more you post around the web the better off you are. This belief is carried even further to suggest that posting anything is better than nothing. Perhaps that was true fifteen years ago, when I started writing books in the late 1990's. I'm not sure. I was writing nonfiction for a traditional publisher and social media, as we know it didn't exist. Blogging was the "new fangled" way to communicate with large audiences.

In any case, it certainly is NOT true now. Readers have a plethora of ways to get information about you, your book, your beliefs, your expertise and the expertise of those who surround you. Competing with that immediate, short form media via a long-form communication vehicle is very, very difficult. The only way to do that is to add true substance that cannot be scanned and digested more quickly. In other words, why should a blog about your cats when I can see a quick picture or a two line post about it on Facebook, Twitter, Instagram, SnapChat, Pinterest..you get the picture.

Blogging is, and has always been, an art form in itself. It is a form that presents interesting information in short articles that are accessible to the public. Notice I used the word "articles" not posts. The difference between blog posts and all other social media is that it is a longer form. To get any decent SEO you need at least 300 words. Most good blog posts fall in the 300-800 word range. Many print and online magazine articles fall in that word count as well, most averaging 500-800 words.

If you think of a blog as writing articles, that means you should give it the same serious attention to topic and structure as you would do writing an article for pay. You should also apply all of your style and writing craft with the creation of each post, just as you would pay attention to a chapter in a book. Yes, a blog post may be less formal, and definitely more brief or compressed, than a book chapter.

However, if you treat it as something you can dash off without much thought—something that is less important—then it is highly likely it will be a waste of your time and your reader's time. Readers will check it out a few times, but then give up.

Just like book writing, editing, and distribution, blogging takes practice and skills at writing concise articles with the right hooks and triggers to draw people in. Also, just like creating books, you have to stick with blogging long enough for it to pay off—minimally a year, practically more like three to five years. In other words, you have to really enjoy this longer form writing required by blogs to keep doing it.

Blogging falls almost 100% in the PR category. It is building your brand, proving your promise for delivering an experience. It rarely results in a sale—unless you are writing nonfiction. And even then, not much.

## WHAT IS MOST IMPORTANT ABOUT BEING A GOOD BLOGGER?

**Planning.** I would guess that close to 90% of people who start a blog have no plan at all. That was certainly my situation when I was told I needed a blog and I could talk about anything I wanted. That readers just wanted to get to know me. I didn't know what to post, how often to post, or who the posts were targeted at. Consequently, though I tried to post weekly, often several weeks would go between posts, my topics were all over the place, and getting above 100 readers on a regular basis was nearly impossible. As if it wasn't obvious I didn't really know what to do, my blog name was "Maggie's Meanderings." At least I was honest about the content.

Only 5% of people who may follow your blog ever comment. It is consistent topic and contents that get you ranked in search engines and makes it easier for people who might be interested in your blog to find it and read it.

Focus on what your audience is already searching for. If you are nonfiction blogger, you may already know what the most asked questions are on your topic. Start with those first. If you are a fiction blogger, think about what happens when you meet a fan face-to-face, or a potential reader at a book signing or other event. What are their most asked questions?

Use a calendar to strategically plan your blog posts to include topics that are the most useful, relevant, and desired by your reader. Focus on your core message and brand with each post. You might consider calendaring according to types of content (e.g., teaching vs experiencing). If you are blogging twice a week, I would plan a minimum of one month in advance. Put up the posts to be scheduled to appear a month later. In that way, if while you are planning you find something that should come earlier you still have some leeway to put it in and reschedule. If you can, plan out your blog posts for a six-month period and then revisit. At two times per week, that would be scheduling out 52 posts in advance. It is much easier to sit down and write to a predefined topic, than it is to sit down and try and decide what your blog post should be tomorrow. Also, by scheduling in advance you can control the mood, the hooks, the satisfaction and build interest over a longer period of time.

**Referencing other blogs and articles.** Spread a little link love by referencing additional helpful articles on the topic you've covered. Use quotes and materials and credit the author by linking directly to their article. No one can be an expert on everything, nor can you fulfill every need of your followers. Carefully chosen references increase the value of your post and get you some good Karma in return for your generosity.

**Clear presentation and formatting.** Use short paragraphs, lists, and bullet points within your article. This helps break up the content and visually draw the reader's attention to critical points. Have at least one image. Make sure the image ties in with the headline. If you have several images within your post, choose one that is the featured image. By doing that, when people share the blog, the featured image is shared with it.

Though blogs are the longest form of most social media—some of the best blogs regularly go up to 2,000 words—they are still frequently scanned by followers. You want to make it easy for your readers to find the content they need. If everything is packed in long paragraphs without white space or images to quickly make sense of the content, they are more likely to skip it.

Ensure the text is easy to read. I like 14 point Times New Roman. No small or fancy fonts. I know a number of writers who think a handwriting font is great because it looks like a handwritten letter. Please don't do that. Those fonts are notoriously difficult to read at any length. Also, contrast between the background and text is critical. Black fonts on white background is the easiest to read. I know that various shades of grey are all the rage, but the lighter the grey the smaller your audience becomes. In addition to people with chronic low vision, there are a lot of baby boomers (like me) who read a lot of books and have a hard time focusing on light grey fonts. Whatever you do, do not try dark backgrounds with light text (e.g., black with white text or yellow text). Also, please don't use picture backgrounds with text. Seeing any font within the business of a background image is a recipe for disaster in terms of building or keeping a large audience.

Make sure all links actually connect to the appropriate material. Don't add a bunch of irrelevant links or mediocre links just to get extra SEO for linking up with someone. Your readers will soon realize not to trust you on sources or your links.

## HEADLINES ARE YOUR READER DRAW

Learning to write great headlines is a skill that will serve you in ALL your marketing efforts, not just blogging. You will need headline skills for tweets, for Facebook posts, for advertising, for blogging, and for your email campaigns. A boring or unclear headline guarantees a poor response and likely little to no engagement.

**Remember:** Readers scan until they find something interesting. Then, and only then, to they stop and read. The headline is their first contact with your post. It is also what is automatically picked up in search engines. It needs to be accurate, yet interesting. It needs to deliver a promise of value if someone takes the time to read further. According to Kissmetrics only 20% of people who read your headline will go on to read the article. Part of that is because the person reading it realizes it's not of interest. Unfortunately, another huge part of that is the headline didn't draw them in—even if they were in your reader demographic.

**So, how do you write a good headline every time?** The first step is to work on your headline first, not as an afterthought. Begin with a working title that accurately describes what you will write. The working title doesn't have to be pretty. For example, I might have a working title for a nonfiction article that is: "Explaining the importance of Facebook Chatbots." For a fiction article, I might have a working title like: "The interaction between villains and heroes in fiction."

The reason you want a working title is because that is going to guide your article. As you write, you are going to focus on including only those things that relate directly to your title. So, in the one on chatbots, I am not allowed to talk about FB chatbots vs Twitter follower growth tools. In my fiction article, I am not allowed to bring in secondary characters to the discussion about the interaction between villains and heroes. A title provides boundaries, and those boundaries help to keep your article concise.

Once you have completed the article, and applied some of the formatting tips I mentioned above, you might see some great actionable items in your article. Think about those actionable items. Is there a way to convey those actions in the headline? Headlines make a promise. The stronger the promise the more likely it will draw someone in.

In my nonfiction article about chatbots, I probably shared some statistics regarding reader engagement. Or maybe I shared my sales figures after using the bot for a certain period of time. As my working title used the qualifier "important" I would look at my primary arguments for most important points. Choose one and make that the headline. Just like taglines, headlines are always a confident statement of experience or what the reader will get out of the article. Here are three possible headlines that might emerge after I finished writing the article.

1. Get 90% Engagement Without Paying for a Facebook Ad
2. Increase Book Launch Sales by 25% with a Chatbot

3. Are Facebook Chatbots the New Panacea for Reader Engagement?

Which one would you choose for your headline? All three are good headlines. Two make an actionable promise—more engagement or more sales. The third declares this is likely an opinion piece. The one to choose depends on how the article is written and the readers you serve. My brand for teaching other writers tends to be around technology and marketing, so I would choose the first headline. However, if my brand were around significantly increasing sales—and I had the million dollar a year income to prove it—I would likely choose the second headline. If my brand is as an analyst then I might choose the third one.

Let's look at the fiction headline now. My working title was: "The Interactions Between Villains and Heroes in Fiction." Oh man. Yawn! That sounds like an essay assignment given out in a creative writing class where I'm expected to cite critical work.

Writing fiction articles for your fiction readers (not other writers) is definitely more difficult than writing a non-fiction article where you know the audience is likely more homogenous. I know my fiction readers don't want a dull lecture or analysis of interactions. They definitely want something emotional. Given that I might refocus the entire article. I might choose one emotion (e.g., anger) and how that is played out in each character. Or I might tell a story of each person's background and ask my readers how they would handle that (e.g., perhaps both had an abusive childhood yet they chose different paths). Or I might focus on how the hero can't resolve his own inner turmoil until something happens with the villain (Killing him? Saving him? Or something in between?)

Here are some headlines that might come out of that brainstorming session, again each makes a different promise.

1. When Anger Kills
2. Abuse and Recovery, a Tale of Two Children
3. Does Killing the Villain Save the Hero?

Again, these are three very different articles. And in reviewing my article, they would lead to a lot of cutting and changing. The key is keeping it within the context of my story. In fact, I could write at least three articles given these headlines based on the same story or three different stories.

Whether you are writing nonfiction or fiction articles, once you've settled on your headline, go back and review your article again to make sure the new headline is the focus of every thing you share in the article. That will likely cause some editing, removing certain sections and perhaps adding different ones. Below are some tips about how you might approach that editing beyond the general focus of the article.

**One Final Tip:** If you want your post to rank well in search, focus on keeping the headline under 70 characters so it doesn't get cut off in search engine results. My longest one in the above examples is 60 characters. Remember, it is actual characters AND spaces when counting to that 70 benchmark.

## THE LEAD PARAGRAPH IS CRITICAL

Consider your lead paragraph as important as the first few lines in Chapter 1 of your novel. Grab your readers and lead them through each sentence until they're hooked and can't walk away. You successfully got the reader past your headline, now you have to deliver on that promise in the first paragraph or you can lose them. Here are two ideas for how to do that.

Ask a question or two. A reader may pause long enough to consider an answer, and then want to compare their answer with yours in the article.

Evoke a trigger emotion that will make them NEED to continue reading. Awe, surprise, anxiety, fear are all typical emotions that keep people reading. This doesn't mean you need to engage in hyperbole. Similar to good fiction writing, you don't need to start a war to make people scared or willing to follow you. You can engage surprise, anxiety or fear in small ways and draw them in. For example, you don't need to tell a reader they will become a pauper if the miss the opportunity to use chatbots. However, you can still talk about the importance of being at the front end of the movement before it is saturated; or how communication is moving away from static posts to dynamic one-on-one communication like messenger. For those who value being first or satisfying individual readers they will still have enough surprise and anxiety to see if you are blowing smoke or not.

In the villain and hero article you don't need to begin with the killing or with a bomb going off. You can begin with a interesting telling of the backstory of each character (one paragraph or a couple lines each)—one that will make the reader immediately empathize with both of them. Then end with a surprise statement like: "Ten years later, Billy was in jail for murder and Kevin was running a Wall Street financial firm." That's the hook. How did two boys, who grew up friends with difficult pasts take such different paths? If I reading that I would immediately wonder how that happened. I might even wonder if Billy isn't as bad as the picture paints and Kevin isn't as good.

Now, don't back off after the first paragraph. Just be sure you are continuing to stay with the core message, delivering on the promise you made with every paragraph. Continue to engage your reader's emotions and employ techniques that will make them want to ask questions each step of the way. End with a call-to-action that will make the reader want to engage as well. People tend to share and comment more if you activate emotions and have actionable steps, than they do if you are lecturing or simply providing information.

## THE CALL-TO-ACTION

Your lead paragraph has done its job of evoking emotion and your reader is blissfully carried through to the end of your intelligent, emotional, and valuable content. She pauses, her finger hovering over her mouse, ready to do something—to act. But there is nothing to do. Sure, she sees the comment box, but what should she say? What do you want? She doesn't want to make a comment you weren't looking for, and she doesn't want to be fawning, or sound like a know-it-all. To avoid this reader anxiety, you need have a call-to-action. Otherwise you will lose all but the most extrovert, confident reader (or someone who already knows you well).

You may be thinking: "It's obvious. They are supposed to comment on the blog. Everyone knows that!" Actually, not everyone knows. Furthermore, people like to be encouraged. People prefer to have a prompt for their response rather than dive into the entire pool of possible comments. Only those who love posting and sharing their voice are going to do so, the rest need a reason beyond reading your amazing article.

If you have no call to action—no encouragement from you to join your blog community—the majority will leave for the next social media item beckoning them in the notifications bar on their computer or phone. A potential fan, supporter and reader lost. The Call-to-Action is YOU telling your reader what the next step is after they finish article. It may be as simple as asking a question: "Can you see yourself taking one or both paths given those character's backgrounds? Join the conversation by leaving a comment." Or, for the nonfiction article: "Have you interacted with a chat bot yet? What do you think of using this on your Facebook author fan page?"

Another call-to-action may be to ask them to share your post with their friends. If you were using a specific book as the context for your article, ask them to sign up for your email list which, of course, is going to guarantee them content as interesting and exciting as the post they just read. Or offer them something as an incentive (e.g., get the first book in this series free and see how these two boys grew up and became enemies). For nonfiction articles, offer a cheat sheet of the steps you outlined or a cool infographic of the process.

But what about my book? You may also give a link to the book sales page. However, don't forget that the primary purpose of your blog is to engage readers in conversation not to sell to them. Yes, you will let them know when a book is available. You might do that with a cover image and a link to the book sales page, but you won't use your call-to-action to sell. Instead, use your call-to-action to engage them in the book's world. If they enjoy engaging they are more likely to buy AND tell their friends.

## BE THE AUTHENTIC YOU

Most people like to know who is penning these articles. It is much easier to trust the source if you can see the author via a picture. It also makes reader's feel more comfortable in posting a comment when they see there is a real person behind the blog. If your blog platform allows for you picture (often called an avatar) to be shown next to every post and comment you make, take advantage of that. It makes it more personal.

Write like you are talking to a friend throughout the article. This is not where you want to be very formal or teacherly. Though you want the writing to be well-written and clear, you also want it to feel personal and open. Most people do not read author articles to get a lecture. The read them to learn how and why the author is talking about this. What is the real impact on that author as a person.

If you have a guest article on your blog, be sure to do a brief introduction of the guest before their post. Again, make it friendly. Be sure to explain your relationship to this person. It could be it's someone you know well (like a critique partner or an author you've known and shared similar career growth), or someone you admire—even fan girl over. However you decide to introduce the person, the reader is still looking for why you are letting this person on YOUR blog—what is your relationship and why should your reader care about someone else's post. Always link to more information about your guest so that readers can learn more (e.g., guest bio on her blog, an About page on her website, a Wikipedia link if she has one). Readers shouldn't have to search for your guest's information in order to decide if they want to tune in that day.

## MAKE POST SHARING EASY

Most platforms have some way to easily share the post, whether it is through social media icons available on your page or through a special plugin provided by your platform. Many WordPress themes come with a social media plugin. In addition, WordPress has hundreds of free or low price plugins.

The one I prefer is *Ultimate Social Sharing* plugin https://wordpress.org/plugins/ultimate-social-media-icons/ . It comes loaded with lots of options, templates, and configurations. You can start off with the default or make changes. It is easy to choose where you want the sharing icons to be placed (top, bottom, right, left, or a specific place on the page) and also choose what will show when it is shared. The FREE version is very robust. If you want some support and even more features you can sign up for a premium package, ranging from $15-$30 per year based on your specific needs. However, most people are more than happy with the FREE version.

**Consistency is critical!** This means consistency in how often you post, and consistency on what you post. To gain any kind of following, you should commit to *at least* two posts every week. When you start blogging, a higher frequency of posts is better—even three to five times a week. Once you gain traction, you can cut back to twice a week or once a week. You should not do less than once a week.

**Consistent topics/genres are also important.** Remember, your blog is PR. That means it is all about your brand. Think of every blog post with an enticing subject head that directly connects to your brand. If you are writing nonfiction about chimpanzee education, every header should reflect that focus. You should not also take on whale education, gorilla education, or human education unless it is to compare similarities to chimpanzee education. By the same token, if you are writing cozy mysteries, you should not suddenly talk about your best friends steamy romance release, your child's wedding, or the latest thing your cat did, unless you can directly relate it to your cozy mysteries.

Many bloggers start off with this disciplined approach and then, within about four months, they get bored and start veering away. Or, they mistakenly believe their audience will be bored. Your audience won't be bored if you keep it interesting. Traction is all about discoverability. Discoverability is all about SEO and finding your blog based on interests. When people do searches, they do not enter in "any topic" in the criteria. Consistency is key.

If you cannot maintain a once per week schedule, consider joining or creating a blog with several authors who are writing in a similar genre. I would not suggest joining or creating a cross-genre blog because no one part of your audience sees enough posts to become regular followers. Remember: Readers are looking for a weekly post on the genre of their interest.

This means that all of you chimpanzee educators should not invite your elephant trainers and dog tightrope walkers to guest on your blog. This will not help you and it will not help them. If you are writing cozy mysteries, you don't want the other authors to be writing romance, science fiction, or thrillers. Those audiences are very different. The only way you can make a multi-author, cross-genre blog work is if you are posting at least once per week within each of the genres represented. That could mean making sure one or more blogs are scheduled to post EVERY day, so that each genre gets at least one post per week to satisfy the readers in that group. To me, that would be a scheduling nightmare.

I know it's really hard to set up a blog with fellow authors and not include your friends who don't write in your genre. This is one of those times where business decisions need to trump keeping all your friends under one tent. You can plan other things with your friends that are more beneficial to both of you.

## SHOULD FICTION WRITER'S BLOG?

The first question to ask is do you enjoy blogging? If the answer is yes, then you should blog. If the answer is no, don't do it. There is not enough reason, from a PR or Marketing perspective to do it if you don't like it. Whereas nonfiction writer's can use a good blog to build an expert platform, most fiction writers don't benefit from that. It can happen, but it's rare. So, fiction writers need to enjoy blogging even more than nonfiction writers to make it successful.

Again, you need to think of your fiction blog as posting a well-written article, like you might provide to a magazine in your genre. And you need to plan your posts just like you plan your book. Take a look at the places your readers go to find books and book reviews. What types of articles accompany those sites or magazines? Usually it is articles about what inspired an author to write the book, how did the author come up with the world, who were mentors for the author, or what their daily writing life looks like? All of these would be fodder for your own blog.

As with nonfiction blogs, your posts need to pertain to your brand and be proving you are delivering on your promise of a specific experience. Do NOT do what I did starting off, writing whatever you feel like or using the blog to post links to Facebook, Twitter and other platforms. Every platform on the web has a specific purpose and type of content and post type that works best. Blogging is no different.

The primary difference between nonfiction bloggers and fiction bloggers is the focus of the articles. Nonfiction bloggers are writing articles to teach, to explain, to make their expertise accessible. Fiction bloggers are writing to entice people into a world of experiences and emotion—to fulfill a desire.

The one mistake many fiction bloggers make is that they write about the work in progress (WIP) trying to build anticipation for a book that is yet to come. Works-in-progress are only of interest to loyal fans who already know and love your work. It is best to provide that information through emails, on your Facebook fan page, or on Instagram.

People who don't know your work, don't care about something that can't have or experience. They engage with you through a book that already exists. The only time you might consider blogging about a work in progress is if you can directly connect it to a work that already exists (a previous book in the series or world). Your most effective blog articles are not about what is to come. They are about what exists (a launch book, backlist books, characters in backlist books, or new stories (short stories, novellas, boxsets) that emphasize books that currently exist. In other words, your posts should accompany and highlight a book or series.

Here are some ideas for content for fiction blogs. I've divided it into five major sections: 1) Share your fiction; 2) Talk about your fiction; 3) Talk about other fiction that is not yours, but similar; 4) Talk about who you are, why you wrote a particular book or series; and 5) Create nonfiction that relates to your fiction.

## Share Your Fiction

*Post Excerpts of your book.* Choose specific scenes and then write some commentary, and/or share images, illustrations of the scene.

*Serialize your story.* If your book is written in short scenes or chapters (1,000 words or less), you can start sharing it on your blog. Make sure that each new post has a hook for the next one so people will want to come back.

*Share short stories.* If you've been writing in a particular world or genre for quite some time, you may have short stories, better yet flash fiction (fiction under 1,500 words) you can share with your readers. Again, make sure this is your best work. You want people to be excited about your writing.

*Read your fiction aloud.* If you like your reading voice and feel comfortable reading aloud, this is a great way to connect on two levels. First, sharing your fiction and second letting readers hear your voice and connect with you on a more personal level. You can make it as simple or fancy as you like. You can use free software, like Audacity http://www.audacityteam.org/ to record you reading and then upload the audio file directly to your blog or to YouTube or Libsyn and link to it. You could film yourself reading, if you have a camera and feel comfortable with being seen. If you have some facility with basic video editing, you could upload you reading and add pictures pertaining to the story instead of a video of you reading.

## Talk About Your Fiction

*The inspiration.* Every story begins with a kernel from somewhere. It may be a personal experience, a newspaper article you read, something you saw while drinking coffee in the park, a movie you saw, a book you read, and often a mashup of several things. Readers love to know how you came up with the ideas, plot, characters, themes of a story. You can stretch this into several blog posts covering each of those elements.

*Author commentary.* This has become popularized for movies and DVDs, as well as certain series on television. Many films and television series now also produce out-takes to share as a bonus, or a Director's cut, or interviews during or after the movie or series. This is where actors and directors talk about the scenes, what they learned, how it changed in the process, or how satisfying or scary it was.

Authors can do this too. Taking a chapter for each post, you can talk about the writing of that chapter. Were their challenges during the chapter? Did a character run off with the story and you had to reel her in? Were you afraid to write that climax scene? OR did you have to rewrite the dialog five times because it wasn't sounding right? Again, readers love a peek behind the magic of writing a novel.

*Special Features.* Again, taking notes from the film world, it is popular to provide special insights into parts of the story—themes, the hero's journey, the villain's journey, setting the scene or mood. Taking each of these insights as one blog post creates an entire month of blog posts. Not enough for an article? Compare your themes, heroes, villains, settings to that of another book, similar to yours and well-loved.

*Deleted Scenes.* Every movie and every book has scenes that had to be removed—sometimes with great angst from the author. Readers love to know what these were and why they were removed. If he scenes are long enough, you can sometimes turn them into a short story or a special freebie option for your fans. Involve your readers by asking them if they think the scene should have been deleted.

*Character Interview.* Instead of interviewing yourself or another author, interview a character. You can even make this a serial in itself. For example, in a romance you might interview the hero and heroine right after the first meet. Ask them about the event and how they feel about that person. Then interview them again later, maybe after the first kiss, or after the first breakup. You get the idea. In other books, you might interview the villain or the dotty aunt, or the detective in a mystery. This allows you to provide some backstory and insights into the characters thinking that you may not have provided on the page.

### *Talk About Other Fiction*

*Author Interviews.* Interview one author a month who writes books similar to yours. This requires more work than coming up with a single sheet of questions that is asked of every author. You want to have some familiarity with the author's work and ask questions that are unique to that person and her work. You might even ask the author what she wants to bring out in the interview.

These are great for two reasons. 1) It associates your work with another successful author; and 2) It's good Karma. When you promote someone else's work they feel good about you and may be helpful in your own promotion in the future. Though never invite them with the expectation that they will return the favor. Some will, many won't because doing interviews is not something that works for them or is not something they feel comfortable doing. You should be doing the interview because you really do love the author's work and want to share it with your readers.

*Reviews/Shares*. Reviews and sharing of books, movies, other blog content similar to yours is always helpful. This is generosity at its best, again building a network of like-minded professionals. Like the author interview, it shows that you read beyond your own books. In fact, it let's readers know that you are more like them than not. You also read, go to movies, like other non-writing content.

You can also share reviews you've received for your books and how they motivate you. I love sharing good reviews because they truly do make me happy and motivate me to write more, particularly those where someone really needed to read that book at that time in their life. I think that sharing some of these and commenting on their impact to you is a very positive thing to do in a blog post.

Some people advise sharing your best and worst reviews. I don't like to share bad reviews because no matter what I say about them, it can be taken negatively. If I say: "I know my books aren't for everybody" it can be taken as sloughing off the reader's opinions. If I say: "this review helped me to be a better writer" It may give permission for readers to do critiques of my work via public reviews. If a review is particularly mean spirited, I find it hard to say anything worthwhile about it. I don't find those reviews helpful and if I say anything about the reviewer's intentions, I'm on shaky ground. However, share reviews however they best fit your needs and brand.

### Talk About Who You Are

This goes directly to the reader wanting to know the person behind the books. The key here is sharing that part of you that you feel comfortable sharing—and more importantly, that part of you that relates to what you write.

*Share a scene related to your real life.* All writers can't help but put emotions, incidences, descriptions in their books that come from their own lives. For example, though you may not have experienced being on a generational space ship seeking out new planets to colonize. You may have drawn from your own experience of moving away from the only home you knew to somewhere else—whether that was across the country or to another country and different culture.

All of us experience the emotions of love, despair, triumph, fear, and many others. If you can relate your experience of one or more of those emotions to your character's experience of it in a scene it makes it very interesting to a reader.

*Interview Yourself.* Just like you asked probing questions of other authors, you can ask the same of yourself and post it. Or share an interview you did on another blog. Again, focusing on your brand and your work.

This is another time that audio or video can also work well. If you were interviewed for a radio show, a podcast, at a conference, any of those are great to share with your blog audience.

*Answer fan questions.* Readers love asking questions of authors. You can use this technique for questions about a book, a series, or about you personally. Gather the questions with the promise of posting answers. If you get lots of questions, it can add up to many posts.

*Share a picture of your writing space.* Whether you have an entire room to yourself, a separate office or unit outside your home, or you work on your dining room table, readers are interested in how you work and manage other things around you. Talk about what is there to provide you inspiration, and what is there that you find challenging. Better yet, how you overcome those challenges day in and day out.

*Your favorite book(s).* Talk about your reading life. This can take the form of several posts. Your favorite book as a child, as a middle-grader, as a teen, as a young adult, in middle age, etc. Talk about how those books inspired you, scared you, got you to where you are today.

*Assistants/Supports.* If you have an assistant (virtual or personal), feature him or her and talk about how they help you with your writing and career. This is particularly important if this individual (or several) interact with your readers. You might also want to talk about other professionals in your life that make your writing business work and feature or interview them. Cover designer, editor, webdesigner, agent. If you employ or are very supported by a member of your family, and feel comfortable sharing/interviewing them, that is great too.

*The Writer's Journey.* Many people love to write about this, and many authors believe this is a good thing to share with readers. My concerns about this is how to be different from all the other writers, and to be cognizant of who my audience is. Yes, some of my readers are writers as well. But are they engaging with my fiction as a reader or a writer? How will sharing my personal writing journey lead them toward my fiction?

I do write nonfiction for writers, as evidenced by this book. However, at least so far, my books tend to be more step-by-step instructions or informational than they are about the general emotional and daily challenges and triumphs of writers. So, I would more likely blog along the lines of what I write—teaching and learning—than blogging about me and my emotional or physical journey related to writing on a daily basis. There is no right or wrong answer here. Again, look to your brand. Look to the audience you are trying to attract and make your own decisions.

### *Create a Non-fiction Article*

This technique is a natural for those who write historical fiction. Many historical fiction authors do a lot of research and the sharing of that research is a great way to create a non-fiction article (a teaching and learning article). However, historical fiction writers aren't the only ones who do research.

Here are some things I've researched for various books:

- Cultures and their practices that are different than mine
- Locations where my characters live, travel, get lost
- Variances in laws in other states or countries
- Specific professions of my characters
- Science principles—particularly in biology, agriculture or physics
- Commentary about possible futures
- Philosophy
- Myths based in diverse cultures
- Different types of guns and their use
- How to repel down a mountain
- How to poison someone or provide an antidote
- How long it takes a body to recover from a horrible car accident
- How long it takes a mind to recover from trauma

In other words, anything you researched for your book is a great subject for a nonfiction article.

## HOW TO ORGANIZE AND CALENDAR YOUR POSTS

With a minimum of 52 posts a year, and more likely 100 or more, you need to find a way to organize your posts into categories and to tag them to make it easy to find. In large organizations that need to manage hundreds of articles or books or stories, this process is called an *editorial* calendar. That means that topics and publications are scheduled for an entire year. This helps to control releases (posts) by seasons, by what the readers are most interested in at different times of the year, and by popular or trending topics.

Once you have your editorial calendar down, you also want to share it with your readers and have an obvious organizational scheme (categories and tags) that can help your readers to find past and future articles along the themes of most interest to them. If you are a single genre writer, you might consider categorizing by subgroups related to you and your books (e.g., character-related posts, general uplifting posts, writing journey posts, etc.)

If you are a multiple genre author, you might consider organization by genre or by themes that hint at content affinity across genres. I've recently begun the latter approach for all my social media and blogging efforts. For example, one of my themes is called "Mutual Mondays." Mutual Mondays are when posts on my blogs and social media features other authors or professionals in my writing life. This helps my readers to know that every Monday's post is going to be about someone else, not me. Your theme names don't have to be alliterative, they just have to be clear. Perhaps you have an Excerpt Friday where you regularly post a book excerpt; or Serial Saturday where you post the next chapter in your book.

Use your imagination. Look at ways to make your blog both enticing and consistent. The easier it is for your readers to remember and have accurate expectations of content from week to week and month to month, the more likely you will grow your readership at a faster pace.

## LAUNCHING YOUR BLOG

Setting up a blog should be done with some of the same attention to detail as setting up a website. If your blog is part of your website (e.g., WordPress) then your setup will be done already. However, if you are using a platform separate from your website, then you will need some additional setup because the information won't already be available (e.g., bio, contact, website link).

If your blog is separate from your website, then your blog needs a title and tagline. The best way to go with this is to use a title that is your name and the same tagline you are using on your website (if you are using one). As I described previously, don't make the mistake I did in naming your blog something that has nothing to do with your brand (e.g., Maggie's Meanderings) or that makes the blog sound as if it's an afterthought, not important to you. The title and tagline help to make it clear what kind of content will be on this blog. And that title and tagline is what shows up in search engines consistently.

**About Page / Bio.** Just like your website, you will want to be sure to include an about page and/or bio on your blog. If your blog content is interesting, people will want to know more about the person behind it. Don't make them search for this or, worse, not provide it at all. Nothing is more frustrating than to be reading an interesting blog and look at the profile to find there is nothing except a name—no picture, no bio, no contact.

**How to Contact You.** People encounter you in different ways. They may find you through your blog but never go to your webpage. So, wherever you are on the web, you want to be sure to make it clear how to contact you. If you are comfortable with sharing your email as your contact, that is all you need. Personally, I don't do this because of all the bots and email scrapers that look for this and then start spamming me. You should include a separate contact page with your blog and a form, or make it obvious in the sidebar.

**Comments.** A blog is designed for reader interaction. However, you need to decide how easy or difficult it will be for people to comment. Just like those page scrapers to get emails, there are bots that look for open comments with the intent of leaving links to their sites or blogs usually for the purpose of selling something or getting emails to spam people.

Your first decision is if you want your blog to have some type of captcha device. This is a small program that requests the blogger to verify they are human before a comment can be posted. You've probably seen these around the web. The first type displays a word or number via a graphic (not readable by bots) and the user must enter it in exactly. This has proven to be difficult for a number of people. People with vision difficulties (even me getting older) find the pictures hazy and often hard to decipher. And the voice option sometimes doesn't work well. I know I've given up commenting on blogs many times when I encounter one of these.

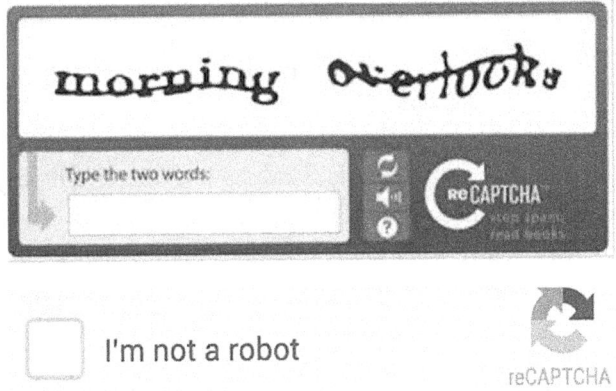

The second type, and the most common in use today, is the checkbox asking you to verify you are not a robot. I love this one. It is easy to use and just as effective. You might wonder how checking a box is safe. Couldn't a bot do that? Surprisingly, Google says it can examine cues every user provides (e.g., IP addresses and cookies) to verify this is the same friendly human Google knows from other places on the Web. In addition, they have algorithms that examine tiny mouse movements (hovering and approaching the checkbox) that can differentiate between humans and bots. If the Google software is unsure, it can still fall back to a secondary test like showing a grid of different animals and asking the human to identify which one matches a specific picture. For example, the picture may show a black and white cat, and you must pick out another cat (though different colors) in the grid. Again, easy for humans, hard for bots. Humans can distinguish between cats, dogs, monkeys, horses in pictures but bots cannot.

**Moderation.** You also need to decide if you want to moderate your comments. Depending on the blog program and plugins you might be using there are different levels of moderation. The highest level is that no comment is posted until a human (usually you) approves it. Though this sounds wise on the surface, it can become frustrating for both you and your readers. Readers tend to become concerned if they don't see their comment posted right away. They think something went wrong. For you, it means you need to stay on top of things all the time to make sure there isn't a long period of time between someone posting a comment and it appearing on your blog.

A lower level of moderation provides a rule that can be automatically checked first (e.g., if there is a link to another site it get's kicked to the moderator, otherwise it is automatically posted). The problem with this is that you may appreciate people sharing legitimate links. If you are talking about the impacts of running as you get older, a reader may have a related article to expand on the discussion they would like to link. Again, that person would have to wait until you were able to get to the comment and determine if it is acceptable.

Another level of moderation is to let people through without moderation for a specified period of time (e.g., 3 days or one week). Anything that comes after that time period is put directly into moderation. I like this level because I find whoever is going to comment will likely comment in the first couple days after the blog is posted. All of the blog bots that look to post links tend to follow a week or more behind. I've had bots trying to comment on a blog post that is more than three years old on a blog I no longer use.

Then there is the no moderation level. If you assume the person is human because they got past the reCaptcha test, you might decide you will let them make a comment. Choosing this level is one that requires some comfort and trust in people in general. My experience has been that the new reCaptcha (clicking I am not a robot) works well and that I rarely see someone purposefully trying to spam my list or act out in the comments. If I do spot it, I remove the post with a message about not adhering to the rules of the blog. This, of course, means you need some type of statement as to what's acceptable or not.

A typical statement I use is: "This is a public blog that welcomes readers of all ages and diversity. Therefore, swearing, racism, sexism, bullying and other incivility will not be tolerated. Any comments deemed to contain these triggers will be removed without warning."

Unfortunately, some very large blogs—particularly those with political or religious commentary—have stopped allowing comments at all because of the hundreds of ugly posts they receive. I'm truly saddened by the rise in incivility in public discussions. So, I understand why they made that decision. There is only so much time and resources.

Perhaps I've been fortunate. In a decade of blogging I haven't had any incivility in comments. Before good captcha controls, I did have problems with spammer links. However, since these controls have been in place I no longer have that problem either.

Only you can decide what you want to do about comments. Most blog platforms allow you to mix and match your rules as well. For example, you may use the reCaptcha to clear most people, but also add a rule about everything goes to moderation after one week, or no linking allowed.

Chances are you won't get many comments for months, or even years, depending on how quickly you develop a following. Rule of thumb is that less than 5% of people who come to your blog will comment—even people who love reading it or have subscribed to get in their email inbox. That means it takes a thousand loyal followers to regularly get 50 posts, which is significant to most bloggers. However, if you can build up your readership and actually get people to engage in the comments, it can be a rewarding experience.

## Chapter Eight
# BOOK GROUPS AND CLUBS

Book clubs as a marketing tool can be controversial among authors. If you are an author who has participated in book clubs yourself, you may feel more comfortable with this effort than those who never have. I think that book clubs are a great way for authors to raise awareness of their work, possibly increase sales, engage directly with readers, build a fan base, and definitely garner more reviews.

From a personal interest perspective, I also think that book clubs can be insightful, help allay fears that you aren't a "real writer", and give you insights into your own work that you may not have considered. Generally, book club readers are avid readers and have a good network of people who value their advice in recommending a book.

Many writers think that book clubs ONLY read NYT bestsellers, or only read literary fiction. That's not true. Bookclubs come in as many varieties and tastes as there are readers.

### START LOCAL

Finding book clubs, outside of the one or two you may participate in yourself, can be difficult. There is not a single registry of book clubs for you to contact. Start by asking questions of your inner circle and your fans. Well in advance of a title release, let your personal network know that you're interested in speaking with book clubs about your newest title or perhaps a title that is at the beginning of that series.

Your fans are your biggest ambassadors for getting into a book club. Many book clubs schedule what they are reading at least months in advance, and sometimes for the entire year. They tend to ask members in the club what they want to read. In the case of my local book club, the rule is any member nominating a book for inclusion must have read the book and vouch for it in terms of being a good book. This is where your fans can be critical.

I've had two of my romance books considered at five different book clubs in the Portland area. One of them was the book club I belong to. I didn't nominate myself (I felt that was gauche). But someone else in the group did and they all agreed to read it. I was nervous but pleasantly surprised when many people in the group told me they were so happy to read a genre book. People in that group went on to purchase my entire series after reading the one book.

The good news is that once you have your book read in one book club it is easier to interest others. You also have a reference source so other book clubs can call on the one you've already done to get questions answered about you as a speaker, or even if your book was "that" good or enjoyed by the group. Don't stop with just your local area. With technology today you can easily connect virtually to answer questions via Google Hangouts, Skype, or any number of other web conferencing software connections.

## HOW DO YOU FIND BOOK CLUBS BEYOND YOUR LOCAL AREA?

Contact libraries and bookstores first. I've found that it is rare a library or bookstore isn't also running a book club. In addition, churches, community centers, and schools are other places where book groups are formed. As to meeting places, they can be coffee shops, bars (I did talk to a group that met in a bar over beers), and people's homes. Try searching through sites such as Meetup.com https://meetup.com Some of these venues work well only if you can physically meet with them—particularly restaurants and people's homes—as they may not have the capability for virtual connections.

Once you learn who the contact person is, let them know where book clubs often meet and ask the proprietor if they can give you the contact information for the club's organizer. If they're not comfortable doing so, leave your name, contact info, and book materials with the owner to share with the organizer.

The major online book communities are Goodreads, Onlinebookclub.org, and Librarything. These are not run at all like the smaller groups mentioned above. Toward the end of this chapter, I'll talk specifically about Goodreads—the largest online book community in the world—and what you can do to leverage your visibility there.

## PITCH YOURSELF AND YOUR BOOK

If you're pitching a book club through a personal connection, like a fan or you know the organizer, you might not have to work too hard to pique the group's interest. Many book clubs LOVE to speak with authors, particularly local authors. More than talking about the book itself (e.g., plot, characters, black moment) the groups are interested in your approach, how you learned the craft, your inspiration for the story. In other words, they are interested in the creative side of writing rather than the exact finished product they just read.

Book groups where you have no personal connection will likely require some convincing and some homework. First, do your research before making contact. Look at what books the group read over the past year or two. Books associated with organizations—like libraries, bookstores, churches—will often have a list of past books or upcoming books on a website or a Facebook page. Make sure they actually read in the genres you write.

If you are already popular, a known NYT or USA Today bestseller, start with that in your pitch. Many clubs want to read the book with the most buzz, but not all of them. Some tend to move toward certain types of topics that are a reflection of the group. For example, the book club where I belong reads a number of literary and genre bestsellers. However, they also like to include at least three or four books that are in line with trending news like the experience of certain disenfranchised groups or a futuristic book about the impact of environmental neglect or controversial medical advances. In other words, look for any pattern that tells you about the books that you can use to pitch your book.

If you write sweet or inspirational books, look at religious organizations where those books would be welcome for discussion. In all cases, contact the organizer to introduce yourself, provide a book description, and explain you're interested in participating as a visiting author. If possible, prove you've done your homework by explaining how or why you believe your book will be a good fit based on their past reading lists.

Don't get discouraged if the organizer expresses immediate disinterest. There are many reasons a group may never want an author to attend. They might be intimidated to host an author or they might not read your genre. The group may be small enough that they value the friendship and camaraderie as much or more than the actual reading and discussion process and are not open to an outsider. Of course, they also may not read in your genre.

Keep in mind that book clubs plan their reading lists months—sometimes a year—in advance, and many of them rely on your book being in the local library so they don't have to buy them. If this is the case, give them your contact information and ask that they keep you in mind when selecting their next round of titles.

*Tip:* For one book group, where my book was not available at the local library, I offered to send them five copies to be shared IF they agreed to give it to their local library when they were done with them. With 25 people in the group it was a good return for me. I did give up five free copies of paperback books for the groups use, but 16 people in the group bought their own paperback copy to read and share.

Some organizers will ask if you have prepared discussion questions for your book that they can use for the discussion. It is great if you do because you are saving them time developing the questions. Typical questions are around themes, character motivations, and ways that readers may or may not relate to the plot or story arc of the characters.

Don't be surprised if more than half the group does not read your book. Though people are asked to read prior to the meeting, many groups have a rule that if the person didn't have the time to read it this month, or perhaps someone started it but couldn't finish it, that they come to the meeting anyway and participate in the discussion as best they can. This is particularly true when a guest author will be present.

## YOUR ROLE DURING THE MEETING

You've made the connection with the organizer and scheduled the meeting. Be sure to find out what expectations they will have of you and how the organizer anticipates the meeting will run. Some will discuss the book in front of you, just as they would if you were not there. Others will discuss the book before your arrival and then use the time to ask you specific questions.

If they do discuss the book in front of you and find problems or inconsistencies, do NOT try to talk them out of their opinions, just say thank you. Let them know that you appreciate hearing what their experience was with the book. If someone is brave enough to say they hated the book, again don't take it personally. My response to that is always: "It sounds like it didn't meet your expectations. That's okay, I know that my books aren't for every type of reader. There are many books I read too that I just don't like. Thank you for your feedback."

## COMMON PLANNING COURTESIES FOR MEETING WITH READERS

Be on time. You don't want to show up late to your own book club discussion.

Be positive and as cheerful as possible. Don't come to defend your work. Come to listen and thank them for valuable feedback.

Know what you want to discuss in case people are shy or don't have any questions. I usually make notes for myself just in case I draw a blank too. I almost always like to discuss my inspiration for the book, as well as anything that was happening in my life while I was writing that impacted the way the book turned out. If you've incorporated deep themes in your work you might wish to discuss some of them in detail and talk about why these themes were important to the story structure, the character arc or to you personally.

If no conversation seems to be flowing, be prepared to ask questions of the readers. I always ask the following questions if I get the chance.

***What was your favorite section?*** This is a good question because people who may not have had a chance to finish it can still answer for a part they did read.

***Was there anything in the book that was confusing or you didn't like?*** This signals that there is no expectation of people loving everything you wrote. Typically, I might get a response about disliking something a character did or said—especially the villains. It's a good question that other readers will chime in to say how they hated that character too but it also made them root for the hero even more.

***If you were the hero/heroine would you have made the same decisions when faced with that challenge?*** This is another way of getting to how much or little people empathize with a character or their situation, or how realistic they found it.

## FINAL WORDS AND SAYING GOODBYE

During the discussion don't do any self-promotion or mentioning of other books you've written unless someone asks you directly if there are more books in the series. The time is devoted to what the participants want to know. Also, don't plan to sell any books afterward unless the organizer specifically tells you they wish to do that. I've never had someone request this. Though I guess it's a possibility. I would never mention it or suggest it.

After the discussion is over, let people know that you are happy to sign any books they own. Point out any promotional material you have if they are interested in learning more about you and your books (e.g., business card, bookmarks, sample pages, other books in the same series). Some authors do a fun giveaway of one or more books as a thank you for having them. I don't do this but I can see how it might be fun and even get you a call back in the future.

Do let everyone know how they can sign up for your author email list to get updates on future books, and ask them to consider leaving an honest review on any book sites they frequent.

Some book groups like to take photos with authors. If they do, ask for a copy to include on your social media sites. Sometimes, specific individuals in the group also want photos with you. I always do that and encourage them to let me know if they post it anywhere on social media so I can like it.

## FOLLOW UP AFTER THE EVENT

Send an email to the organizer thanking them for their time and expressing what a great time you had and how much you appreciated the discussion from the group. Let them know you would be happy to return again with another book if they have an interest in the future.

## VIRTUAL BOOK GROUP MEETINGS

If you do the book group guest author slot virtually, all of the above still applies. The difference is that you need to also practice using the virtual meet up software and equipment. If at all possible make a dry run for connection with the organizer in advance of the event. Nothing is worse than spending half an hour trying to get connected.

Personally, I don't do a lot of book club events. They are time consuming and don't end up making a lot of sales. However, I do enjoy the ability to have insightful discussions with avid readers. I find them more fun than going to a typical book signing at a bookstore or festival because the time allows for more discussion.

If you are unsure as to the efficacy of spending time on contacting or networking with book groups, you might be interested in this Publishers Weekly story about how one author worked very hard to contact 100 book clubs across the country to leverage her new release. As an introvert, I wouldn't personally choose to do this, but I can see how some authors would find it fun.

https://www.publishersweekly.com/pw/by-topic/columns-and-blogs/soapbox/article/68539-how-one-author-turned-the-internet-into-a-giant-book-club.html

## BOOK CLUBS AND SOCIAL MEDIA

With the rise of social media, book clubs are showing up in new formats and places—particularly in Facebook groups, and in live discussions on Facebook, Twitter and other places. Instagram has become a place for celebrities to talk about books they are reading. So you can too. You might want to begin with fans or start your own book group.

In addition to Goodreads, which I'll discuss at the end of this chapter, there is a nonprofit designed to connect readers and discussions that is interesting. They are supporting something called Reading Circles. http://www.readerscircle.org/ The concept is that instead of requiring everyone to read the same book and discuss it, the nonprofit let's people bring whatever they are reading to discuss. There are ways for groups to gather around a particular book or topic and then disperse. In other words, no requirement to continuously attend with a specific group. There are options for authors to participate by "sponsoring" their book for $70 and making themselves available for a virtual book group author spot on a particular day.

I haven't tried this yet myself, but I do find it an interesting option and have it on my list for 2018.

## GOODREADS FOR BOOK CLUBS AND AUTHOR MARKETING

For those who haven't heard of Goodreads, imagine the world's largest social networking site devoted exclusively to discussing books. With 55 million members and over 50 million reviews it is the largest book club in the world.

Goodreads is a place where readers can share what books they have read, discover new books, learn more about books and the authors who write them. For authors, the site offers an opportunity for you to make sure your books are in the Goodreads catalog, to share a little about yourself and your books via an author page, and to participate in a variety of promotional opportunities.

It seems that the Goodreads reputation among authors is not in the middle of the spectrum. Authors either love them or hate them. I was a member of Goodreads as a reader before I started publishing novels. I've always liked the ability to rate and review books and see what other readers thought of a book I was considering. I have personally never experienced the "trolls" that some authors have discussed. As a reader, I'm perfectly satisfied with my experience.

As an author, I'm not convinced that Goodreads is a place to make sales. I've tried a number of different promotional things over the past five years, including giveaways and ads and have never seen any significant bump in sales. However, I DO find it to be a place where I can get readers to leave reviews when they won't or can't leave them on vendor sites. I also find it a place where I can get people noticing my book. Not buying it, but talking enough about it to take notice. Just this talking can be viral if enough people are adding the book to the TBR (to-be-read) list.

## So, what can you do at no cost to leverage Goodreads?

The best way to learn Goodreads is to sign up **as a reader** at https://goodreads.com and then start exploring. The website will walk you through the process of getting started.

It is important to establish yourself as a reader first. The easiest way to do that is to look for books you have already read (I added about 300 when I first started in Goodreads). Rate each of them, and for those you feel strongly about start putting in a review. The review doesn't have to be really long, explain the plot and all the charcters. Short and sweet is fine. Say what you loved or hated about the book, the writing, or if you want to see another on by this author.

*Caveat:* Because you ARE an author, I highly recommend you do not post a review about a book you hated. Though one might think all authors understand not every book is universally loved, there are those who take all reviews personally and are particularly mean-spirited with other authors. So avoid that scenario by not reviewing those books.

How much time should you spend establishing your "reader" credentials. As much as you can spare and feel good about posting ratings and reviews for books you've already read. If you can only do 50 or 60 that's fine. If you can do more, that's even better. Goodreads is primarily for readers, and there are some who will put you in the "outsider" category if you are only there to sell and not participate as a reader.

On the other hand, there are many authors who do no reviews or ratings, but put up a passive author page and perhaps establish their blog there. They also don't participate in any part of Goodreads, including selling, so they are safe. My personal opinion is that if you aren't going to participate at all, don't bother putting up a profile or anything else. Without driving traffic to your page, no one is going to pay attention anyway.

Once you have your reader profile set up and at least a few books rated and reviewed. It is time to set up an Author page. **Note:** You can Only do this if you have books already published. If you are just thinking about publishing a book, or it is not yet published, then you cannot request an author page. You will be required to prove you have at least one book published on a major vendor site (e.g., Amazon, B&N, Apple or Google).

**Setup a Goodreads Author Page**

Getting an author page is the first step to connect with your readers on Goodreads. Creating an author page will allow you to claim all the books you've written, provide some basic statistics about your books, and will give your readers a place to see what you are up to and what you are reading.

You can find out how to join the Goodreads Author Program at https://www.goodreads.com/author/program. This page has step-by-step instructions on how to get approved and the options for setting up your author profile and taking advantage of a variety of promotional programs.

*Tip:* Think of your author profile as containing the same type of information you include on your website—a bio, a listing of your books, access to your social media and blog platforms. No need to make up new information when you already have it all on your website. Just copy and paste.

One of the options on your Author page is to connect your blog feed to Goodreads. Definitely do this! Goodreads will automatically email your fans once a week with all your new blog posts. This is a great way to increase blog readership and, if you are a regular blogger, it shows readers that you are actively thinking of readers. Just set it up once and let it run automatically.

**List Your Books on Listopia**

The Listopia section of Goodreads has a list for every kind of book imaginable. Make sure your books are on the appropriate lists. You can find this section at http://www.goodreads.com/list. Find a list your book would fit in and then click the "add books to this list" tab. Make sure to add more than just your book to the list. Pick your top 10 books in that category and vote for each book. Your readers want to know what books you like to read.

Often the difference between 30th and 10th on these lists is only a few votes. So feel free to invite your readers to vote for your books as well.

**Lead a Q&A Discussion Group About Your Book**

Goodreads allows you to host a book discussion about your book. This is called an Author Featured Group. You set the date and the time you will be available to answer questions. It is smart to make sure that some of your followers commit to being there. You arrive and then ask the group to pose any questions they have about you or the book. You participate for the set period of time.

Readers may choose to continue the discussion after you leave. The viral part of this is that when you set up a group, Goodreads will list it in their Authors and Groups section and they select certain groups to be featured in their newsletter. Well after the time of the group, the Q&A that occurred is still available for people to read.

If the conversation was interesting, this is a way to turn people who have your book in their TBR pile into wanting to actually reading it and perhaps making a purchase. You can read more about how to set up this Author Group here https://www.goodreads.com/author/featured_groups .

**Ask Fans for Reviews on Goodreads**

Because Goodreads has no requirement to prove purchase of a title and it is not outwardly associated with a vendor—even though it is owned by Amazon—getting reviews on GoodReads is often easier than getting reviews on vendor sites. This is particularly helpful if you later want to run ads in newsletters or ask for a BookBub featured deal. Though you may only manage 10 reviews on Amazon, you might see 30 on Goodreads for the same book.

An easy way to ask for reviews is to message individuals readers directly on GoodReads. The data Goodreads shows for each of your books includes who has marked it as read, who has rated it, and who has done a review. Consider mentioning those who have marked it as read but neither rated or reviewed it and ask for them to do it. This is the primary reason being on Goodreads is important. Every time someone encounters your book and reports on it, that action is getting shown to all of that person's friends. That means your book is continuously in front of people you may not know.

You can also reach out to groups dedicated to doing book reviews. There are many groups on Goodreads who do this in exchange for a copy of the book. Of course, these groups are hit with a lot of requests so don't have high expectations.

**Connect Goodreads Reviews to your Website, Blog, or Facebook author page**

Goodreads provides "widgets" that can be placed in a variety of venues around the web to display Goodreads review on a book. This allows you to have reviews displayed in each of these venues which provides social proof that your books are well-reviewed. The technology for the implementation of this is a little more technical than other things. However, Goodreads does supply step-by-step instructions. If you have a paid web designer for your website, providing them the information can also get it implemented quickly.

The widget allows you to set a number of parameters in terms of what is displayed. For example, you can say you only want reviews displayed that are 3s or higher, or only 5 star reviews. I always select all of them. You can select the total number of reviews displayed (e.g., 5, 10, or all of them in a scrolling box). If you prefer you can only display a summary of reviews—the portion that says 25 reviews and a 5.8 average. You can also set the size of the display. The one pictured below is the default size. Though you don't se it in the static picture, it is scrollable. Though I have over 30 reviews on this book, I chose to only show 10. Below three are shown and the user would need to then use the side scroll bar to see the other seven.

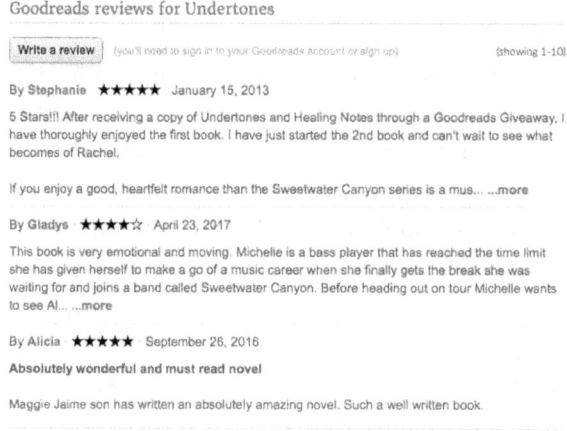

## Can't do it all right now? Just get started

Begin by building a foundation. Establish a profile, share books that you have reviewed (you need to post around 20 books to get traction on the site), and add any other basic information to get started. Share your books as you read them, add events, and take part in discussions. Work on establishing yourself as a reader.

If you have one or more published books, make sure to request and set up your author profile. You want to focus on beginning to build your network. Add "friends" to your Author page. Link to your Goodreads Author page from your website and any social media profiles that provide you that opportunity. Link your blog to your Goodreads Author page.

If you are an author with more than three books, you want to focus on claiming all of your books on your Author profile and begin targeting your audience by building relationships with readers in the network. Actively promote your Goodreads page through your social media and on your blog. Consider setting up a Author Group to discuss your newer releases as they come out. Continue to grow relationships.

# ENGAGING WITH READERS BEYOND BASIC COMMUNICATION

Social Media Overview
Facebook
Facebook Messenger
Twitter
Instagram
Pinterest
You Tube

## Chapter Nine
# SOCIAL MEDIA OVERVIEW

There are hundreds of possible social media platforms, and new ones seem to become available every month. I suggest considering five questions when choosing which social media platform you want to expend time and energy (and perhaps money) in learning to use. Remember, you will be building your specific audience of readers on this platform and you don't want to put in that effort for a year or two and then decide to drop the platform.

1. Which platform provides the largest possible reach for your audience?
2. Which platform has the highest penetration in the geographic areas you are targeting?
3. Which platform has the highest engagement with readers?
4. Which platform has a proven positive ROI for paid advertising.
5. Which platform do you actually enjoy using?

Notice that I put "enjoy" using at the end. I am well aware that a great number of authors don't enjoy using social media. Whenever I've spoken about social media during a workshop, at a conference or even among author friends, I frequently hear: "I hate social media. I don't enjoy using any of them. Do I really have to do that to be successful?"

Of course, it is your choice whether to do it or not. I've heard many speakers say you don't have to use social media. If your book is good enough it will find it's audience. If you are J.K. Rowling, Nora Roberts, John Grisham—name your famous author of choice—you don't have to use social media. You have already built your audience and it is large enough (in the millions) that you'll be fine. However, the rest of us don't have that luxury.

Ten years ago (in 2007), you could get away without using social media. Ten years ago, in the U.S. only 7% of American households used at least one social media application. That means it was likely a lower percentage in other countries. In fact, probably until 2011 or 2012 you could get away without using social media to stay in contact with your readers. However, in 2017, a whopping 81% of of adults in the U.S. have a social media profile. (https://www.statista.com/statistics/273476/percentage-of-us-population-with-a-social-network-profile/ ) Furthermore, the trend is for people to engage on social media more than they do in email. I've found this true in my own family. From my 84 year old mother to my 32 and 35 year old children, I'm more likely to hear from them on Facebook than to get an email with a quick note and pictures. Grandchildren, nieces and nephews are all on social media beginning around age 12. Whether you agree or disagree with social media usage, the reality is that is where readers are and from current trends will be more often. Ignoring social media is a sure way to stifle your reader growth and engagement.

Let's look at the answers to the first four points with some actual data to back it up. I don't want to bore you with lots of statistics and percentages, so I am going to summarize the data below. However, if you love reading about the statistics, how the research was done and seeing cool graphis presenting it, I highly recommend becoming a basic member (FREE) at Smart Insights. They keep on top of this across many research studies. The summaries I provide below are from data presented at Smart Insights which analyzes numerous research reports and provides insight on the statistics and what it means for businesses. https://www.smartinsights.com/social-media-marketing/social-media-strategy/new-global-social-media-research/.

## WHICH PLATFORMS PROVIDE THE LARGEST POSSIBLE REACH FOR YOUR AUDIENCE?

Facebook, and it's additional owned apps definitely provide the largest social media reach of any platform. Facebook alone provides two times the outreach of the next biggest app (QZone, a Facebook-like App developed in China that serves the chinese-speaking population. Facebook is banned in China).

The current registered user base for Facebook alone is over 1.8 billion individual accounts worldwide. Facebook-owned additional apps include What's App and Facebook Messenger, each with 1 billion users. It's most recent purchase, Instagram, already has 600 million users. Of course, Facebook encourages you to use all of their owned apps and provides a somewhat integrated environment for doing that.

However, you might feel about Facebook personally, what this data tells me is that choosing to ignore Facebook is choosing to ignore the largest user base in the world. It is the equivalent of an author choosing not to load her books on Amazon.

Below these Facebook apps are three platforms that were unfamiliar to me prior to doing research for this book: QQ, WeChat, and QZone. Those three apps have 632, 846, and 877 million users, respectively. These platforms are most popular in what is known as the Asia-Pacific and Oceania region of the world. That includes: Australia, China, Japan, India, Sri Lanka, New Zealand, and many smaller islands. For a full listing of countries see https://en.wikipedia.org/wiki/Asia-Pacific#Main_countries_and_territories_data

Next up is Tumblr at 550 million users. Far below the half million mark are applications I've heard many authors say are important: Twitter is at 315 million, Snapchat at 300 million, and Pinterest at only 150 million. If you enjoy using any of these lower reach platforms, certainly continue to use them. Even at 150 million users for Pinterest, it's more than I can ever imagine reaching. However, if you are feeling overwhelmed, I would stay with the largest audience reach until you have time to consider or try other platforms and see how they work with your brand. With the reach of Facebook, it is highly likely that your readers on Pinterest or Twitter are also on Facebook (particularly in english-speaking countries).

## WHICH PLATFORM HAS THE HIGHEST PENETRATION IN THE GEOGRAPHIC AREAS YOU ARE TARGETING?

Total number of users is one measure. However, as we saw in the brief summary above, platforms that are used by the western world are different from platforms used by the eastern world. This means, an author will want to consider **penetration in your geographic area of choice**. If you are trying to open up markets in Asia, you may wish to use a different platform than you would use to get to markets in the U.S.

Based on research data from 2016, in the U.S. 79% of adults use Facebook, 32% use Instagram, 31% use Pinterest, 29% use LinkedIn, and at the bottom is 24% using Twitter. This is important because even though apps like Messenger and Tumblr had more registered users than the rest, the penetration doesn't match that. I would suggest, at least in the case of Messenger, that the end of 2017 research will show exponential growth because Facebook is pushing that platform very hard among its users.

If you want more detailed data about these platforms (e.g., breakdowns by gender, age, urban vs rural, etc.) go to https://sproutsocial.com/insights/new-social-media-demographics
Sprout Social has taken the 2016 Pew Research data and put it into easily readable graphs that let you get a sense of the demographics quickly. These is particulalry useful if you already know your reader demographics.

For example, from my Facebook advertising in the U.S. I know my romance and women's fiction demographics skew 90% female, of which 55% are over the age of 55. I've been thinking about investing in some advertising in the U.K. to build my audience there. However, I see that of all Facebook users, 12% are in the U.S. and only 2% are in the U.K. That might stop me. However, upon further research into the U.K. market I learn that though it is only 2% of the worldwide market, it is still the number one app used by social network users in the U.K. in fact over 89% of U.K. users use Facebook. That is higher than U.S. penetration.

Don't jump to conclusions about a market based on scanning a couple of graphs or statistics, particularly when they are given in terms of worldwide use. Asia-Pacific markets are currently growing the fastest and that may skew your perception of markets that have stabilized, like the U.S. and the U.K. Also the populations in China and India dwarf populations in other countries, including the U.S. So, when thinking about a smaller country (the U.K. at 65 million or Germany at 82 million) you know you need to dig deeper to discover how social media works in those geographic locations. Let's face it, I don't want to miss out on a chance to reach a possible 30 million+ readers in the U.K. that speak English, the language I write in, just because they are only 2% of all Facebook users.

## WHICH PLATFORM PROVIDES THE HIGHEST ENGAGEMENT WITH READERS?

It is one thing to have users and penetration. However, what really matters to authors is engagement. Just because a reader exists doesn't mean they are likely to engage with you. On each platform, the more engagement you see, the more your content is put in front of your readers for them to see. Sometimes that means it is moved to the top of their feed. Sometimes, as with Facebook author pages, it means more followers actually see the content. Without engagement you have your content being shown to less than 5% of your followers.

PEW Research does not provide engagement data, as it requires constant monitoring of sites. However ComScore, a cross-platform measurement company that precisely measures audiences, brands and consumer behavior has provided engagement data for the U.S. and the U.K. for the 18-34 year old demographic. The two charts look at engagement on one axis and penetration on the other. The number of minutes represents actual time on the platform when someone uses it. The percentages along the bottom represents the percentage of people who use social media who are using that particularly platform.

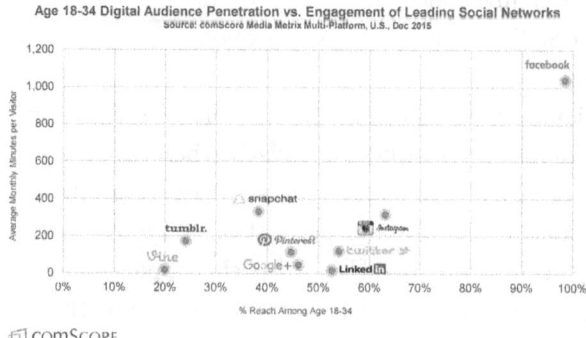

In the U.S. it is clear that Facebook, which as a penetration of 100% among social media users, has the highest engagement at more than 1,000 minutes for each time (session) someone is on Facebook. That is a little over 16 hours.

*Caveat:* A "session" does not necessarily equate to a day. A session is the time the app is open and active. Unlike most websites and other apps, Facebook doesn't log you out when you're idle. However, it does end your session when you close the browser if you don't enable the "Keep Me Signed In" option on the Facebook sign-in page. Some users keep their browser open over night, and Facebook if they are logged in.

According to the above graph, the next highest engagement per session is Snapchat at around 370 minutes, ~6 hours. However, Snapchat only has a penetration level of 40% of all social media users. Close to Snapchat is Instagram at about 350 minutes, 5.8 hours, and a penetration level of near 65%. On the penetration level difference, I would probably opt to invest in Instagram reader building before Snapchat. It's also important to note that this data snapshot was taken in Dec. 2015, and other research indicates that Instagram has grown by 100 million users each year since. It is likely that the penetration is even higher now.

## SECRETS TO EFFECTIVE AUTHOR MARKETING

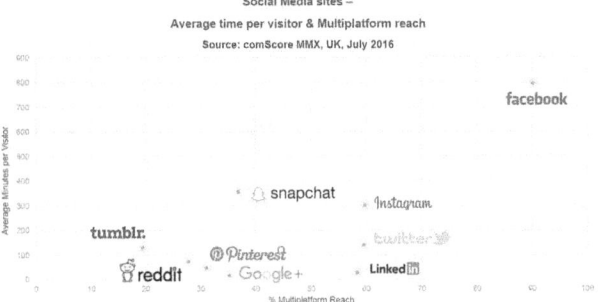

How does the U.K. compare to the U.S.? Again Facebook is well ahead both in minutes per engagement as well as percent of penetration in the U.K . market. Snapchat and Instagram seem to hold a similar pattern in terms of engagement and penetration as it does in the U.S. A big difference is that Vine doesn't appear at all in U.K. engagement whereas Reddit is doing better than Pinterest, Google+ and LinkedIn. However, it's penetration is slight lower.

Let's look at one more piece of interesting data. That is the increase in people who are using their phones, instead of interacting on a laptop or desktop computer. The average smartphone user spends in excess of 2 hours per day looking at their screens, either texting, browsing the internet, scrolling through emails and often using apps.

The chart below compares the reach of social media, as well as the average number of days per month and the sessions per day.

*Source: Forrester's Mobile Phone Data, December 2015*

Once again, we see that Facebook is the app accessed the most, with an average of 15 days out of a month being accessed in 8 sessions per day. For the first time, we now see Facebook Messenger in the number two spot with almost 8 days out of the month being accessed on the phone and usually 3 times per day on those days it is accessed.

## WHICH PLATFORM HAS A PROVEN POSITIVE ROI FOR PAID ADVERTISING

Although all the above platforms have millions of users engaging, to date only one continues to show promise for providing positive ROI (Return On Investment) for paid advertising for authors. That one is Facebook. If you want to access Facebook's immense user base, you must have a profile account on Facebook AND a business account (an author fan page). I'll talk about how you set those up later in this chapter.

Though large advertisers, like Sony or Nike or a large Big 5 publisher, might use many other platforms. In order to get economies of scale on platforms that are not Facebook, your ad budget needs to be at least in the tens of thousands per month because of the niche market of books and an even smaller audience on a per author basis.

Because of the other platforms owned by Facebook (What's App, Messenger and Instagram), I believe we will see advertising viability happen on those platforms fairly quickly. For the past year, when I have done a Facebook ad, I am given the opportunity to include that ad on Instagram. And I have had some success by including that platform—both in drawing new readers to my Instagram account and in getting actual book sales. So, that is already implemented. As of the writing of this book, I've seen a couple of emails from Facebook about their development of advertising for Messenger. I have not yet seen what that entails and if it is worth an investment. However, I predict it will be. (More on Messenger later in this chapter).

Sadly, as much as I have personally enjoyed using Twitter and Pinterest, I see no reason to spend advertising dollars on either of those platforms.

## WHICH PLATFORMS SHOULD YOU INVEST THE MOST TIME LEARNING TO USE?

I hope I've convinced you of the importance of Facebook. So, I will assume you will learn to use it, if not love it. Of the others, which you use depends on how you like to communicate.

I grew to like Twitter because of the short form of 140 characters, including spaces, to communicate with followers. It is a challenge to say anything of consequences in that space. However, it is also a relief because I don't have the space to expand on my message. (Note: in November 2017, Twitter doubled it's maximum characters allowed to 280).

In terms of building audience, I have found that at least one-third of my feed are people from businesses that have no relation to my business as an author. For those people in my feed twho MAY be readers, the nonfiction readers are the most responsive to me in Twitter. Though I have fiction readers, I have not found them to engage on Twitter as much as they do on Facebook.

I also like Pinterest as an idea and dream platform. It does have a much higher gender bias toward women, and the few actual readers I have who like me on Pinterest tend to be my romance readers. Even though I will continue to use Pinterest for myself, again I don't see it as that viable of platform for gaining new readers or getting sales. However, because I enjoy being on it I may gain a few. It's not something I invest a lot of time in.

I'm growing to like Instagram. I've only had my account for about 6 months as of the writing of this book. It has proven to be effective for ads as well as a quick personalized engagement device.

Finally, I am learning to like Messenger. Another app I've pretty much ignored except to watch it's growth. With the advent of chatbots, I see Facebook Messenger is the next big avenue for growing readership in the same way I grow my email readership. Those who engage on that platform appear to be even more loyal than email list readers. Early reports from other authors is they are getting 90% engagement on a regular basis and sales in the 30-50% range on book launches or notfications of backlist deals. Those percentages are definitely intriguing. I will talk more about this briefly in Chapter 9 when

I compare the use of Email list building and Messenger Chatbots for individualized communication. They follow similar principles but speak to two different audiences in terms of how they prefer to communicate.

Let's take a look at each of the platforms most commonly used by authors for engaging with their readers. In the next six chapters I will cover Facebook, Facebook Messenger, Twitter, Instagram, Pinterest, and YouTube. I will share resources beyond what I write for each of these platforms. At the end of the chapter, I will also share a curated list of links to learn more about other platforms that I don't cover.

Each platform will include an overview of the platform and its use, as well as a description of how to use that platform to grow your audience, engage your readers, and eventually sell to your readers if the platform is appropriate for sales. I will also provide some good resources for step-by-step instruction if you need it. Because this book is about marketing, I am focusing on the use of the platform for marketing rather than providing step-by-step instructions on how to set it up and use it. There are many good resources online for technical instruction that includes tutorials, videos, and written instructions. For each platform I will look at: how to grow followers; using the platform for brand building (PR); and using the platform for marketing (product awareness and sales).

**TIP:** All social media platforms are focused toward images and videos, in addition to words. Two excellent resources will help you with understanding how images should be delivered and where you can find images without having to spend hundreds of dollars to do social media posts.

**Image Sizing.** The first place many people stumble is knowing what size the image needs to be. Each platform is slightly different. Some want a landscape image (rectangle that is wider than it is tall). Others (e.g., Instagram) want a square image. In addition, the size of the ideal image in a post varies from platform to platform AND it seems to change every couple years. To keep up with this I highly recommend bookmarking Hubspot. They provide an up-to-date infographic for social media image sizes ranging from your header image (sometimes called a cover) to your post images. https://blog.hubspot.com/marketing/ultimate-guide-social-media-image-dimensions-infographic

Finding images to use without spending a lot of money is also difficult for many authors. I recommend beginning with images that are free via a Creative Commons license. Because you are a business person, you will want to look for images that carry a CCO license (Creative Commons, Can be used for Commercial uses, and does not require a credit to the originator—though a credit is always appreciated) I use Pixabay. https://pixabay.com/ They have thousands of images that you can search in the same way you can search at paid sites. The difference is that these images are available for free under a variety of Creative Commons Licenses. I love Pixabay particularly for backgrounds, seasonal images, and conceptual art. When you choose an image to download you are given the opportunity to send some money to the artist. Though you can download it for free, I highly encourage you to send something if you can—even $1 or $2 helps to keep artists and photographers sharing their work with others who may not have the means to pay at all.

## OVERVIEW OF SOCIAL MEDIA MARKETING

Now that you have a general understanding of the differences in the platforms, how do you use them for organic marketing. This book is all about unpaid PR and marketing techniques, or the occasional low cost (under $100) paid marketing.

Most PR and Marketing folks like to come up with pithy mnemonics to help you remember the steps. My memory aid is the word ACTS.

A – ATTRACT
C – CONVERT
T – TRANSFORM
S – STEADFAST

Before you have any chance of making a sale, you have to have an audience. Each social media platform has a different audience, different demographics, and different ways in which they are used. It is important to know those difference to attract an audience to that platform. One of the biggest mistakes that author's make is to use a post that is good for Facebook, and then link Facebook to Twitter. This means that all their tweets give a header and then a link to Facebook. Twitter users HATE that and, unless they already support you on both platforms, will not click that link. It's worse the other direction. People who tweet something on Twitter and then autolink that to Facebook. Now all the Facebook posts are character limited and the link goes back to whatever was on Twitter (e.g., an image).

Each platform audience needs to be treated with same kind of separateness that you might treat different genre audiences. Just as a mystery reader may never cross over to romance or fantasy. It is the same with loyal social media users. Those who prefer to get their content through a limited text platform, like Twitter, don't want to be sent to Facebook to get their content.

There are, of course, some exceptions to that inter-linking. The biggest exception is when a platform owns other platforms and purposefully wants you to link between the two. In this book, the only platform that applies to is Facebook. Facebook also owns Messenger and Instagram. As you read the discussion in those three social media platforms you will see there are times that interlinking and sharing between them is really effective.

Outside Facebook and its subsidiaries, you need to use each platform separately and be aware of the unique demographics, expectations, and uses of that platform. As you digest the ideas under each of the ACTS steps, also consider how that might be implemented differently in each platform.

## A - Attract Your Audience to Your Platform

### 1. Make it Helpful

When your target audience is perusing their platform of choice, they're consuming content for entertainment, learning, or social networking. They are NOT looking for a product to buy.

Think about what content appeals to your reader on that platform, the things they likely want to find out before every being shown a book to buy? You are a reader. What do you want to know about a new-to-you book or author? Even when you want to support a new author, there are still reasons people don't take that step. What are the reasons YOU default to a known author or a known series? That is what marketing people call "pain points" and you need to use your posts, tweets, pins address those proactively. And how does that match your brand with the content you're creating and publishing on social media?

Let's look at potential reader pain points

*1. Limited time to read.*

- Talk about your short novels or novellas instead of a 75K+ book
- Ask or suggest your audiobook or talk about a discount if they buy both audiobook and ebook.

*2. Past bad experiences when trying a new author.*

- Highlight good reviews.
- Talk about your professional editor.
- Point to number of reviews and star rating.

During the Attract stage, position your social channels as a knowledgeable resource or a hub of entertainment and news around themes that relate to your brand, rather than a place to sell your books.

## 2. Connect with Your Influencers

One of the best ways to attract an audience is to leverage influencer marketing. By working with established industry thought leaders or celebrities, brands can amplify their social content immensely.

When Hewlett Packard ran a new Star Wars-themed commercial, they tapped influencers to help promote it. One influencer, Rudy Mancuso, has 2.5 million followers on Instagram. Compare that to

HP's 357,000 and you understand why influencer marketing was a huge opportunity. HP worked with Mancuso to recreate the "Star Wars" theme song and, in turn, Mancuso drove his followers to HP's Instagram page.

Who are the influencers for readers? In reality it is other readers—particularly those who regularly share what they are reading and why. This could be celebrities like actors, politicians, TV anchors. If you have those contacts certainly use them. However, most of us don't have those contacts. The most likely influencers for readers are book bloggers and reviewers. Look for those contacts to connect with and offer mutually beneficial exchanges to draw new readers to both of your platforms.

### 3. Experiment with Multichannel Mulitmedia

Focus on content that's shareable and entertaining for people who may not be familiar with your brand. That way, when fans share the content to their circles, other potential customers will discover you and your books. One way to do that is to push beyond product and industry-related content and explore new territory.

Macy's is one of the most recognizable clothing and apparel brands in the world. When it comes to music, they aren't as well known in that industry. That's why Macy's first digital summer music festival, Macy's Summer Vibes Concert, is so interesting. By creating video content with upcoming musical artists (who were often wearing Macy's outfits), Macy's was able to build up a substantial social following across channels like Instagram and YouTube.

Video content is highly engaging, especially if it's about an interest that might be relevant to your audience's lifestyle. Overall, the Summer Vibes video on YouTube, featuring 45 minutes of music, got 1.5 million views.

What can authors do that is similar to that? Think outside the box. If write stories that feature characters who are musicians, why not consider partnering with musicians and sharing the love for both creative endeavors. Are your characters police officers? Athletes? Cowboys? Again, look at influencers with other products that also target those same interests in their customers. You won't know the possibilities until you ask. It is these creative partnerships that put you above all the other authors who are doing exactly the same thing.

## C – Convert A Passing Interest to a "Warm Lead"—someone who is likely to buy.

So, you've built and published social content that attracts potential buyers to the top of your funnel. The Convert stage is all about turning those fans and followers into leads. You can start doing that by offering an incentive. The incentive you offer (e.g., a free book or short story or character dossier) needs to be something that will get rid of their fears that your books aren't as entertaining, emotionally satisfying, or fun as the content you've been sharing on social media.

Offering a "taste" of your work is the best way to move them from warm leads to buyers. Whatever your incentive be sure to get information that allows you to easily contact them again. Typically this is done by asking for an email address so that you can get them an ebook download. This is where email marketing takes center stage.

With some of the new technologies, like Facebook Messenger, you might do the same thing without an email address. Instead, they become a willing subscriber to your Messenger chatbot where you will deliver more content and set up your sales funnel. Whatever technology you use, you want to be sure it is easy to continue the conversation with your readers on all the channels they frequent.

### 1. Create a Great Offer

One of the best ways to Convert your social audience is to create remarkable content that solves the problem your buyer is experiencing. By offering something like an ebook, Google Hangout, video, free course, webinar, consultation, or free giveaway in return for an email address or contact information, you can convert your social followers into interested leads that your product or service can help them with

### 2. Intrigue Your Audience with Exclusive Research

In B2B marketing campaigns, research means a lot. Businesses are constantly looking for the latest industry trends when it comes to the behavior of their target market. By creating Convert campaigns that preview premium content, you can entice people to learn more.

*Think With Google*, for example, is a division of Google that builds a lot of resources for digital marketers. The end goal is to get people to use Google Ads in their own campaigns. But before they introduce their product, they've built their email list by offering educational tips targeted toward people in the digital marketing fields.

What might you do to provide exclusive research your readers would be interested in receiving. Certainly, if you are a nonfiction writer the answer to this is easier to conceive. You are an expert in something and you can offer tip sheets, cheat sheets, dossiers, or whatever fits your topic.

Fiction writers, on the other hand, have it a little more difficult—but not impossible. Most writers do research while writing their book. Historical authors research time, location, clothing, cultural changes, and much more. However, contemporary authors might do the same. A book that takes place in the southern United States likely has differences than a book that takes place in New England. Even more a book that takes place in Paris has a lot of differences than one in Rekjavik. Sharing your research on people, places, and things that relate to your story is one way of providing exclusive research that readers may at least find interesting, and maybe valuable.

### 3. Retarget with Relevant Events

Most marketers use retargeting to sell products. They'll target website visitors by placing product ads next to search results. But you can use retargeting to target fans and followers. Try promoting a personalized offer or event to improve conversion.

Northface ran an Instagram campaign that promoted an upcoming event featuring a videographer and a professional climber. This aligns with the Northface brand of the outdoors lifestyle, while creating a real connection that converts potential customers by driving them from Instagram to an event page.

You can do the same with your brand or your books. Do an interview with someone who has the same background or job as one of your characters. Do you feature a former special forces member? Do an interview with one and make it a live event. What about a firefighter or a singer? Pair that with a movie or another event that features people like this.

Your book is SF and takes place on a planet we haven't yet explored. No problem, share an article about exo planets or one from a futurist discussing likely scenarios for deep space exploration. It is rare that a writer creates a world or characters that have no context for the reader to understand them. Most writers draw from their own expertise or things they've read and learned over time. You can be creative and plan online events and shareable content that compliment those aspects of your books.

## 4. Invite Your Audience to Webinars & Live Streams

Live streams are becoming a popular way to connect with your fans and followers across channels like Facebook and Twitter. Likewise, webinars, panels, and other digital events have always been a huge asset to brands because you can create a more interactive and immersive experience for potential customers.

Authors have many options for doing live events on the Internet. If you are the kind of person who is very uncomfortable with this, consider who you can partner with to still create an event—actors? Bloggers? Other more extraverted readers? There is always a way to involve others and still take advantage of this rich experience.

## T – Transform Your Audience from a Warm Lead to a Buyer

Most sales people call this the Closing stage. You attracted a reader, you took away most of their hesitation by addressing pain points, and now you need them to actually buy something.

To move your audience down the funnel into the Close stage, build targeted deals and promote them strategically. If some of your social media followers have passed through the Convert stage, you'll have other ways to contact them. When it's time to actually sell them your book through a marketing campaign, you should be able to reach your readers across multiple channels that you've built.

At the end of the day, this is where you need to closely track the revenue from your efforts. While in the Attract and Convert stage you've been tracking growth and engagement, the Close stage is where you should track dollars spent and dollars earned.

You've built a social community during the Attract stage and nurtured them with great offers during the Convert stage. In the Transform stage, it's time to put some dollars behind targeted posts and help your leads turn into customers.

## 1. Feature Your Readers

You can't beat a bona fide reader testimonial. Companies can create great targeted social ads if they feature current customers. By showcasing what your customers already love about your brand, you can help close the deal via social channels.

Authors get testimonials primarily from reviews. Most of us are fairly adept at featuring these. But it doesn't hurt to do it more often through a variety of social media posts, images, and inclusion in distribution channel copy. Beyond the written review, there are now other ways to promote testimonials. There are book bloggers who do video blogs where they animatedly praise a book. If you have any of those, they are great to feature.

Even something as simple as asking your fans to post a picture of themselves reading your book (print or ebook). Just make sure the picture includes your cover. These can be shared all over your social media channels.

I recently asked people on my street team to share a brief favorite quote from one of my books they read. I was pleasantly surprised at what they chose. I then took those quotes and made quick marketing images with the quote and a picture of my book. I then paired that post with my reader blog where I run an excerpt of the scene in the book where the quote appears. Both the images shared in social media and the longer blog post with the excerpt link to buy pages for the book.

## 2. Put Your Price Upfront

A social ad in the Transform stage should offer transparent pricing and product benefits that directly solve the problem your buyer is experiencing. That will narrow down who clicks to take the next step, in effect making sure that only truly interested customers go to the landing page.

I know that many authors believe they can't market a book unless it is free or heavily discounted. I think that is not only inaccurate but also dangerous. If that is the only time you market, you are training your readers to only purchase at a discount. I believe that the majority of your marketing should be at full retail price. This not only improves your income, but it also proves there is VALUE in your book. Your work is worth more than free or 99 cents.

Save the special deals for truly special occasions (e.g., Christmas, to celebrate your birthday, or to match a season or holiday that pertains to that specific book). Then when the deal is announced, it REALLY IS A DEAL because your readers should know the normal value of that book.

## 3. Show the Product in Action

Authors typically show books by themselves, as a cover or a three dimensional image. Instead, focus on photos that show how your product can fit into the reader's day-to-day lifestyle.

How many ways can you show someone reading your book? It may be more than you realize. Someone reading the book on their tablet with morning coffee. Someone reading on their phone as they stand in line to get into an event. Someone snuggled into their favorite reading nook with a paperback. Someone with headphones listening to the audiobook. Someone sharing a passage of your book with a friend. Again, this might be a way to get your fans engaged in sending pictures of all the places they encounter your book from finding it online, in the library or a local bookstore to all the places they read it and take it with them.

If fans don't participate you can do some staging yourself.

## S - Steadfast Loyalty to You as An Author and/or to Your Series or a Type of Book That You Consistently Deliver

A customer who just bought their first book from you does not automatically become a steadfast customer—even if they loved the story. They already expected a good book, because of the previous steps they took to convince themselves to actually make a purchase. They expected a good book, because you promised not to let them down. But now you have to prove to them that this wasn't a fluke. YOU need to continue to do things that show it wasn't a one-time promise and know that you hooked them you will be selling to them all the time.

After the sell you need to build that steadfast loyalty by continuing to create a great customer experience with more non-sales content. You need to prove that you care about them as a reader, not just as a buyer.

### 1. Respond & Personalize

A survey from Sprout Social found that brands respond to just 11% of people who reach out on social media, despite the fact that social media is now the favored way for people to contact companies. http://www.mediapost.com/publications/article/275848/

It might not be realistic to personalize a response to every person on social media, but it doesn't hurt to try. Authors should invest resources in their relationships with their most vocal readers. Those are the customers that can become brand advocates or brand detractors. And it all depends on if they feel they are being treated as a valued customer.

This doesn't mean you have to buy them presents and do everything they ask. But it does mean you need to thank them for their feedback and give them opportunities to help you get the word out.

Make it easier for those who already love you to share the love and get some modicum of recognition for doing that.

## 2. Loyalty, Revamped & Retargeted

Want readers to keep coming back? Think about how you can empower your loyalty program with your social media campaigns. This is a key piece of the Steadfast stage - don't just create content that targets potential customers; think about how to educate, entertain, and, entertain current customers beyond offering more books to buy.

One of the best ways to build a social media loyalty program is by using retargeting pixels from Facebook or Twitter. This enables you to show ads to visitors who have already been on the website, so they're likely familiar with your brand - if not customers already - so you can target your messaging accordingly.

## 3. Inspire Readers in their Day-to-Day Lives

If you've ever seen a motivational tweet or a quote overlaid on a Facebook image, you probably know the power of inspirational content. Think about what your brand can provide that can help energize your audience as they go about their day-to-day lives. The more targeted the content, the better.

## Chapter Ten
# FACEBOOK

As I've already discussed, Facebook is the number one social media platform used around the world. To ignore it is not advised. Facebook is Facebook is a social networking website that can be accessed via any device that can access the Internet. On a laptop, desktop you access Facebook through a web address. On other devices (tablets, phones) you access Facebook through an App.

Facebook allows users to post comments, share photographs, link to news or other interesting content on the Web, play games, chat live, and even stream live video. Shared content can be made publicly accessible (meaning anyone on the Internet can see it), or it can be shared only among a select group of friends or family or a group you've created. You may even elect to share it only with one other person.

Three independent types of Facebook "pages" are available: a Profile Page, a Business/Interest Page (I refer to this as your Author Fan Page); and a Group Page. According to Facebook Terms of Service you are allowed to have only ONE Profile page and unlimited group pages and business pages.

**Profile Page.** This is a page associated with you as an individual and serves as the core account for your Facebook use. To set up your account you are required to enter certain information. That information is your first and last name, a valid email address, a password, your gender, and birthdate. By default, Facebook will display your name and birthdate. However, you may choose to hide your birthdate if you like. Facebook asks for birthdate in order to determine whether to show you "adult" information. This doesn't only refer to potential content that includes sexy images or violent messages. It also refers to anyone doing advertising for a product. Facebook does not condone direct selling to minors.

You have the opportunity to complete other information about yourself to be displayed: a brief bio, places you went to school, jobs you've had or relationships to other people (e.g., a spouse or other relative). Completing this helps people to find you who may have some of those shared experiences.

**Key Point to Profile Pages** – Every post you make can be seen by everyone you are friends with on your profile page. Facebook does not withholding those posts.

Authors make one of two choices about using a profile page. Some authors set up a profile that is the "real" person. Others set up a profile that is only their author self. I use my profile page as the real me, and it is the same page I use for talking to friends and family. Though I do allow some readers and other authors to be my "friend" on that page, I am also conscious that I have an extended family that consists of people from young children to elderly adults who communicate and share with me via that page. I've instructed them how to be careful in what they post and make sure, in the case of pictures of minors or things they really don't want the general public to know, that it is going to only Friends. In that way, I will see it but no one else on my page who is not their "friend" will see it.

Others choose to set up a Profile page as their author persona. This works if you have an email address just for your author contact that is separate from your email address for your personal contact. Then you can successfully have two Profiles—though Facebook does NOT like this and it is against their Terms of Service. They specifically state you are allowed ONE profile page per individual. However, they haven't cracked down on this.

One other thing to be aware about your profile. Anything you have in your profile that have you agreed to display to those who "friend" you becomes part of the data about you that will be shared anytime you engage with an advertisement. That is why Facebook has more information on what people do and buy than any other platform.

**Business Page (Author Fan Page).** Once you have a Profile account, you may set up any number of business pages. Most authors only set up one. However, you could choose to have a separate page for each penname or a page for a particular series. Though I have three author names, I only have one business page. I figure I don't need to take even more time to keep up with three pages. But other authors are fine with multiple pages.

The primary purpose of your business page is to represent your author business. This is where you really want to be sure your branding is clear and available. The information about the "business" is information about you as an author. You also have many more opportunities for drawing readers to your books through a business page. You set up your page by choosing which category your business is associated with. I suggest you choose Artist, Band, or Entertainer.

You can set up an online book catalog that readers can use and then link to a sales page. Within the Facebook header you can set up what is called a "call to action" button. That button might be to join your email list "Sign up". Or it might be the "Shop Now" button where they go directly to your bookstore—on Facebook, on your website, or somewhere else. Other options are "Book Now" (good for courses or services), "Contact Us," and "Watch Video." I haven't found a good way to use the Watch Video on a regular basis. But with Facebook pushing videos, I'm sure there is something interesting. The video can set up the visitor for all kinds of other options on the page. Facebook has a straightforward tutorial on how to set up your call-to-action button on your cover page. https://www.facebook.com/help/977869848936797

## HOW TO GET FOLLOWERS

There are four things you need to do with any social media account you set up to help gain new followers.

1. Fill out your profile completely on your business page (fan page)
2. Share a link to your profile via your other networks and via email
3. Place follow links and widgets on your blog or website
4. Add your new social profile to your email signature

Facebook is no different in those steps. The first step is to make sure you complete all the information about your business. Remember YOU are the business. Think about making it interesting and drawing the reader in—just like you would think about writing the first couple paragraphs in your novel or nonfiction book.

It begins with choosing a friendly page title. I've already indicated you should use your name. Your name is your brand. If you use a pen name for your writing, then that should be the title of your page. What if your name is already taken? Then alter it in some way. I was surprised to learn how many Maggie Lynch's there are in the world. I ended up taking maggiewrites as the name of my page. People still find me when they search for Maggie Lynch. There are a number of variations I might have chosen: maggielynchauthor or maggie-author or maggie-amazing-author. Okay the last one is not one I would have chosen back then.

Next write a catchy description in the short description field. Think of this like a tweet. It's not very long but it has to be interesting. Lead with the most important part about your business. If you went through the earlier section of this book on creating your press kit, you will have already gotten through this. Below is a screenshot of the information associated with my Maggie Lynch business page.

Fill out EVERYTHING you can on this business page with your brand in mind. Notice in the screenshot, how I also completed the Personal Interests section and the Story section. The Personal Interests is your opportunity to show you are more than a business. Readers love to know about writer's personal life too. They want to relate to you. Whatever you put there, know it serves as a list of possible future posts too. The Story section is designed for the business to talk about their origin story. For writers, I see it as a great place to talk about your story in terms of characters and the tagline/story brand that threads through all of your books.

Once that is complete, it's time to start posting interesting content. What is interesting? Anything that fits your brand, your personality, and the work that you are producing. In the beginning no one outside of close friends and family will be even looking at your posts. Don't worry about that right now. Spend some time getting five to ten posts in there over about a week. Ask everyone you know to go look at it and at least give it a thumbs up if they think it is worthwhile at all. Of course, if they want to comment that's even better.

Once you've accumulated some posts, it's time to invite everyone you know to come and LIKE your page. The quickest way to do this is to let Facebook invite everyone you are "friends" with on your personal page. In fact, Facebook will remind you to do this fairly early on. If that doesn't happen or you just want to get it going, here are the simple instructions.

1. Click below your Page cover photo.
2. Select Invite Friends.
3. Click Search All Friends.
4. A list of all your friends on your regular profile page will appear. Click Invite Button next to the friends you want to invite.

The downside to a Facebook Business Page is that, unlike your personal profile page, not everyone gets to see every post. In the beginning they do (for a week or so). But after that, Facebook stops showing your posts if that person has not "engaged" with that post. How do they engage? In one of three ways: liking the post (thumbs up click or other icon associated with that); commenting on the post; or sharing the post with their Facebook friends.

The reason Facebook does this is because they know that with more than a billion people posting on Facebook every day, customers would quickly become overwhelmed with the stream of content. In the end, they would stop paying attention. So, Facebook decided they would try to ONLY show information to customers that the customers want to see. Though it may seem so at times, no software can read your mind. The way they decide who will see the post is by that person having shown an interest in getting that information. This means the onus is on you to post things your readers really will be interested in. If you aren't reaching as many people as you like, then you do have the option to "Boost" a post and pay to reach them. I'll talk more about that in the Paid Advertising section of this book.

So how do you get fans to see all your posts without buying ads? Teach them how to turn on **Get Notifications** for your page.

Turning on the Get Notifications feature for a page is easy.

1. Go to the page you from which you want to get notifications.
2. Hover over the **Following** button (the person must have Liked your page to get notifications)
3. Select **Get Notifications**.

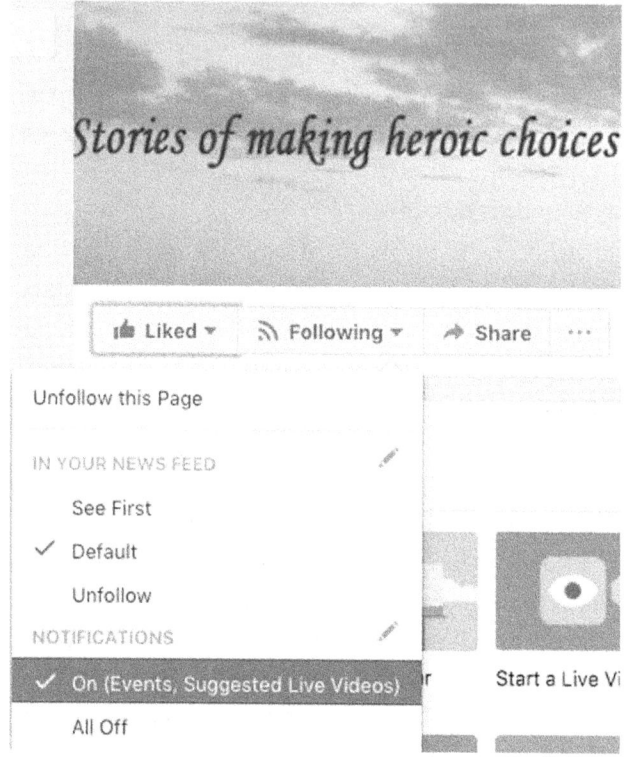

Anyone who does this will now see all your posts in their newsfeed. Unfortunately, only your superfans will likely to take the time to do this. So, let's look at ways to set up your posts to entice people to engage with you.

## SHARE RELEVANT CONTENT

Share content that your fans expect to see in your page. This goes back to your brand and your audience. If your books are science fiction with your characters living on other planets, using cool technology, and using genetic modification both in agriculture and on themselves, you can share short posts about what is happening in genetic modification today. If you are a fantasy writer who built a world around the ability to use different kinds of lichen for food, look for pictures of lichen and teach your readers how to identify them. Link to articles on lichen and food. No matter your genre there are interesting things you can share and post.

The other part of relevant content goes to your brand. Anyone who has made it this part in the book and skipped "that branding stuff" as not being helpful, you should go back now. It will be coming up in every section of this book.

If your brand is humorous, you can post humorous pictures, jokes, or pithy quotes. You can link to humorous videos on YouTube. On the other hand, if your brand is heartwarming stories of family and love. Look for quotes and pictures that depict that. Select you tube videos or news stories that reinforce the goodness in people or the way people overcome challenges. Even though none of these pictures or quotes relate directly to YOUR book. They still relate to your brand.

Readers love to know how authors live or work on a day-to-day basis. That also leaves you open to lots of posts about your daily life. Again, be careful that you aren't posting everything. For the most part readers don't want to know what you ate at every meal—unless your books are all about food or you are chef, or your characters love dumpy diners. But they do want to know about your day-to-day life *as it relates to your brand*. Again, if you are writing humorous books, relate humorous things that happen to you. If you are writing heartwarming books, relate heartwarming things that happened to you.

You can share books you are reading or authors you like. Again, you want to share books in the genre you write. If you are writing sweet, inspirational romances. You want to talk about books like that or authors who write that. You do not want to share the latest big erotica book—even if you did read it and love it. Sharing other books and authors in your genre creates a connection, in the readers mind, between your book and their books. That's valuable in the long term if those readers like that author's books too.

## PROMOTE YOUR BOOK(S) NO MORE THAN ONE TIME FOR EVERY 7-10 OTHER POSTS

Sharing promotional content about your book all the time will drive your fans away. It is true that one of the reasons they Like your page and watch posts is to see when you are releasing a new book or have a deal for them. However, they don't want to see you talking about the book every day for weeks. Or having something to sell them every day. It eventually becomes too much of the same and they will ignore you. Keep it up and you are consigned to the "sleazy salesperson" category.

Outside of an actual release or great deal, when you do talk about your own books do it in a way that provides valuable content. One of the popular ways authors do that is to share a quote from their book with a related picture. You can further connect that quote with a blog post that shares an excerpt where that quote is located. Here is an example of how I did that with a Facebook post connected to a blog post. The picture below is connected with the excerpt here: https://maggielynch.com/heart-strings-excerpt/

How does this differ from actual selling? First, it offers something of value to fans at no cost—an excerpt of the book. Second, in the Facebook post itself there are no words about buying the book or how to buy the book. Third, even when the reader goes to the blog post there is no request to buy the book. There are links to the book page where the reader would see buy links, but she would go there because she was interested in the quote and/or the excerpt.

Keep posts short. Readers often see hundreds of posts and pictures in their timeline every day. Two things draw them to pay attention to yours instead of others. 1) The purpose of the post is stated clearly within one active sentence. For the above, I wrote: "Every Thursday I share an excerpt based on a reader submitted favorite quote from a book." You can see the excerpt here. LINK. 2) The image is attractive, easy to scan and can quickly be judged whether it is of interest. As I've talked about before, social media has become image dependent. You don't want images to be too busy or too wordy. Readers scan and move on quickly. The image above has an interesting but not distracting background. That draws attention to the primary image, the book. The quote is in large type to make it easy to read. My website is always at the bottom. Whenever posting an image you have created, include your website. It is a help for someone who wants to go there, and it is a constant reminder even if the person doesn't click on the link.

For me this makes sense because people that see a title and image in their timeline may not 'Like It' since it provides no value to them (don't forget that the average user is presented with hundreds of postings in their timeline every time they login to Facebook).

Often a fan will click LIKE on an image without ever reading the post. Though your website visits didn't improve, just clicking that like increases engagement on Facebook and that engagement with that fan means he/she will see your next post without you having to pay.

## SELECT IMAGES AND VIDEOS THAT DRAW EMOTIONAL RESPONSES

The most popular posts on Facebook pages not only have great images, but the image engenders an emotional response. Why do cat pictures get so many likes? Because cats tend to be inherently cute and people love to equate the picture with human actions and emotions. The same goes for any other picture. When someone has an emotional response to an image—whether its laughter, sadness, warmth, hatred, or love it will likely get a click and a share, and sometimes even a comment.

## SHARE YOUR POST WITH YOUR PERSONAL PROFILE PAGE

On your personal profile page *everyone* who is a "friend" does get your post in their news feed. Often, people who are your "friends" are also on your fan page. However, they pay more attention to your posts on your profile page because they see them all.

By simultaneously sharing your fan/business page post in your profile page you will increase engagement numbers for your fan page. Even though, the engagement takes place in your profile page, if that person is also a member of your fan page it means it will count. Should you then later that week put a post in your fan page but not your profile page, that person will get it in their feed.

***Post regularly and consistently***. The primary thing that keeps up your engagement is to post regularly. Whenever an author tells me how hard it is to get anyone to engage on their fan page, I always ask: "How many times a week do you post there." Invariably they say once a week or once a month, or whenever they have something to sell (which may be twice a year). That won't work. With the hundreds of posts people receive in their feeds, they are likely to skip over yours unless they see your name again and again and they've clicked or noticed enough valuable content that it signals them to take a look.

***Post at least once per day.*** Some marketers suggest posting three to five times per day! Whatever you choose, make sure its valuable, quality content. Pick something you know you can sustain (even if it's only three times per week) and post on that schedule for at least three months consistently. I know you will see a substantial difference in your engagement numbers and in the number of people liking your page.

**_Invite People to Engage_**. Just like with other marketing efforts, you need to have a call-to-action. In this case the action is to engage with you. You need to ASK for this or at least invite them with every post. One way to invite people to engage is to present them with something to click, like a button or a link. Another way is to extend an invitation, e.g., "Join in the Discussion." You might also ask a direct question. For example, when I post a personality quiz link, I always say tell my results and then ask: "How about you?"

I've never directly asked people to like or share a post. To me, that is the equivalent of saying "Buy My Book." I want people to like and share posts because they find them interesting or valuable. However, I definitely include a call-to-action as mentioned in the paragraph above. My personal style is to be a bit understated. Yours may be different. I do know some authors who regularly ask people to Like their page or to Like or Share a post and they do get follow through, at least from their superfans. So, it can work. It's a matter of what feels comfortable to you.

## THIS SOUNDS LIKE A LOT OF TIME-CONSUMING WORK

It can be if you are trying to think of things each day without planning. And once you get on Facebook, it is easy to be sucked into the social milieu and forego the time you set aside for writing. There are two things I do to lessen the amount of time I spend.

**_I have a theme for each day_**. This way I don't have to think about what I'm going to post. It also sets a goal for me to post at least once per day. This also builds up an expectation with fans of what I might post that day. Here are my themes. You can choose your own that fits your brand.

- **_Mutual Monday_** – I post about an author I like using that person's picture as the image. I also link to a longer blog

post about that author and his/her books. I only choose authors who write in the genres I write in.
- **Terrific Tuesday** – I post an image or video that is positive and uplifting. This matches my brand as a heartwarming writer of characters who overcome major challenges to live a better and happier life.
- **Wacky Wednesday** – I post something amusing. For the most part I am a dramatic writer. However, every story has some amusing moments and maybe even humorous or snarky depending on the character. This is my chance to show that side of me. Humor is very personal, so if you do this be sure it still matches your brand and doesn't offend.
- **Title Taste Thursday**—This is when I use the quote images I discussed above and then tie them to an excerpt I post on my blog. This is the one consistent time each week that I'm actually talking about my books. Not selling—just talking.
- **Fast Fridays**—I post a quiz or poll that I think readers would enjoy. I favor the personality or fun quizzes created by places like buzzfeed. Again, it needs to match your brand. Most of my books have characters who are trying to figure out who they are, what is the purpose or meaning of their life, or how they relate to others. In reality, this is also what many people are doing in their day-to-day lives. This is a way to explore that and talk about it that is fun and not too revealing if you don't want it to be.
- **Caturday Saturday**—I have two rescue cats myself and I frequently feature a cat in the stories I write. This is an opportunity to share a bit of my life and to get all those cute-cat clicks that are so popular. It also seems to encourage my fans to post pictures of their cats too.
- **Sundry Sunday**—This is my free post day with no specified theme. I tend to share meditative thoughts from the week, an image of something I loved that week (e.g., a hike or walk I took, a bird in the tree, something I read or a

movie I saw that spoke to me, or some statement or meditation on the way I view the world).

Many of the posts you've now labored over can also be cross-posted on other social media (your blogs, Twitter, your VIP reader group, Google+ and sometimes on Instagram or Pinterest depending on the images). That means do the work once and then spread it around to all the platforms.

One of the things I learned early on is that it is NOT good practice to feed Twitter from Facebook or to feed Facebook from Twitter. A lot of people do that and both platforms make it easy. However, the feeds are the lowest ranking posts. The reason is that consumers on the specific platform do not want to leave and go to another social media platform to see your link or what you said unless it is really enticing.

So, how do you get the same posts everywhere without doing a forward from one platform to the next? By using a scheduling tool. My favorite tool for this is Buffer http://buffer.com Buffer is a web-based social media app that allows you to quickly schedule multiple posts to a variety of sites. Each scheduled post is being posted as native to that specific platform. This means when someone sees the post in the platform they don't have to leave just to read it or act on it.

The best part is you can schedule these posts well in advance, including the day, time of day, and exactly what the post says. The posts are automatically formatted and images are automatically sized for scheduled postings based on your choice of sites for that particular post. The free version gives users the ability to schedule five social accounts: Twitter, Facebook, LinkedIn, Google+ and Instagram. That means one Twitter account, one Facebook account, etc. You are also limited to schedule up to 10 posts each month per site account. So, in the scenario I described above, I could plan 10 days of posts for each of the five platforms.

Buffer also has several paid plans ranging from $10 per month to $399 per month. I'm using the $10 per month plan. That allows me to have up to 10 social accounts. In addition to the above I include my Facebook profile, my Facebook group page for my VIP reader group, Pinterest and access to Windtree Press Facebook and Twitter accounts. The $10 per month also allows me to post up to 100 posts per account each month. That averages out to 3 posts a day for each account.

For me, it is unlikely I would exceed the need for more than 3 posts per day for each account. However, should I later need to do more significant posts, I could move up in pricing to the next tier ($69 per month), which then allows for 25 accounts and up to 2,000 posts per account per month. The more expensive pricing also provides for adding team members who can access your account and run it for you.

## HOW TO GROW YOUR FANS AND FOLLOWERS IN FACEBOOK

Initial followers come from your friend list and from them sharing your posts with their friends. However, this can be a slow build unless you are posting amazing content that regularly gets shared a lot and is easily traced back to you and attributed to you. Beyond those methods you have to find ways to drive traffic to your page. You can do that through paid advertising on Facebook—boosted posts and other ads; or you can do it by other means that send people from one place (e.g., your website) to Facebook. As we are covering Paid Advertising toward the end of this book, let's look at other more organic methods of growing your followers.

### *Invite People Who Have Engaged On Your Page to Like Your Page*

Many people are unaware of this simple way to get likes from people who already enjoyed some of your content. How does someone even see a post if they didn't already like your page? The miracle of social media is viral networking. If a fan shared your post with a friend outside your sphere, she would see it in her news feed and would have the option of liking the post. Also people outside of your page might see things their friends are doing in their "Activity Feed." That's the stream on the right hand side of a desktop where they can stalk their friends. For example, they might see that friend, Maggie Lynch, just liked a post about the next Star Wars movie. They can then click on that post too.

This is a time-limited option that I missed for quite a while. The option to invite people who liked a post lasts for only 3-4 months, unless that post continues to get engagement because it is still being shared. This makes sense because inviting someone who liked a post a year ago is unlikely to generate a positive response as they may not remember that post. So, it is best to check at least once a week and do those invites right away. Even better is to do it within 24 hours if you happen to be hanging out on your page anyway.

To access this feature, click on the number of **likes** under any post on your page. You'll automatically get a list of every user who has liked the post. To the right of each user's name, you will see a button that shows if the user has already liked your page. For those who have not yet liked your page, there will be an Invite button. Click the button and Facebook will automatically send them an invitation to like your page.

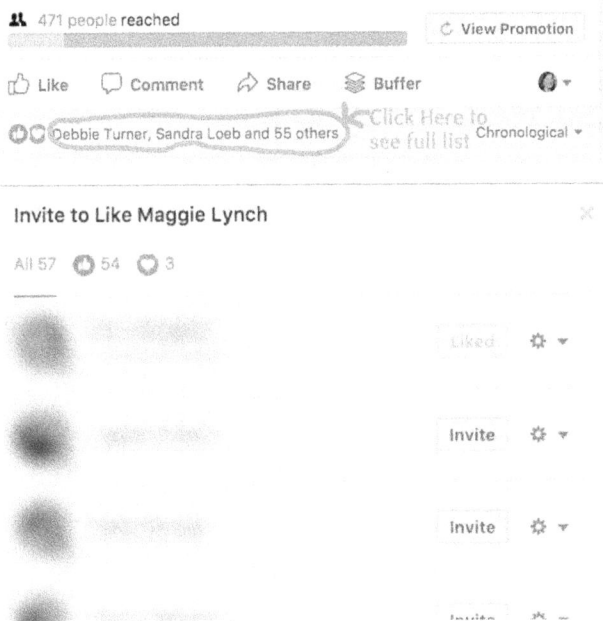

This is particularly effective after you have run any kind of an ad like a boosted post or any other Facebook ad where people, not already affiliated with your page, saw the post and liked it. Depending on the post and how closely it matched your brand and offerings, you can see between 20% to 50% conversions of these people to Like your page from that invite.

In the screenshot above you can see that 55 people liked this particular post. Out of that 38 were people who had not already liked my page. I invited all of them and within 24 hours 17 people had accepted the invitation. That's a 45% conversion rate!

**Caveat1**: If you run an ad and have thousands of new likes on the ad, Facebook will stop your ability to invite them after 500 invites. This is because after that the Facebook algorithm thinks you might be a spammer. Of course, if several people on your invite list reports you as a spammer before the 500 invites are sent, they will limit you earlier. My advice is for you to spread out your invitations over several days. Let's face it, most people do not want to spend all day manually clicking invites for a thousand people anyway. Consider scheduling only 100 or 200 each day.

**Caveat 2**: Once your page likes go over 100,000 likes you will no longer get the option to invite people to Like your page. I don't know about you, but I'm currently not worried about the limitation.

### Run a contest

Contests are used to send traffic to lots of places—to build an email list, to become aware of a book, and they can be used to gain LIKES on your social media pages.

There are several contest apps that include additional entries if the person LIKES your Facebook page. Some of these are Gleam, King Sumo, and Rafflecopter. This does drive traffic to your page. However, you need to be careful as to if the people are liking your page just to try to win the contest or if they truly want to see your posts and engage with you. It looks great to have 5,000 people who have liked your page. But if only 50 of them are engaging, it will keep the number of people being shown your posts to those 50 and never go above that without paid advertising.

### *Participate in a Live Facebook Event*

These can be anything from a video event that happens live within Facebook to a multi-author social event. Video is picking up followers more quickly than any other method. You might use this to talk to fans on a regular basis, read from your book, interview another author or some other person your fans may like to meet, etc. A multi-author social event is also live, in that readers must participate during a specific period of time (usually two to three hours). The event is somewhat like an online party, in that people socialize, usually authors give away something readers want (free book for example), and the event highlights specific authors at different times during the party. If you make an impression on a reader during these events they will go LIKE your page.

### *Provide specialized content in exchange for liking your page*

Similar to providing a free book in exchange for getting an email for your list, you can also provide something for people who LIKE your Facebook Page. Facebook does record all the likes. To see who has liked your page, click on **Settings**. Then click on **People and Other Pages** in the left column. In this way, you can verify who liked your page and then send a link to whatever you are giving away.

### *Place a Facebook Like Box on your Website and/or Blog*

This can be a big box that shows latest posts on your website along with some of the people who have liked your page, to as small as a LIKE button displayed along with other social media icons readers can click to contact you or engage with you outside of your website. Equally important, the like box or button, along with displaying your Facebook Business Page name also provides information to search engines. It allows them to associate your website with a Facebook Business page.

Facebook doesn't index personal profile pages because they aren't public. Though it may show a specific post in a personal profile if it is shared as "public." In general, anything you are putting on your personal page is shared for "friends" even if some of them are fans, but it is not helping your search engine status or ranking. However, Facebook does allow search engines to index Business pages.

### *Promote your Facebook page in other social media networks*

For me, this is controversial. We already know that people have favored social media networks. A number of fans are annoyed by being asked to "like" you in another platform while they are in the platform they prefer to use. I don't think, for example, that responding to a new Twitter fan with a thanks and a request to also like you in Facebook is effective. You are asking the person to leave Twitter to do this.

On the other hand, a number of fans are on multiple platforms and it may be the one they encounter you on (e.g., Twitter) is not their favorite. And the content you provided is valuable enough they are willing to leave Twitter and check out your Facebook page.

An effective way to get people to check you out from a non-Facebook platform is to offer an incentive. e.g., I'm going to be giving away my entire series to one lucky fan on my Facebook page. Go there now and like me and I'll be sure you have an invitation to the party.

### *Promote your Facebook page in your newsletter and email campaigns*

With any newsletter or email you send, make sure to include a link to your Facebook page. (I personally include all my social media links at the bottom of every email I send) Again, you can use it to drive traffic there for certain content or events. For example, I might announce to my email list that I am participating in a Facebook party on a certain date where authors will be giving away books. Another possibility is to plan a specific deal that will only be available to people who have Liked my page. In other words I'll boost a deal announcement post for $10 in Facebook but target *only* people who have liked my page. No one else would get notification of that deal. I'm sure there are a lot of other ideas for getting people to your page without specifically writing the words "Please like my page." Get creative.

**A Final Note**

Facebook does offer paid advertising opportunities to specifically get people to Like your page. I do NOT endorse this. There is no reason to buy ads only for this purpose. Any paid advertising you do, for any reason, gives people an opportunity to Like your page—whether it's a boosted post, a post to gain email subscribers, a post about a deal or a book sale. The option to also Like your page is there and easy to find. And for those who don't Like your page but like the post, you have the option to Invite them as discussed above.

If I'm going to spend money on a Facebook ad I want it to do something more than asking for likes. I would rather people like my page because they find the content valuable and make that conscious decision. Those people will then prove to be more likely to respond to posts in the future and to buy books in the future.

**A Great Resource Based On Research**

Buzz Sumo researched the actions of over 1 billion posts on Facebook to analyze what works best to increase engagement. This slide share of only 12 slides is very insightful. I learned a great deal I didn't know and some of it is counter-intuitive—like sharing an image from Instagram gets higher engagement than sharing an image natively. Check it out.

https://www.slideshare.net/buzzsumo/how-to-improve-facebook-engagement-insights-from-1bn-posts

*Chapter Eleven*

# FACEBOOK MESSENGER AND CHAT BOTS

At its core, Messenger is a texting app, for both one-on-one and group messaging, but it can also send images and video. Because it is attached to Facebook you don't need to know a person's phone number to text them, which is critical to authors and their marketing. No one wants to give out their phone numbers anymore.

From a user perspective, Messenger allows them to connect with more than friends and family. It's a kind of instant connection with anyone you might know on Facebook who have allowed you to connect. It could be that you can text with thousands of people if you want.

A major feature of Messenger as a texting tool, is that it's not limited to being used on your phone (though many people do interact with it that way). You use it on the web, therefore you can setup, receive, and respond to messages using a laptop or desktop. That means I don't have to fumble with the small keyboard on my phone. Messenger includes lots of built-in emojis, stickers, and GIFs that you can use within your messages. Also, like Facebook, Messenger saves all images, videos, and icons in a collection of media files that you can easily sift through to reuse again if you like. This can also include PDFs if you like to send cheat sheets or work sheets to readers.

If you are in live mode, Messenger includes a typing indicator to see when the person is writing something. When it is sent, the date and time is included with the message. This is also great if you are looking at your messages long after the person sent the requests.

There are many other features that I won't get into here because I haven't identified how they are useful in general book and author marketing. However, understanding all these features helps to explain why over 1 billion people are using Messenger and it has become the hub of their communication platform. Here are some of those features.

- Make voice and/or video calls for free (similar to Google Hangout), including a saved audio clip.
- Send money to people by connecting your debit card
- Play games that are within the Messenger app—some of them are multi-player games.
- Schedule event reminders (e.g., appointments, meetings)
- Request a pickup from Uber or Lyft

In other words, Facebook Messenger is aiming to provide a lot of the most common apps we use on our phones and make it available within the Messenger app not only for phones but for tablets, laptops, and desktops too. Because the reach is farther and easier—not having to know other people's phone numbers—the uptake has been much faster.

**How does this impact author marketing?**

Previously you could only receive and send messages with Facebook "friends." That means from your profile page and people who selected to "friend" you. If a person was not your "friend," and you sent a message it would end up in a separate place called "Other inbox." Few people knew about this place and, more important, it wasn't accessible from the smart phone apps—iOS or Android.

In late 2016, Facebook began allowing messages to Facebook users who are NOT friends. Those messages now go to the same inbox as the "friend" messages AND they can be seen on phone apps. It arrives as a "Message Request." By accepting the "Message Request", the person is agreeing to allow you to text them without the need of ever becoming a "friend."

Users may also ignore or delete any request, and they can stop allowing you to text by typing "Stop" or "Unsubscribe". Facebook has also put in some time gatekeepers to help make sure marketers can't get permission to message once and then start spamming whenever they feel like it. For example, if the user hasn't accepted your request within the last 24 hours, you cannot sell anything to that user until they take action to accept a request again. I'll talk a little more about that later, when I discuss the possibility of providing some automation for common questions and product sales via Messenger Chat Bots as part of your overall communications plans with your Facebook fans.

Though it is exciting to have that one-on-one interaction with fans, to keep that up is again very time consuming. I currently use messenger to respond to fan questions, talk specifically with a VIP reader where perhaps I am gifting her something for a contest or a birthday.

The question is, how can you use Messenger to be available to answer questions about you and your books while being available 24/7 and attracting new fans to your Facebook page. The Answer is Messenger Bots.

## WHAT IS A MESSENGER BOT AND WHY WOULD I WANT ONE?

A Messenger Bot is like having a virtual assistant available 24/7 to both your fans and people simply checking out your Facebook page. It provides an appearance of immediate access to get some general questions answered. Think of it like an automated receptionist but more fun and interactive.

If you know the most common questions people ask, you can have a bot answer for you. Here is a list of common questions I often hear readers asking authors online.

- What genres do you write in?

- When is your next book in X genre coming out?
- Are you ever going to write sexier? Sweeter? More suspense?
- What was your inspiration for writing X book?
- Do you have any new series planned?
- When are you going to be visiting my area of the world so I can meet you?
- What books do you have on sale or free?
- Do you have any book bundles?
- Do you have audiobooks?
- Where are your books distributed?
- How can I get a signed paperback book?
- Is there other author merchandise available for me to purchase (t-shirts, coffee cups, specialty items)

You can probably imagine hundreds of other questions that you answer over and over again. A bot can answer these questions for you in a friendly way, while also drawing your customer toward a book or series that is one they are likely to purchase because of the qualifying questions the bot has asked.

If you also teach classes or do events, you can use bots to announce events, qualify attendees, and even do the registration all within Facebook with a friendly, helpful voice that never gets tired or snippy.

## HOW TO CREATE A MESSENGER CHAT BOT

First, if you've never seen or tried out an author chat bot, go check out the one on Katie McAlister's Facebook page. Follow it for several screens by answering the questions for you as a reader. Nothing is more illustrative than seeing a well-designed bot in action.

Katie McAlister – author of historical, contemporary and paranormal romance books. Click on the SEND MESSAGE button in her Facebook cover image to engage her chatbot.

Fortunately, there are a number of programs that have fairly user-friendly platforms for you to use in creating a bot. The top two are Chatfuel and ManyChat. I prefer ManyChat http://manychat.com based on costs and ease of use. I chose it because the pricing is reasonable--Free or $10 per month for a little more complexity in the branching. No coding is required, as it provides forms for you to fill out, including what you want the bot to say. It also comes with a visual editor that helps you to see what the interconnections look like and where they point to reused content or skip a logic step.

Typical of the types of actions you might enact from a conversation or selection are: go to a page, go to another set of questions/conversations for further qualification, or go to a URL outside of Facebook (e.g., your book buy page). At every step along the way, it is important to provide an easy out like: "I want to talk to Maggie." Or "Bye, no more questions." Or you can use some keyword processing for words people might use to get out of the flow.

One of the considerations when thinking about using a bot is what kind of "voice" does it have. I don't mean a recorded voice, but character voice on the page. Is it light hearted and humorous or does it "speak" with the deferential language of a serious butler. Again, that choice would go back to your brand and your author persona.

## CONSIDERATIONS WHEN PLANNING AND MAPPING YOUR CHAT BOT

Bots are great for welcoming people to your Facebook page, guiding them through any common issues, and maybe asking two or three questions to help them find the best book in your catalog. If you only have a few books, then you probably don't need the questions to help them find a book because they options are limited. However, if you've been writing for a while and have several series, maybe in different genres, then those questions can help lead a reader to the type of book they really want and it is more likely then to get a sale. If not right away, the in a future contact. The bot can also be helpful in providing an interactive opportunity to sign up to your mailing list without them ever having to leave Facebook. And later to use your sales funnel to actually launch or sell books to those who use your bot regularly.

The reason I am so excited about bots is the data authors have been reporting about its use. Whereas in email campaigns it is normal to see open rates at 40-50% for good qualified lists. Messenger Bot engagement rates are being reported at 70-80%. Even better are the book launch and sales numbers authors are reporting. My email conversion to sales numbers run between 20-30%. Authors using bots are reporting closer to 50%. That is a huge payday difference!

## GET STARTED WITH THE BASICS OF PLANNING YOUR BOT MAP

It really helps to map out a basic tree structure for what you want your bot to do. This helps you to know, in advance, the types of navigation you want to connect. You don't have to do this in a fancy piece of software. It doesn't even have to look pretty. Below is a picture of my initial bot planning tree with coffee stain and all.

The top level is the Welcome message when a user first encounters the bot. Then it branches into various genre books and writer books. This was the initial thought process. As I worked with it more, the branching became more complex. I've described all of that a little later in this chapter.

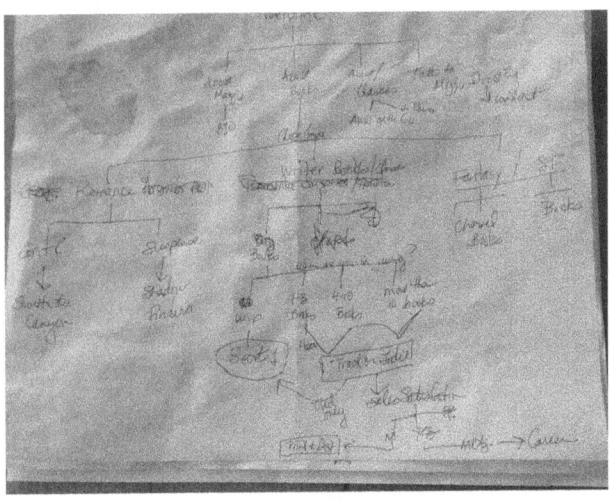

I took the easiest structure possible. Begin with a welcome message that anyone encountering the bot gets. This message briefly explains what the bot is and it's job. I don't want anyone to think they are actually talking to me and then get angry that I don't understand their questions.

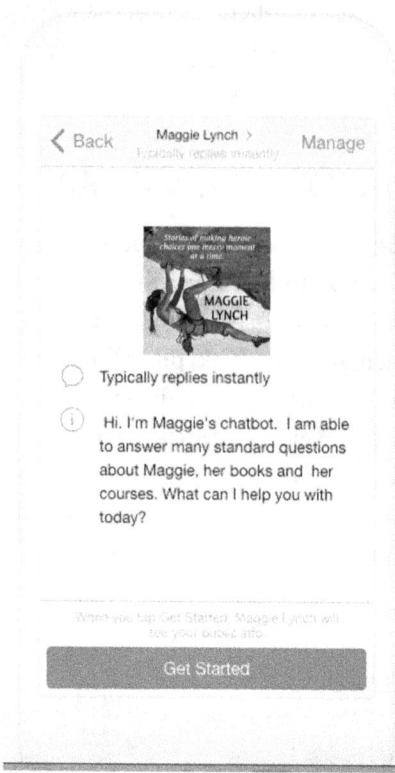

Let's look at some questions to ask yourself when you begin to plan how you want your bot to function. When you plan your chat bot conversations and scripts for the first time, you want to ensure that your bot can answer some basic questions. A conversation tree based on what you drew up for moving people from one branch to another based on their responses. Remember: You do not want to try to sell to them off the bat. You want to offer valuable content that makes the reader feel comfortable that the bot is really there to help, not just scream, "Buy! Buy! Buy!"

Your chatbot represents YOU with its online presence. It is the only face a customer may see at midnight or 4:00am. There are three basic things the bot needs to be able to do: 1) explain it is a bot and what it can and cannot do; 2) contact you directly so you can get on messenger and engage with the reader when you are available; and 3) provide information about your bio and your books.

The first two are fairly quick and straightforward. It is something you can set up quickly by filling in forms in ManyChat and doing one action. The third item, however, takes a bit more planning and thinking. However, a lot of that thinking has probably already been done if you have a basic website already active. Most authors have a website menu that consists of an About page (letting the reader know who you are as an author, a Books page (featuring your books and series and other book products), and a Contact page. In effect, what you are creating in your Facebook Messenger Bot is a similar navigation that provides that information without the reader having to go to your website and look it up.

Yes, you can have your bot simply connect to the website. However, if readers were willing to do that they probably would have done it already because your website is available in your Facebook bio and maybe even pinned to the top of your page discussions. The reality is that reader's do NOT want to go to your website when they are in Facebook. In fact, they prefer not to leave Facebook at all. In addition, the reason they are using Messenger is because they want to have a one-on-one experience where they can ask questions and get answers and not have to look up anything.

The beauty of that desire for readers to have a one-on-one experience is that you can seize that opportunity to guide them to the books that are most likely to make them happy based on some fairly basic qualifying questions and choices. Of course the books they want will be your books. In the meantime, you'll learn all kind of things about who your reader is and the path they took to select the right book for themselves.

Below I'll share how I began handling the scripting and actions for each of those three basic questions.

## 1) Who Are You?

It is important to establish from the start that the user is speaking to a bot with limited capabilities. This sets the right expectations. You have a number of opportunities for doing that with your script. First, let your bot introduce itself right at the beginning and explain its limitations up front.

**Example:** *Hi. I'm Maggie's bot assistant. I am a work in progress. I'm available 24/7 and able to answer common questions about Maggie, her books, and her courses. When I don't have an answer I send an email to her and ask her to contact you directly. So, how can I help you today?*

Following this initial text I present clickable buttons as choices that will lead to the next step. Here are my choices.

- Talk to Maggie Directly
- Learn More About Maggie
- Learn About Maggie's Books
- Learn About Maggie's Online Courses for Authors

For every option, there is an action that must happen when the user selects that option (clicks a corresponding button). Typically those actions are:

- Send an email
- Send a scripted message back to the user
- Start a sequence—this can be a combination of scripted messages and more selection buttons
- Send the user to another part of your Facebook page (e.g., your catalog or shopping section if you've set that up)
- Send the user to a URL outside of Facebook (e.g., a book buy page on your website or a vendor site)

### 2) Contact You Directly

There are plenty of times when the person messaging you wants something different than your bot can provide. For example, the person is a friend and just wants to say Hi or wish you a Happy Birthday. The person is already a fan and is corresponding with you about an ARC or a review or something else. OR the person just doesn't want to use a bot to get their questions answered. You want to make it easy for anyone encountering your bot to make this selection quickly and easily.

When someone selects **Contact Maggie**, my bot sends an email to me letting me know someone wants to talk in messenger. The bot response to the user is something like this.

*"Okay, I'm sending an email to Maggie right now. She usually gets back within 24 hours unless she is traveling. Is there anything else I can help you with while you are waiting?"* Options are Yes and No. If the person selects yes, I present the same options again. If the person selects "no." The bot says: *"Thanks for stopping by and letting me help you. I'm here 24/7 and happy to answer as many questions I can."*

It may take a couple of tries before people actually believe the bot contacted you, but once they see you really do get back to them they will trust in using this method again.

## 3) Provide Information About Your Bio and Your Books or Other Products

This is the more time consuming part of your bot to plan and is the primary reason to have a bot running 24/7 helping potential readers. Just as in the examples above you are responding to the selection with a friendly acknowledgment and then providing choices for the user to select to get closer to the answer they seek. Here is how I have chosen to handle these steps.

**Learn more about Maggie** – The bot says: *"Here is her brief bio to get you started. Let me know if you want to know more."* Then a 100-word bio is presented, and below that bio are options to go deeper or to return to somewhere else (e.g., learn about Maggie's books). This option can be as short or complex as you want. The beauty of building your own bot is that you can also change it whenever you want. You might start off with a short official bio, like you would have on your website or at the end of a guest blog post. Then, at a later date, come back and add additional options for learning about inspirations for series or books, or more about the writing journey, or anything else you care to share.

**Learn About Maggie's Books**—Selecting this option sets up a multi-tiered sequence of questions to lead the reader to the types of books they are most interested in seeing. Each tier is prefaced with a scripted response that includes an intro to that tier. For example, once the reader selects **Learn About Maggie's Books** the script says. *"That's great! Maggie writes in many different genres. First, do you want to know about her fiction or nonfiction? Don't worry, if you want both you can always come back and try the other category."* The buttons below the script are then to select either fiction or nonfiction.

If the user selects **Fiction**, again a friendly script introduces the next options.

*"Great selection! One of Maggie's fans told me she'll read anything Maggie writes because of her characters and the realistic problems they face. This fits Maggie's core story: men and women making heroic choices one messy moment at a time.*
*To get started, please select the genre you are most interested in learning about and I'll provide information and titles for you. Don't worry you can always come back and select a different genre later."*

Again choices are presented through buttons. For fiction the reader selects between romance, suspense, fantasy, science fiction, and women's fiction. Once a button is clicked the bot provides a little scripted information and presents all the titles in that category. Depending on how many books you have available, you may want to limit this or again guide the reader to a subcategory or specific series based on more questions.

Currently, I've chosen to provide all of my books within a selected genre with that click. ManyChat provides this with a "card." A card allows you to show a picture of the book, provide a brief description and then an action. I've chosen to take the reader to a Universal Book Link (UBL) provided through Books2Read https://books2read.com that provides the full blurb and vendor selection/buy options. For readers who have used Books2Read before, and made a vendor selection, it will take them directly to their vendor of choice (e.g., Apple, Amazon, B&N, Google) to buy. At a later date, I will investigate setting it up so that the reader can buy direct within Facebook. I understand that is possible, but not something I have taken the time to investigate or set up as of the writing of this book.

My script for any selection is similar. I say something about the genre and then a brief intro to what I write in that genre. The script below is for my suspense novels, which are a cross between thrillers and romantic suspense.

*Maggie's thriller/suspense novels are full of twists and turns and they take place at different locations around the world. Her current series,* **Shadow Finders***, is about an organization formed by a group of retired Marines. Their specialty is to find and save people who seemingly don't exist, or at least governmental agencies won't recognize them or expend resources to help them. Enjoy!*

***Tip:*** The beauty of bots is that you can reuse content whenever you want. In my case, my books tend to be cross-genre so they are categorized in more than one place. However, I'm giving the reader the chance to choose by how they see the genre and then deciding if my books fit in the parameters of their perception or not. For example, my contemporary romances are also categorized as women's fiction because they are as much about friendships with women or family relationships as they are about romance. So, whether the reader selects romance or women's fiction they will get the same listing of books.

## THIS SEEMS LIKE A LOT OF WORK

Yes, it is, but you can start small and then add to the bot over time. Or, if you have the financial resources, you can pay someone to set it up for you. Typical costs are similar to costs for building you a website, ranging from $500-$600 for a basic bot with welcome and a single tiered menu with 3-5 options to $2,500 for a more complex bot.

As with all recommendations in this book, you need to determine where you are in your career and at what point you have the time and resources to invest in a particular marketing option. The nice thing about starting a bot early on is that you don't have as much to set up. If you only have two or three books, you can set up your bot in a short period of time. Whereas if you wait until later, when you have 20 or 30 books or more, it takes a pretty big chunk of time to plan what you want it to do and get all of that information into the bot.

## Chapter Twelve
# TWITTER

Twitter is considering a "microblogging" platform. It was conceived as a way to broadcast daily, short-burst interesting messages to the world. The appeal is ideal for our modern world where attention is less than 3-5 seconds. The size restriction—now 280 characters including spaces—makes it easy for users to scan and track hundreds of interesting tweeters and get a sense of their content at a glance.

The tweet size limitation also makes it that much more difficult for an author to stand out in the crowd. Understanding the of copywriting headers and key phases is critical on Twitter, as is being engaged every day in both writing content and retweeting (sharing) content you deem interesting and something that your readers might like as well.

Unlike Facebook, where your posts on your author page are only seen by a small percentage of your followers, Twitter feeds are public for anyone to find, read, and comment on. There is no such thing as a "private" post. You may be thinking: "This sounds like an impossible marketing venue. How can I even begin to compete. What do I have to say that is interesting enough to stand above the thousands of other tweets? I'm not sparkly or interesting."

There are two reasons for Twitter being an important platform for you. First with 330 million active users around the world, it should not be ignored. Second is the demographics. Twitter users skew younger than some platforms with close to 50% being in the 18-49 year old range and the gender demographic is fairly evenly split between men and women. Even with a younger skew, still 21% are in the age range of 50-64.

In spite of the downside of Twitter, I definitely see it as a PR platform—a place where you can get eyes on your brand. In terms of sales, I've found it to be better for my nonfiction books for authors than for my fiction. I have a lot of authors in my Twitter feed, so it seems to be natural place to let them know about books geared toward helping them succeed. Of course, I also have readers in my Twitter feed. But they are rather diverse and, unlike Facebook, there is not a very good way to segment them and deliver messages to specific readers for my genres.

Let's start with the basics of setting up your Twitter account to maximize exposure and opportunities for people to become your reader.

## COMPLETE ALL PARTS OF YOUR TWITTER PROFILE

This begins with crafting a great bio. This is the first thing people see when deciding whether to follow you on Twitter and you **only** have about 160 characters to tell them everything they need to know. <big gulp> If you did some of those exercises in the beginning of this book around writing a short bio of 100 words and then narrowing it even further you'll have a running chance at getting this write.

Your bio should accurately convey who you are, excites the user, attract readers to your niche, and invite them to follow you. No pressure right? Chances are you won't get it right the first time. Most important is to get something up there. You can back and tweak it later. If you get all your keywords in, you don't need to worry about hashtags. Here is my current bio.

*I'm a multi-published author with over 20 titles. Fiction in romance, suspense, fantasy, and SF. Nonfiction is books to help authors succeed.*

What are the keywords here? Author, romance, suspense, fantasy, and SF are all decent key words. I could do better with the "help authors succeed" part, but I haven't yet decided how to state that without being too obvious with keywords.

Definitely take advantage of adding your website URL and upload a picture of yourself and a cover photo like you do on all social media. The more consistency you can maintain in these items, the more likely readers are to remember you across platforms.

**Pin a tweet to the top of your feed.** This allows anyone who comes to your profile to see this first. It should provide further provides information as to your primary focus. If you are giving away a book for free or some other incentive to collect emails, this would be the place to put it.

As you can see in the example below, I've put a nice graphic in my pinned tweet that matches the same section on my website. This graphic invites people to get to know me by trying a free book. This does three things: 1) Lets the person know there are at least three genres in which I write (in case they didn't read my bio) which is emphasized with hashtags in the text of the tweet; 2) Entices them with something free; and 3) Emphasizes my profession as a writer.

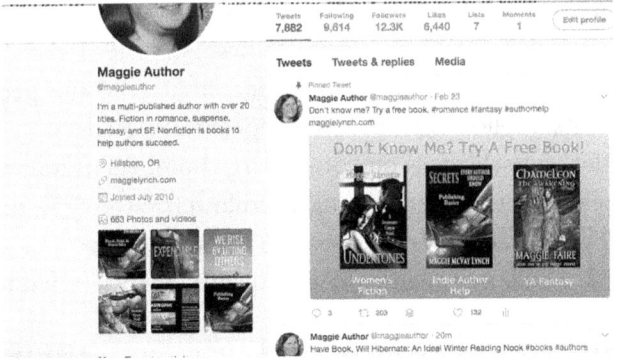

The image links to my website home page where the actual offer is presented and I can collect the email before delivering the free book(s). As you can see from the data, this has been re-tweeted over 200 times and liked 132 times. This is a pinned tweet I've been using for about 6 weeks now. I believe the actual follow through from Twitter to my email list has been about 25%.

**Share a link to your Twitter Profile.** Wherever you are on the web, you should provide a link to your Twitter feed. This includes your website (e.g., a follow button). Share with your Facebook friends that you've started a Twitter account. Add an announcement to your next newsletter. Include it in your regular email signature.

**Find relevant accounts to follow.** The first step in growing your followers is to find them and follow them. Many users on Twitter will follow back those who follow them. There are a number of ways to do this. One is to look at who follows a particular hashtag (e.g., #mystery). Simply put #mystery in the search box and you will see a listing of posts which have used that hashtag. Mouse over the person's name and you will be given the opportunity to follow them.

**Note:** In the beginning, you want to limit yourself to under 100 new follows in a day. If you go much above that, Twitter thinks you might be a spammer and bans you from following. So choose wisely when you are starting out.

Another way to find potential readers is to go to an author, who writes in your genre, and check the followers on her twitter account. Simply click on the word Followers and it lists all the people who follow her. Start following those who appear to be readers.

Don't let yourself focus on getting large numbers of followers right away. Instead, focus on getting quality followers—the type you believe will actually be your readers and look to be building 20-50 people a day. Believe me, you'll get plenty of non-quality followers without even trying.

There are some free tools to help you identify potential followers and manage your list. The two most popular are Tweepi https://tweepi.com/ and Followerwonk https://followerwonk.com/ . Both of these use some artificial intelligence to identify followers in your niche and to analyze their networks to gain more followers. They also analyze activity and unfollow people who are not engaging with your account. Using tools like this can save you significant time and build your list more quickly.

## USE RELEVANT HASHTAGS WITH ALL POSTS

Whenever you use a hashtag people outside of your network can find those tweets and decide to follow you based on how much they like your content. Twitter will suggest hashtags to you just like search engines suggest keywords. As you type in the pound sign (#) followed by a keyword, Twitter will show you the most common word. You can select that or do your own. Just remember whenever you select the most common option, you are opening yourself to a wider group of followers.

Of course, there are also tools to help you select the best hashtags to use. Once you've identified good hashtags, they will work for many social media tools including Twitter. Focalmark is one of the popular apps to generate relevant hashtags based on the topic or theme of your tweet.

## POST REGULARLY AND CONSISTENTLY

Just as discussed with Facebook, it is critical that you are posting new content and retweeting content relevant to your brand every day. Most marketers indicate you need to post a minimum of 5 times a day. My current tweeting consists of one to two original content postings and 10 to 20 retweets.

As discussed in the Facebook section I use, and highly recommend Buffer as a tool to manage and schedule posts for your multiple social media sites. This makes a huge difference in the time needed to post original material to each site.

**Tip:** To really grow and manage your list, and tweet as much as is recommended on Twitter, you need to have one of two things: 1) Endless time to manage Twitter; or 2) Some good automation and management tools. Here are the tools I recommend with a brief description of each.

## TWITTER AUTOMATION

The first thing to understand about automation for any social media tool is that you want it to still reflect your brand and your choices. There are numerous options for growth tools on most platforms and some automations. You want to choose ones that allow YOU to configure the app so that it is doing what you would do if you had all the time in the world to make the choices one by one. If you don't stay on top of your automation you can find yourself liking and retweeting or sharing things you would never choose were you doing it yourself. In other words you can't just set it and forget it or it will become like HAL in 2001: A Space Odyssey, making decisions that do not follow your logic.

Also, remember there is NO tool that can generate original material for you. You must still do that. Simply retweeting everyone else is not enough in Twitter to maintain a following that cares about who you are or your brand. And, if they don't care, they won't engage and won't buy your books.

Let me share a cautionary tale of where automation went awry for me. I've used a tool called StatusBrew https://statusbrew.com to manage my Twitter followers and engagements. The tool was originally designed as a Twitter management tool, called Unfollow and, though it has grown to be a tool for multiple platforms, it's strengths lie in managing Twitter. One of it's capabilities, similar to Tweepi and Followerwonk is the ability to tell it what types of people or companies you want to follow and retweet based on hashtags they use. Once it follows those people it checks that they follow you back. And if they do, it will retweet what they tweet if they use your chosen hashtags. All of this is normal and recommended behavior for members of the Twitterverse.

One of the genres I write in is romance. So, I chose to follow people who read romance using the hashtags #romance and #romancebooks as a way to grow my audience. It actually did that pretty well. However, I didn't pay attention for a couple of weeks when I was particularly busy catching up on projects and one day I noticed that "I" had retweeted the announcement of a pornographic book, and on further investigation "I" had also retweeted a group of pornographic comicbook recommendations (not erotica but actual porn). Of course this wasn't really me retweeting, it was my automation tool. But my followers wouldn't know that because it looks like me retweeting.

In a panic I looked up the #romance hashtag for all my tweets and found I had also retweeted a status for a store that had a sale on kinky a retweeted some posts by some men who were looking for sex hook ups. Why did this happen, because all of these people used #romance as one of their hashtags. The automation tool cannot tell the difference between MY kind of romance and other people's perception of romance who use that hashtag.

My romance audience skews older (55+) and more conservative. In fact, at least one third of my audience would prefer my books contained no sex at all. They put up with it because they like the stories and see how the sex is important to the character development and the resolution of many issues, and never gratuitous. My brand doesn't even include book covers of bare chested men or half naked women, or what I call the "clutch" pose because my books are at the intersection of contemporary romance and women's fiction. When I noticed these automated follows and retweets—fortunately there weren't a lot yet—I was very concerned my actual audience of romance readers would drop me.

The lesson I learned is that though automating by hashtag is useful, not everyone uses a particular hashtag in the same way I do. And romance isn't the only one that can have problems. #thriller can get some interesting people too, as can #mystery and #fantasy—all hashtags that reflect the genres I write in. I needed to go back and select narrower hashtags that better reflected MY audience, and also include some logic for not selecting certain types of status posts.

Fortunately, I caught it early and had no complaints from my readers but it was a hard lesson to learn. I either needed to manage my own follows and retweets or be significantly more careful on how I told the app to do that job and check it more regularly to make sure it was doing it in the way I would.

Here are other things Status Brew does that I find saves a lot of time as long as I've been specific as to how to do the job. Engagement and reciprocation is very important on Twitter and with thousands of followers it needs to be managed somehow.

**New Unfollowers.** When people choose to unfollow you, it is important for you to do the same to keep your account clean. That person made a choice based on you not providing the content they needed which means you are not a match. Sometimes people do unfollow me that I DO still want to follow because I like THEIR content. So, again you want to either do this yourself or make sure your configuration can smartly do it for you.

**Search Twitter Accounts and Targeting.** Statusbrew.com is great for creating targeted searches and finding the right people to follow.

### Automate Welcome Messages

It's really hard to hit every new follower with a personal message—especially if you are getting a couple dozen to a couple hundred new followers per day. A welcome message is a great way to find people willing to engage. Just say hello, thank them for following, and share something of value (e.g., a free book or your cool video trailer or cheat sheet if you are a nonfiction writer). It's a great engagement starter.

**Note:** DO NOT say Hi and then ask them to follow you on Facebook, Instagram, Pinterest etc. They are following you on Twitter. That was their chosen platform. Also do not ask them to buy your book or go to your website to see your books. All of those things are turnoffs to new followers.

### Automate Mentions

Acknowledging your new followers and those who share or like your content is also very important. Again, with thousands of followers it's impossible to catch everyone who mentioned you or liked your content. Automated systems can track that and @mention the follower back with a thank you. which gives them a shout out. It can also be helpful to automate your retweets if it matches the criteria you've set forward.

## STILL TOO MUCH FOR YOU TO MANAGE? HIRE SOMEONE TO MANAGE IT FOR YOU

If you don't like more software to manage but still want your Twitter account to do all the above things, you can hire someone to do it for you. Just be aware that anyone you hire WILL be using automated services for you. So be sure you and that person have a really clear understanding of your brand, what you want and don't want, and that you can get to them easily to make a change and they will respond.

After several years of doing my own Twitter management and trying various tools I decided to use a service in conjunction with my own original posts I do with Buffer and one other tool in Readerlinks. I use Author Platform Sidekick https://www.authorplatformsidekick.com/ The developer, Ian Sutherland, is a great guy, an author himself, an ALLi member and completely ethical and trustworthy. You pay a monthly fee based on what you want him and his automated tools to do for you. He uses Status Brew and other tools for his clients. You can still do, and should post, your own original tweets too. But if you don't get on Twitter for a few days or a week, you know that Author Platform Sidekick has you covered for lots and lots of tweets and retweets.

## *Chapter Thirteen*
# INSTAGRAM

Similar to Facebook and Twitter, Instagram is a social networking app where everyone who creates an account has a profile and a news feed. Just like other social networks, you can interact with other users on Instagram by following them, being followed by them, commenting, liking, tagging and private messaging. It has been around quietly adding users since late 2010. Facebook bought the platform just 18 months after startup, in mid 2012 and integrated it with the Facebook platform—particularly the ads platform—in 2016. This is why the platform has grown so quickly in the last two years..

What is different about Instagram is that it is a completely app-based program that was designed specifically for your smart phone. It runs on both Android and Apple phones. Since being bought by Facebook, they have been working to make Instagram available on tablets and desktops. So far, it is available in Windows 10 and on the Surface Pro. The key is the platform must have touch screens. It is still not available for the iPad.

Instagram takes the trend of images and video to the extreme. It was designed to be primarily photo and video based. Though you can post text, that is not the focus of the platform. Many people post only an image without text, and others post perhaps a single line to put context around the image.

When you post a photo or video on Instagram, it will be displayed on your profile. Other users who follow you will see your posts in their own feed. Likewise, you'll see posts from other users whom you choose to follow.

Through scheduling programs, like Buffer, you can use a desktop or laptop to setup posts. However, you will ultimately have to post it from your phone. In the case of Buffer, you will install the Buffer/Instagram connector app on your phone. When your Instagram post is scheduled you get a notification on your phone to post. Buffer stores your text ready to be pasted into your post. You do any modification to the image (filters, resizing, cropping) on your phone and then tap to paste your stored text. It sounds complicated, but it's not too awful once you get the hang of it.

## WHY BOTHER WITH USING INSTAGRAM?

More than 600 million people use Instagram every day, and over five million businesses use Instagram to tell their stories visually, connect with their fans, and build their brand. If you're new to Instagram, it might be daunting to think about how you can stand out in such a large crowd. But getting started with Instagram is much easier than it might look. Again, the demographics skew to the sweet spot for adult users—35-55 years old.

**Set up Your Account and Profile**

Download the free Instagram app for your smart phone. It is available at the Apple App Store for iOS phones, at Google Play Store for Android phones, and at the Microsoft App Store for Windows 10 or Surface Pro tablets. Once it is installed the mobile app will guide you through the steps to get your account ready.

As with other social media it is important to complete all the suggested steps for your profile. You will first be set up as a "regular" user. After you've taken the time to get everything ready and made some posts, you will want to convert to a business user. Here are some things to take into account in your profile.

**Profile Photo.** Your profile photo will be displayed as a circle. You will have an opportunity to decide how you want that to look. So, be sure to move your photo so that your picture is centered within the circle. 1All Instagram photos will appear as a square. Your profile photo will be displayed as 110 x110 pixels in phones. So, that is the minimum size you want to upload. However, I suggest you upload it at 180 x 180 as that is the current maximum resolution size for tablets and desktop web views. Instagram will resize to the 110 x 110 for phones.

**Profile Information.** The app will *not* prompt you to fill out your profile information, so it is up to you do this yourself. Go to your profile in the app and tap on **Edit Profile**. The two fields to fill out is your website and your short bio. Also check your Instagram username to something your readers would recognize. By default, you are given ???? Change it to your real name or something close.

Congrats! You have just set up your Instagram account!

## POST PHOTOS OR VIDEOS

Instagram is all about the images. Though Instagram is known to favor the square image (1:1 ratio), we all know that cameras tend to take pictures in landscape or portrait and all other social media tends to favor landscape pictures. You can now show those pictures as long as the longest side does not exceed 1080 pixels.

The best resolution pictures will be ones uploaded from your phone. So, if you do use a program like Buffer to schedule Instagram posts, know the images will be lower resolution. Personally, I don't care because I appreciate the time savings that Buffer scheduling offers. However, if you are a photographer and really care about resolution, you may want to load your photos directly from your phone.

Below is a listing of sizes you can load and the size it actually scales down to display. My recommendation is that you always load images and videos at the maximum allowable size.

- The maximum Instagram image size, as of the writing of this book, is 1080 pixels on the longest side with a preference for the square 1:1 ratio of 1080 x 1080.
- Instagram will scales these photos down to 612 x 612 pixels for the web and tablets, and 510 x 510 for display in phones.
- Smaller featured header images appear as 204 x 204 pixels, and larger featured header images appear as 409 x 409 pixels.

When you want to post a photo or video direct from your phone, just hit the "+" icon at the bottom of the app window. Instagram will show you the most recent photos in your photo library. You can also choose to take a new photo or video by tapping on "Photo" or "Video" respectively.

## TIPS FOR SELECTING YOUR MEDIA FROM YOUR PHONE

If you are choosing photos from your library, you can upload your photo as a portrait or landscape. Select your preferred photo and tap on the icon with two arrows in the lower-left corner of the preview. You can then move and zoom the photo to adjust how you want it to fit within the frame.

You can also upload up to 10 photos and videos into a single Instagram post. Tap on the icon with two overlapping squares in the lower-right corner of the preview and select your media. **Note:** As a rule of thumb, I would not recommend doing this except in cases where you are trying to tell a "story." More about that later. The concept on Instagram is to scan and get a story from a single great image.

When you are taking a new video, press and hold the record button to record your video. If you want to film a few different things, you can let go of the button, point your phone camera at something else, and press and hold the record button again to continue with the recording.

## EDITING AND POSTING YOUR MEDIA

Once you have selected your media for your post, you can add a filter or edit its orientation, brightness, contrast, and more. When your media is ready to go, just tap **Next** to fill out your post details. Here you can write a caption, mention a person, add hashtags, tag people in a photo, add a location, and share it with other social media accounts. Let's look at each of these.

**Write a caption.** The "caption" is the equivalent of any text you want to appear with the image or video. It is actually displayed just below your image when the post is published. As part of this "caption," you can mention another Instagram account by using the @username protocol. You can add hashtags (#) just like you do in other social media. As in other social media like Facebook and Twitter, any accounts you mention will receive a notification, and any hashtags you mention will appear whenever someone searches for the hashtags you used. Mentions and hashtags are ways to grow your following and search for new users who may like your content.

**Tag People.** If you are posting a photo or a collection of photos, you can tag multiple Instagram accounts in each photo. The accounts you tag will also receive a notification about it. To tag people in a photo, tap on the person in the photo and star entering their name or username. If it is someone known to you they should quickly appear in the dropdown menu for you to select. If you don't see their name, tap **Search for a person**. Just as with the @username mentions, anyone you tag will be automatically notified.

**Add Your Location.** To add or edit your location, first tap above your image. Then tap **Edit**. Tap **Add Location**... and enter the location information. Then whenever someone searches for that specific location your post will appear. This is particularly helpful when you attend an event with other readers or authors because many people will be adding their posts and locations as well. It puts you in their company which makes it more likely people will follow you because you are in the same place as their friend or fave author.

**Share with Other Social Media Accounts.** If you have connected other social media profiles to your Instagram account, you can easily share your posts on those profiles. Tap **Share** and Instagram will publish your post. Your post will appear on the feed of everyone who follows you in that account.

**Find People to Follow.** As with Facebook and Twitter, the next step is to follow some accounts to see what they have been posting. If you have not followed any accounts yet, Instagram will prompt you to **Find people to follow** on your feed and provide three ways to determine who to follow.

1. *Connect to your Facebook account.* This will be your Facebook personal profile account, not your author fan page. It will compare everyone who is listed as a "friend" to see if they have an Instagram account. Where there is a match it will give you a list. You can then pick and choose who you want to follow out of that list.
2. *Connect to your contacts.* If you do this Instagram will search all the phone numbers and see if any accounts are linked to that number. They will also suggest other people that those linked accounts follow. This is a way to find accounts for people you know. As to if you want Instagram to do that is up to you. Remember, when you request to follow someone they have to "accept" before you are actually linked.
3. *Follow profiles suggested by Instagram.* This is based on what Facebook and Instagram already know about you. When you are just starting out, the suggestions are fairly broad because it is using your behavior primarily from Facebook. However, after you've been using Instagram for a while, this can be quite powerful. Suggestions are then made based on your actual behavior IN Instagram. It looks at the people you've chosen to follow, the posts you've liked, the searches you've made, and the hashtags you've used. It tries matching all of those things to make best recommendations. The best matches will be at the top.

**Use the Search and Explore Tab to Find People.** In the search and explore tab, Instagram will show you Instagram stories and posts that you might like.

- Type in a keyword that is relevant to your business in the search bar
- Check out the suggested Instagram profiles or hashtags
- Follow the profiles that are relevant to your business
- Check out profiles that are recommended to you when you follow a profile

Ideally, you want to follow your readers. Imagine how excited most of them would be knowing their favorite author was following them. Unfortunately, Instagram does not have a way for you to load your reader list and then see if they all have Instagram accounts. (If someone comes up with a way to do that, please let me know). However, if you do the items mentioned above in sharing on your social network and in your emails, letting your reader know you are on Instagram and would love to follow them. You will slowly grow your list of actual readers on Instagram.

**Comment on Other People's Posts.** Social media isn't primarily about you posting your content for other people. It is primarily about engaging with people, sharing common interests and likes. To comment on a post, tap on the speech bubble icon below the photo or video. You can either leave a new comment or reply to an existing comment.

When your followers comment on your photos, it's a good practice to reply them as soon as possible to show that you're listening to them and noticing that they are paying attention to you. This does not mean just to an automatic: "Thanks for the comment." Try to actually say something meaningful that shows you are paying attention. For example, let's say I posted a picture of me at my beach writing retreat, and one of my followers makes a comment: "Good luck getting lots of words written." Instead of just saying Thanks or clicking the like button, I might say. "Thanks! I usually manage 20K words during the week which is why these retreats are so important to me." In other words, I provide more context and thus more content. The most important part is that it is a real engagement with the reader, not just a quick drive by thanks.

I understand when you have thousands of followers it is not possible to do this with everyone. However, even a single line acknowledging the person behind the post every now and then goes a long way to building loyalty. When you can't take the time to do that, at least DO take the time to click like.

After interviewing more than 1,000 people, Sprout Social found that 70 percent of the people interviewed are more likely to use a brand's product or service when the brand responds to them on social media. When the brand doesn't respond, 30 percent of them will go to a competitor instead.

## CONVERT YOUR PROFILE TO A BUSINESS PROFILE

Once you are set up, have some followers and feeling pretty good about your direction, it is time to convert your basic Instagram account to a business account. It is still free, but with a business profile you get some extra benefits and exposure.

First, you get to add additional information about your business on your profile and promote your Instagram posts through advertising. More importantly, you get additional analytics and insights into your Instagram customers and what is working or not working in terms of posts and conversions.

All you need to convert your Instagram profile to a business profile is a Facebook Business Page (Your fan page). Here's how to do it:

- Go to your profile on your phone and tap on the gear icon.
- Tap on **Switch to Business Profile.**
- Select the Facebook Page that you want to be associated with your Instagram account.
- Fill out your email address, phone number, and postal address.
- Tap **Done**.

## USE THE INSTAGRAM INSIGHTS ANALYTICS TO MEASURE AND IMPROVE YOUR MARKETING EFFORTS

To access your Instagram Insights, go to your profile and tap on the chart icon. Here is some of the data that can provide important information.

- See the changes in your key metrics, such as follower growth, in the last seven days.
- Find out when your followers are most active to find your best posting times. If you are using a scheduling tool this can be done very easily.
- Know which are your top-performing posts and stories, and be sure to schedule more like that.
- Learn about your followers' demographics so you can more accurately target campaigns—particularly any paid advertising you are doing with Facebook and Instagram.

If you are interested in learning more about Instagram analytics, Buffer has a great post that briefly explains the 20 Instagram metrics available to business accounts and how you can act on the data it provides. https://blog.bufferapp.com/instagram-analytics

## REVIEW OF BEST PRACTICES TO GROW YOUR FOLLOWERS

***Post consistently* (at least once a day)**.

***Use quality hashtags.*** Though hashtags are important for several social media applications, it appears that they are even more important on Instagram because the right hashtags actually help you to be featured more often in the suggested people/businesses to follow. Remember, Instagram allows up to 30 hashtags per post. However, the most effective number of hashtags is between 9 and 11 depending on which tracking service does the analysis.

**Resources for finding quality hashtags to attract readers.**
http://www.amreading.com/2016/04/18/the-31-most-popular-hashtags-for-book-lovers/

***Share user-generated content.*** This is the "re-tweeting" of Instagram posts. Whenever you come across something you love on Instagram, you want to share it to your timeline. Be sure to include hashtags with it! You can even make it a call-to-action with your readers. Let them know you would love to see their post Instagram photos relating to your X series. Or photos of which actor should play the hero or heroine in a move of your book. People who already love Instagram and use it regularly are often excited to show you their best stuff and to have you share it with others.

***Ask users to "tag a friend."*** Planning to go to a movie that matches up with your genre? For example, I write SF and have a new series planned that is inter-planetary. I could tell my users I'm planning to go to the new Star Wars film. If they are going, ask them to "tag a friend" they want to attend with—even someone who doesn't live near them. That tag then exposes your post to a lot of people who would never have found you—at least not yet.

***Host a photo contest.*** Instagram hashtags make it easy for to collect photos from followers around a theme, and many brands have had success and fun using this capability to host photo contests. If you are a fantasy writer, for example, ask your fans to create or share photos of what they think your world would like if they could go there. Of course, you should share too.

Be sure to re-share some of the best ones so fans know you are paying attention. Not a fantasy writer? That's okay, you can also ask fans to share photos of a real place: New York, Chicago, London, you name it. Or ask them to share photos of where they would like your next book to be set. Note: Only do this if you are likely to actually pick one of those as a setting.

***Add some emojis.*** I admit, I'm of an age that the whole emoji thing seems kind of crazy to me. Though I am known to use the smiley face fairly frequently. However, emojis have become a universal method of expression. Instagram reports that nearly 50 percent of all captions and comments now have an emoji or two. So, if you like them feel free to include them in your posts as well as your comments back to fans.

***Cross-promote.*** Make sure your fans know you're on Instagram through cross-promotion. Instagram makes it simple to share your images to Facebook, Twitter, Tumblr, Flickr, and Foursquare, which could be a great tactic to get some extra exposure. You can also try embedding Instagram photos in your blog posts or by adding an Instagram feed to your Facebook page.

***Join the Video Revolution.*** Instagram allows users to upload videos between 3 and 60 seconds in length. Though videos are not loaded as often as images, they get significantly more comments. I'm not sure if this is because they are still relatively new or the world really is moving toward videos in social media. In any case, if you have one then show it. However, as Instagram is quality oriented, make sure it does a good job of drawing out excitement, emotion, or really showing a theme.

## THE "NEW" EXCITING THING—INSTAGRAM STORIES

Instagram Stories are all the buzz at the writing of this book. It does seem fun and I can see how it might be a way to create buzz about a book or event. I think it's worth considering or looking into only because I've seen mention of Facebook stories now too. So what is an Instagram Story?

It is a compilation of photos and videos that tell a story and are available for only one day. They disappear after 24 hours. Verified accounts are able to add a link to their Instagram stories to drive people to their preferred website or location. This is handy to use when you are doing a big push, like a book launch or a contest, or offering a special discount deal.

Unlike your normal Instagram posts, Instagram stories do not appear on your profile gallery or your followers' feed. They are hidden behind your profile photo on a separate feed at the top of the app. You might wonder then how does anyone find your story. Good question! You have to let your followers know in advance that it will be running and this is the day. Make it so enticing they will mark their calendars to get to it.

I admit, I haven't tried this myself. Instagram is fairly new to me. I've been on it six months as I end the writing of this book. In general the move to an image or video-based social media world is a challenge for me as I'm not a visual person. My preferred way of learning is listening or reading words, not viewing visual images or videos or even personal cues. Instagram, of course, is all about the visual experience. However, what I've read about the "story" idea sounds exciting and I can see how it might be a great way to engage not only your fans but others if the story is exciting or different enough.

Instead of pretending I know what I'm talking about with Instagram stories, or regurgitating what I've read, I'm referring you to a great post about it on the Buffer blog. This post includes pictures and instructions on how you set one up in Instagram. Inside this post they also offer 10 free, easy-to-edit story templates you can use.

https://blog.bufferapp.com/instagram-stories

If I get around to trying Instagram Stories in 2018, I'll be sure to post it to my DIY Publishing blog. https://maggielynch.com/category/diy-publishing/ In the meantime, I'd be happy to hear from anyone who is using Instagram Stories and how it's worked for them.

## Chapter Fourteen
# PINTEREST

The first thing to understand about Pinterest is that it is primarily used by women. I believe the statistic is about 85%. If women are not a large part of your reader demographic, I wouldn't bother with Pinterest as part of your marketing plan. However, if women are a part of your demographic AND you like the premise of creating a kind of virtual scrapbook of your books and your general interests, then definitely go for it. It can be fun and it is a way to gain followers from venues you normally wouldn't market because you wouldn't know how to target it.

Pinterest was conceived as an electronic bulletin board where people could discover and save ideas. Imagine, for example, that you were planning a vacation to Scotland. This may be your one and only time you will get to Scotland. As you do research on the web about where to stay and what to see, you could automatically save those pictures and ideas to Pinterest for later viewing. The URL to the original picture and idea would always be there for you to easily go back and re-read a post or make more notes.

Eventually, you might actually decide to book time in some of the bed and breakfasts you found, or purchase tickets to a hot Scottish roots music concert in Inverness. You might book a special tour of the

Highlands with a tour agency. It is in these actions that marketers become excited about the conversion from ideas to purchases.

The ideas and pins people use on Pinterest are as varied as the people themselves—everything from recipes to tiny homes, wedding planning to vacation planning and lots in between. Yes, there are a lot of readers on Pinterest who save book covers, character information, share what they've been reading and make decisions on what they want to read next.

It is these readers that authors want to entice to their Pinterest pages and books. In addition to book covers you might share pictures that inspired your world, pictures of characters, and pictures of potential scenes in the book. However, it is expected you would also share some of yourself as well. In other words, people on Pinterest are also interested in what else you save on your board. They want to see if you are interested in the same things they are. Do you search for healthy food recipes? Do you have a bucket list of places to travel? Do you love to dream about fashionable attire? Are you a person who can't have enough pairs of shoes? Do you save inspiring quotes to keep you positive?

**Warning:** Like most social media, Pinterest can become a huge time suck. When I first got on Pinterest I was on there ALL day dreaming. You might want to keep a timer by your side to make sure you return to actual writing on a regular basis.

## PINTEREST CONTENT IS BASED ON "PINS"

Every idea is represented by a "Pin" that includes an image, a description and a link back to the image's source online. When people click a Pin's URL they can find out more about the idea and act on it. Once you add a Pin, people who follow you will see that Pin in their home feed. And people who search for similar pictures or topics will see your pin in their search results.

## BOARDS ARE THE ORGANIZATIONAL STRUCTURE OF PINS

Think of Boards as a category or theme under which you place your Pins. Each person determines what that organizational structure looks like. Some people might sort their boards by interests. Others will do it by themes. Yet others will do it by typical product names. You can have as many boards as you like. I currently have 23 boards, but I know others who have over 100 boards.

My boards are a combination of things that feature my books, as well as other themes around my brand. It also features things that personally interested me . For my books, I have a board that contains all of my books under my name Maggie Lynch. I also have separate boards for each of my series, and boards for each of the genres in which I write. Even though some of the pictures will be duplicated across boards, it's okay. Board titles act as keywords for searches, as does the individual pin names inside a board. I am providing several ways that Pinterest users might locate by books—by my name, by series name, or by genre.

Outside of my books, my overall brand is represented by boards for other author's books I like, boards for positive pictures and quotes, and boards about reading in general. The reading board contains places to read, quotes and memes about readers, as well as pictures of celebrities reading.

The remainder of my boards reflect my personal interests in travel, animals, sharing my cat pictures, and a variety of other themes of interest to me.

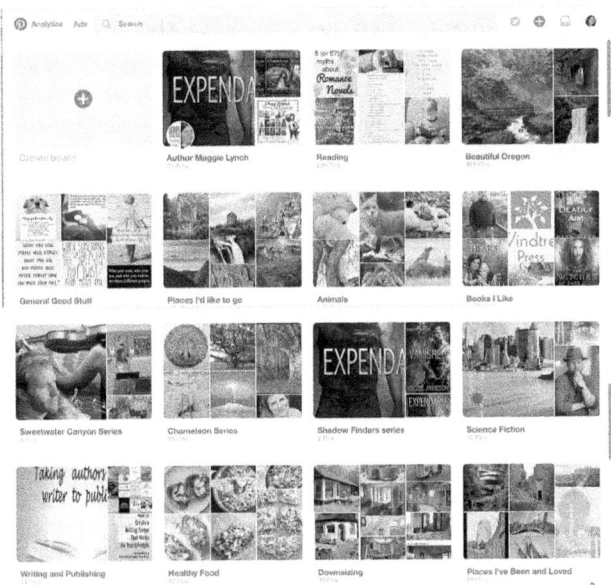

Pinterest users interact with each other through liking, commenting, and re-pinning each other's posts. That's what makes it such a viral social network. It's image based. It's personal. And it's actually fun to do, even if no one likes your pins or follows you.

If you want step-by-step instructions for getting a free Pinterest Account and getting started pinning, you might enjoy this article from Lifewire. It contains screenshots along with the instructions. https://www.lifewire.com/how-to-use-pinterest-3486578

## HOW TO USE PINTEREST FOR MARKETING

As with all the other social media platforms, the first thing to do is to complete your profile. Pinterest creates a distinction between individual users and business users. You can switch your individual account to a business account at any time and then enjoy features like rich pins, customized Pin It buttons and widgets, and more. https://www.pinterest.com/join/?next=/business/convert/

To fully complete the information on your profile, click the gear icon and then **Account Settings**. Clicking the Edit Profile button lets you edit only the basic information. As a business, you will want to do more than that so please use the Account Settings option where you can complete the following:

- Email
- Business type
- Contact name
- Business name
- Profile picture
- Custom username and vanity URL
- About section
- Location
- Website
- Connected social networks

Be sure to select the custom username to make it easy for your fans to find you. The About section is for your bio. Once you enter your website, Pinterest can step you through a variety of ways to verify your website with them. That will allow you to use their Rich Pins services as well as to add a verified icon next to the website on your Pinterest profile. For some followers, that icon gives them more confidence in following you.

## SHARE YOUR PINTEREST PROFILE WITH OTHER SOCIAL MEDIA ACCOUNTS AND IN EMAILS YOU SEND TO FANS

As with the other social media accounts we've discussed, you want to be sure to let your fans know you now have a Pinterest page. Make the announcement fun. Talk about a board that might interest them and invite them to share with you a special pin from one of their boards so you can follow them too. Be sure to include a link to your Pinterest page as part of your email signature.

## INCLUDE A PINTEREST BUTTON ON YOUR WEBSITE OR BLOG

Pinterest offers five different styles of buttons and widgets that you can place on your website.

- Pin It button
- Follow button
- Pin widget
- Profile widget
- Board widget

The Pin It button is helpful for getting the content on your website more traction on Pinterest. There are also some helpful Wordpress Plugins that can help add Pinterest functionality. My favorite is Pin It Button Pro https://pinplugins.com/ which makes every image on your pages or posts potential pins with a single click. The cost is only $29 for a full year of all updates and support or $49 for three sites.

If you're interested in boosting your followers, something like the Follow button may help with that. The Follow button is easy to implement. Enter your Pinterest URL and your full name, and build the button. You get an HTML code to place wherever you'd like the button to appear. If you use any kind of social media plugin already for your links, they will have a space for Pinterest where you simply provide the URL to your page.

## START PINNING AND GETTING FOLLOWERS

Similar to other social media platforms, the first thing to do is to start pinning. Set up 5 to 10 boards that reflect the categories for your books, series, and your own interests. Pin as much content from your website as possible into a selection of your different boards. Add long descriptions (100 words or so) to each pin with 2-4 relevant hashtags. Try to space this out – don't pin too many things at one time or you'll flood everyone's feeds. Try to stick to no more than 10-15 pins in an hour. If you have a particularly robust website, set yourself a task to do 10 pins a day until you have pinned everything from your website.

Next select at least two boards in topics that are of interest to you, but are not your books, and match your branding. Enter a couple of hashtags into the search engine (e.g., quotes about reading) and it will present you with boards using that same hashtag. Within a matter of minutes you can usually fill up a board with at least 20 images.

## FIND AUTHORS IN YOUR GENRE AND FOLLOW THEIR FOLLOWERS.

Now you are ready to start finding some people to follow you. Begin by entering author names in the search engine. Focus on authors whose books you like and who write in your genre. Be sure to create a board that is for your "fave" authors in your genre. Pin some of their books. This will help when you start following their followers.

Go to the first author on your list (Note: Not all authors participate in Pinterest so it may take several tries to find an author with a robust site). Click on the author's followers link. It will present you with a list of their followers. Click to follow around 50-100 of their followers' boards each day. Do take time to at least scan each person's board. If you see things of interest to you on their board, pin it to one of your own boards. This will signal that you aren't a bot, that you are actually pinning things too.

Do this same search for another author and follow their followers. Continue this practice every day for at least two weeks. Depending on how lucky you are and how recognizable you are as an author, you should garner at least 50 people following you back within that two week period—maybe more.

For the next six months calendar in time once a week to go through your own boards and look for new things to include from other boards. The easiest way to do this is to look for the same hashtags you are using. If you can repin at least 10 pins each week, pin from other boards. It doesn't always have to be followers from authors, you might also seek out topics that fit your genre and will still draw people to you.

Think like a reader. What kinds of things besides books would readers be interested in finding or dream of having? It could be cozy items with reader connections—coffee cups, hoodies, blankets. Also look at places readers might read and create a board for that. Nooks, libraries, special snuggly reading chairs, etc. There are thousands of memes and quotes about reading you can also incorporate. If you have a good email list, ask them to suggest pins to you from their boards and go get them and repin.

In the end, Pinterest is social. It is people with common likes sharing their thoughts and pictures. Soon, you will be well on your way to a robust presence on Pinterest.

## Chapter Fifteen
# YOUTUBE

We all know YouTube. Most of us can probably get it on our televisions as well as our desktops, laptops and even smart phones. Though why anyone would watch a video, of more than 30 seconds, on a smartphone is still beyond me. I think I'm showing my age. Prior to 2014, my relationship with YouTube had been in one of three ways. 1) Watching music videos; 2) Watching book trailers; or 3) Watching silly, entertaining videos featuring the humorous antics of animals, children, and adults.

YouTube has always been a good venue for teaching resources. So, if you are a nonfiction writer and an educator, using YouTube for marketing makes perfect sense. But what beyond education is viable for authors? Every conference I've attended in 2017—in person or virtually—marketers are planning to add YouTube as an essential marketing strategy in 2018.

Why? Again it's reach and demographics. YouTube has more than a billion active users, can be accessed in 76 different languages, and video in general is at least competing with if not replacing images in most social media accounts. As an author, this means that at a minimum you need to have a YouTube channel where you can share videos that you like and you believe represent your brand and your readers will enjoy.

If possible, you should also create some videos as well. Typical videos that authors share are book trailers, interviews with the author OR the author interviewing other people (e.g., authors, experts in fields relating to the author's books or brand, the author reading an excerpt from her book, and the occasional travel video). So let's look at what are the initial steps you need to take to get started using YouTube for your marketing.

## CREATE A YOUTUBE ACCOUNT

Before you start filming, editing, or just sharing video content from other sites, you'll need to set up your YouTube channel. This is surprisingly easy, actually. Google owns YouTube. That means to have a YouTube account you need a Google account. If you have a Gmail account, you are already set with space assigned to you for a YouTube account. If you don't have a Google account, then the easiest thing to do is to get a Gmail account. I won't go into the instructions for setting up a Google account here. If you don't have an account, these instructions by GCF Learn Free.

FGC Learn Free is a nonprofit organization that provides free instructions for all types of technology—will get you started. https://www.gcflearnfree.org/gmail/setting-up-a-gmail-account/1/

Even though the YouTube account is available to any Google account holders, you still need to set it up to meet your branding needs and complete some basic information.

To get started, follow these steps:

1. Go to https://youtube.com In the upper right-hand corner, you should notice that you're probably already logged in. If this is not true, click on the blue **Sign In** button in the upper right-hand corner, and enter your Google account username and password. (This would be the same one you use to get into your gmail account)
2. Click on **My Channel** in the left-hand menu bar.

3. Do **not** click on "Create Channel." Click on **Use a business or other name** which appears below the create channel option.
4. Use your business account name (usually your author name) and press **Create**. *Note:* You can update or change your channel name at a later date if needed.
5. Now let's customize your channel by clicking on **Edit Layout**. You are going to work on adding a channel icon and channel art.
6. To add a channel icon, click on the default red profile picture in the upper left-hand corner of your channel. Then upload an image. A channel icon is similar to a Facebook profile picture. It will be used across all of your Google properties like Gmail and Google+. I suggest you upload a headshot. Google recommends uploading an 800 x 800 px square or round image. Please note, it may take several minutes for your channel icon to appear after uploading. So don't worry if it seems to be doing nothing for five minutes.
7. Next, click on the blue **Add Channel Art** button in the center of your page. Channel Art is the same as a header that appears on your page whenever someone visits your channel or searches for you. This should be the same header you use everywhere else on the web—Facebook, Twitter, your Website, etc.
8. Google recommends you upload a 2560 x 1440 px . The image will be resized to fit whatever device users use to see your channel. The reason the image is so large is because many people watch YouTube videos on their television as well. Though Google requests the art to be so large for bigger screens, it is important to make sure that all important information fits within a 1546 x 443 px space. That is what Google calls the "safe space" and is guaranteed to resize all the way down to a mobile phone image.
9. In the **About** section of your setup, complete your configuration by adding a channel description, a contact email,

and links to your website and other social media platforms. Your description should include your bio. However, be sure to add information at the top or bottom of your bio explaining what type of video content you plan to share in your channel. Search engines look at your description when determining how to rank your profile, so be sure to incorporate relevant keywords in your description such as "author," "books," "name of your series," and anything else that you typically associate with your brand and book products.

An advance feature that is nice to incorporate, if you have the time and need, is to customize the way your YouTube channel looks to channel subscribers versus how it appears to visitors. This means that unsubscribed viewers could see different featured content than dedicated, subscribed viewers.

Most fiction authors do NOT use this. For me, my videos featuring my books and my brand are all publically available because I want as many people as possible to see them and then to use them to drive readers into other sales funnels. However, if you are teaching courses or doing a regular video cast on topics of expertise, you may well benefit from this separation of visitor and subscriber experience. In the visitor section you have an introductory channel trailer and perhaps provide some introductory discussion or instruction to topics in your expertise. The purpose of these introductory videos, open to the general public, is to entice them to subscribe to your channel in order to get the extra value. In the subscriber-only section you might do more in-depth discussion or instruction only to those who have subscribed to the channel.

One of the primary ways users differentiate these two areas is to create a **channel trailer**. This is the video version of your description and is shown to all visitors. Your trailer should be about 30 seconds. You can stretch it to a minute if there is a lot of content to highlight but don't go beyond that. Focus on converting visitors to subscribers by highlighting the added value of content they will get if they subscribe. This is somewhat the equivalent of getting readers to sign up for your email list so they can get valuable content from you on a regular basis.

If you are going to focus on having a subscriber space different from the public space, you can learn more about creating a channel trailer and customizing your YouTube configuration here: https://support.google.com/youtube/answer/3026513?hl=en

**Note:** *As of September 19, 2017 you can no longer create PAID content on YouTube.*

For the past couple of years, YouTube had provided a way to manage payment options for users who wanted subscribers to pay to get special content. They are no longer doing that. At the time of writing this book, it is unclear whether there are other ways to operate payment processing outside of YouTube that then delivers content to registered subscribers. It is likely that would be against the terms of service as Google appears to be setting up a vision for YouTube to be a high-performing advertising platform.

If you wish to do paid instructional videos or even discussion and opinion videos, it is best to use products that are designed for hosting courses and include a paywall facility. My favorite platform for this is Teachable https://teachable.com/ . However there are many options. This article from Forbes provides a good overview of the top 10 platforms.
https://www.forbes.com/sites/tomaslaurinavicius/2017/02/22/host-your-online-courses/#2d2735dd63be

## USING A CUSTOM URL FOR YOUR YOUTUBE CHANNEL

The URL for your channel is not very pretty. It consists of a long string of numbers and letters. Here is mine: https://www.youtube.com/channel/UC9m7V6ilyKSYNQt2Oa4Y7cQ/

To change that to a custom URL (e.g., /channel/maggielynch), you need to have over 100 subscribers, a channel icon, channel art, and your channel must be more than 30 days old. To learn more about custom YouTube URLs check out this article from Hubspot https://blog.hubspot.com/marketing/youtube-hacks-tips-features .

## HOW TO OPTIMIZE YOUR VIDEOS FOR SEO & RANKING

Now that your YouTube channel is up and running, let's talk about how people find it to watch your videos. The key to that is search engine optimization (SEO) just as it is for every piece of content you put anywhere on the web. Remember, YouTube is the second largest search engine in the world. Not surprising as it's owned by Google the largest search engine in the world.

The first step is to pay attention to your video's metadata. This includes your video title, description, tags, category, thumbnail, subtitles, and closed captions. Providing the right information in your video's metadata will help to ensure that it is properly indexed by YouTube and appears when people are searching for videos like yours. Be succinct and straightforward when filling out your information about your video. Also be accurate. Your content could be removed if you try to promote it with unrelated keywords. Here are some basic tips for optimizing your video for search.

### Title

The title is the first thing people will read when scrolling through a list of videos, so make sure it's clear and compelling. This doesn't necessarily mean it should be salesy or proise something it can't deliver. For example a title like Sweetwater Canyon Book Trailer is clear and compelling for people who like to watch book trailers. It has the key word "book trailer" in the title. Would something like "Woman Survives Murder Attempt" be more compelling. Probably, but would your video deliver on that promise. Even if your book's plot has the heroine surviving a murder attempt, how does your video portray that and tie it up to deliver on the promise?

Don't worry you'll have plenty of other SEO opportunities to get in the murder part.

Do some keyword research to better understand what viewers are searching for when looking for videos from authors. Include the most important information and keywords in the beginning of your title. Also, keep titles to around 60 characters to keep text from being cut off in results pages.

## Description

YouTube will only show the first two to three lines (about 100 characters) of your video's description, then viewers will need to click "show more" to see the rest. For that reason, be sure to include any important links or calls-to action in the beginning of your description, and write the copy so it drives views and engagement.

Below your primary description, you can include the video transcript. Video transcripts can greatly improve your SEO because your video is usually full of keywords. If you completed the information about your social media channels, they will already be shown as a part of your default channel description.

Though you can use hashtags in your description, I don't recommend it. Research has shown that video descriptions without hashtags get significantly more views. It seems that when viewers see a lot of hashtags displayed in your video, they immediately assume it is spam or salesy. YouTube already provides the opportunity for you to add keywords when you upload the video. They will use those as part of the search words without them having to be displayed in the description section of your site.

## Keyword Tags Section

Using keywords is a way to associate your video with similar videos, broadening its reach. When tagging videos, tag your most important keywords first and try to include a good mix of more common keywords (e.g., genres) and long-tail keywords. Long-tail keywords are three or four word phrases that specify exactly what is in your video. e.g., "emotional book series video" instead of "book trailer." To learn more about the importance of long-tail keywords, check out this article https://www.wordtracker.com/academy/keyword-research/guides/long-tail-keywords

## Category

After you upload a video, YouTube will allow you to choose a video category under **Advanced settings**. Video categories help to group your video with related content on the platform. YouTube allows you to sort your video into one of the following categories: Film & Animation, Autos & Vehicles, Music, Pets & Animals, Sports, Travel & Events, Gaming, People & Blogs, Comedy, Entertainment, News & Politics, Howto & Style, Educations, Science & Technology, and Nonprofits & Activism.

Note there is no "book" or "author" category. I tend to select **Entertainment** for my book trailers and me reading excerpts. I suggest selecting **People & Blogs** for videos where you are being interviewed or interviewing someone else, and for videos of fans or book bloggers talking about your books as those types of videos are people-centric.

## Thumbnail

Similar to a book cover, your video thumbnail will be the main image viewers see when scrolling through a list of video results, and it can have a large impact on the number of clicks to view your video. YouTube will auto-generate a few thumbnail options for your video. Sometimes, one of those will be perfect. However, most of the time that is not the case. If the three selections don't grab the viewer, you can upload a custom thumbnail.

YouTube reports that "90% of the best performing videos have custom thumbnails." See https://creatoracademy.youtube.com/page/lesson/thumbnails?cid=get-discovered&hl=en If you are controlling the filming yourself, think of high-quality shots that accurately represent your video. YouTube recommends using a 1280 x 720 px image to ensure that your thumbnail looks great on all screen sizes.

### SRT Files (Subtitles & Closed Captions)

Not only do subtitles and closed captions help viewers, they also help optimize your video for search by giving you another opportunity to highlight important keywords. You can add subtitles or closed captions by uploading a supported text transcript or timed subtitles file. You can also provide a full transcript of the video and have YouTube time the subtitles automatically, type the subtitles or translation as you watch the video, or hire a professional to translate or transcribe your video. Adding this file is handled in your **Video Manager**.

### CARDS ARE THE BEST MARKETING ADD ON YOU TUBE PROVIDES!

Cards are small, rectangular notifications that appear in the top, right-hand corner of both desktop and mobile screens and allow you to provide a linked call-to-action at the end of the video. You can include up to five cards per video, however all marketing gurus advise to focus on a single call-to-action. The more options you give, the more likely the customer will do nothing.

The two most common calls-to-action used by authors are: 1) Invite viewer to download a free book to try you out; and 2) Provide a link to a buy page to purchase the book or series.

**Remember:** To Add Cards you MUST have verified your website through Google Search Console and YouTube. This was discussed earlier in this chapter.

### Adding a Call-to-Action Card to Your Video

After your website is associated and verified, you are then allowed to add up to five cards to one video. The type of card most authors want to add is a **Link Card** which sends the viewer to an external URL.

1. On a computer signed into your YouTube account, go to your **Video Manager.**
2. Select the video you want to add cards to and click **Edit**.
3. In the tab bar at the top, select **Cards**.
4. Select **Add Card** and choose what type of card you want. Your choices are Video or Playlist, Channel, Poll, or Link card. Authors most often choose **Link Card**.
5. By default, YouTube adds the card at the top right corner of the video. However, you may drag the card to the spot in the video you want it appear. Your changes will be saved automatically.

## END SCREENS

End Screens are another means for inviting viewers to do things related to your channel. It allows you to extend your video for 5-20 seconds to direct viewers to other videos or channels on YouTube, encourage viewers to subscribe to your channel, or promote external links, such as ones that direct to your website. End screens encourage users to continue engaging with your brand or content.

To add an end screen, go to **Video Manager**, click the drop-down edit arrow, and choose **End Screen & Annotations**.

Then choose which elements you'd like to add to your end screen. You can add elements by importing an end screen you used in another video, using a template, or creating elements manually. It's important to keep in mind that YouTube requires users to promote another YouTube video or a playlist in part of the end screen.

## PLAYLISTS

Are you creating videos around a few specific themes? Playlists might be the perfect tool for you! Playlists allow you to curate a collection of videos from both your channel and other channels. Not only do playlists help to organize your channel and encourage viewers to continue watching similar content, they also show up separately in search results. Creating playlists provide you with more discoverable content.

To create a new playlist, go to a video you'd like to add and click the under the video. Next, select "Create new playlist." Type in the name of the playlist you want to feature and click "Create."

## HOW TO CREATE VIDEOS FOR YOUTUBE

This could be an entire book on its own, so I will send you to resources on this instead. As an author, my primary job is to write books. Though I do create some very basic videos, like interviews or excerpt readings, for the most part I leave video creation to the experts. My book trailers are created by Book Candy because I love the cinematic feel they give focusing on theme and emotion rather than plot.

Unless you are a video or film professional yourself, realize that competing on YouTube with professionals and getting a wider audience is extremely difficult. Of course, you can definitely drive your fans to your videos and for many authors that is enough.

Here are some resources for those of you who really do want to film, edit, and master your own videos.

Inspiring Video Marketing Campaigns from Hubspot
https://blog.hubspot.com/marketing/lovable-video-marketing-campaigns

8 Types of Videos based on importance and effectiveness – article from the Huffington Post http://www.huffingtonpost.com/vala-afshar/how-video-marketing-will-_b_8962102.html

## HOW TO MARKET YOUR YOUTUBE CHANNEL & VIDEOS

While ranking high in search results and having a large subscriber base are ideal, those goals can be difficult to achieve when you're just starting out. That's why it's important to always spread the word about your YouTube channel and videos across other platforms.

**Use Social Media.** Sharing your videos on social media provides an opportunity for you to additional insights to your video and engage with viewers. YouTube makes it easy for you to share videos across your social networks. Just click the **Share** tab underneath the video. There you can select where to market the video. YouTube also provides a shortened URL to your video for convenient sharing.

Simply sharing the video on your timeline or feed may not be the most effective option. Express excitement about the video and its release. Talk about why you made the video. If you are sharing the video as part of a larger marketing campaign be sure to include relevant hashtags to ensure your video is included in the SEO for your campaigns.

***Blog Posts and Your Website.*** Market your YouTube channel and videos on your website and blog. Here are several ways to do that.

1. Add a YouTube follow icon to your website and blog so your readers can easily find your channel.
2. Embed videos on your website in a special page that features all your videos.
3. Consider embedding a video as part of a specific blog post. This may be a video you've created about your book or series (book trailer, excerpt reading, interview) or it could be a video someone else has made that is appropriate to share with the post.
4. If you have a Wordpress site, there are several plugins that make it easy to add videos from your channel to your website or blog. My favorite is: Video Gallery by Huge-IT. It makes it easy to add YouTube videos by providing the URL, then adding a brief description. There are several options for how it is displayed and you can display several videos on a single page.
5. You can also display videos on your website manually by including the "embed code" YouTube provides. Beneath the video in your YouTube channel is the link and then a square the contains **Embed Code.** Copy and paste that code onto the website page or blog where you want the video to appear.

***Talk about A Video or Your YouTube Channel in Emails.*** Though we all want to find and attract new customers to our video content, don't forget about the readers you already have. Share your video content and channel in your email campaigns. Encourage your contacts to check out a blog post where you've embedded a video or the place on your website where it is easy to find. Don't forget to provide a link to your YouTube channel in your email signature line.

***Add Video to Your Goodreads Author Page.*** Earlier I talked about having a presence on Goodreads. In addition to sending your blog feed to your author page, Goodreads also has a section where you can add videos. Be sure to take advantage of it.

***Collaborate With Others.*** Network with other authors or people related to your brand to collaborate and share each others YouTube channels. Do some guest posts or email swaps to feature your videos. Consider creating a video playlist together. There are a lot of options to creatively collaborate with other brands, just make sure that their audience and goal is similar to yours.

***Engage With Viewers.*** Don't forget to engage with your viewers by responding to comments on YouTube. As with other social media, do more than say Thank You. Include some additional information or recognize a good insight they made or feedback for improvement. Definitely answer any questions. This is task that is easy to forget, so it might be helpful to calendar dedicated time to check on all your video interactions and respond to users. Certainly, if you are running a special push or campaign featuring your video, be sure to check every day during the campaign and for several days after the campaign.

## YOUTUBE ANALYTICS HELP YOU IMPROVE YOUR VIDEOS AND YOUR CHANNEL PRESENCE

Analytics are provided by video. The analytics link is found in the **Studio Creator** section of the new YouTube interface. Select the specific video where you wish to see the analytics. YouTube tracks how viewers found your content, how long they watched it, where they are located in the world, and how they engaged with it.

After selecting the video you want to analyze, all the analytics charts are provided on a summary screen. I suggest you then click on each chart to open it and study the information more closely. Below are brief descriptions of how to interpret the data to help you improve.

**Watch Time and Audience Retention.** Watch time reports the *total number of minutes* your audience has spent viewing your video content. A video with a higher watch time is more likely to rank higher in search results. YouTube provides a line item report on watch time, views, average view duration, and average percentage viewed for individual videos, location, publish date, and more.

This view duration and percentage viewed charts are most important to me. It tells you, by viewer session, at what point viewers are leaving your video. If they are leaving early on, it may mean that your introductory section needs work to entice them to continue viewing. If they make it most of the way through but leave in the last 10-15 seconds, it may mean your call-to-action isn't valuable enough to keep them watching. Wherever the majority of viewers stop watching is a section to consider revising and making better.

However, don't get carried away with perfection. As in all marketing efforts, there are some people who will come to your video because you made it intriguing but in the end are not your readers. Instead of leaving because your video is bad, they may be leaving simply because they realized these books are not of interest to them. Also, don't make changes based on a small number of viewers. Anything under 25 views is likely not statistically significant. Once you approach 100 views or more and you still see the majority of people leaving before the end, it is time to discover what is happening at that section to stop them watching.

**Traffic Sources.** The traffic sources report shows how viewers are finding your content online. This provides valuable insight on where to best promote your YouTube content. For example, you can see if viewers are finding your content through YouTube searches, Twitter or other social media feeds, or from your website. To view more in-depth traffic reporting, click on the overall traffic source category. This data can help refine your YouTube marketing strategy. Be sure to optimize your metadata based on your findings.

**Demographics.** The demographics report helps you understand your audience by reporting on their age and gender. You can then break down age groups and genders by other criteria like geography. This report will help you better market to your YouTube audience and understand if your content is resonating with your target audience.

**Engagement Reports.** Engagement reports tell you how many viewers are clicking, sharing, commenting, and promoting. You can also see how your cards and end screens are performing in your engagement reports. If Cards and End Screens are not getting good clicks then you may need go back and look at how to optimize your calls-to-action in future videos.

It appears that video is definitely on the rise. YouTube makes it easy to upload videos and provide calls-to-action within them. They are easy to share around the web and most social media and blog platforms seem to crave more video. Do consider what you can do in this space and see how it helps grow your brand presence and your sales.

# BUILD A MAILING LIST OF TRUE FANS

Purpose and Importance of Mailing Lists
Selecting a Mailing List Provider
Set up and Qualify Names
Drip Campaigns
Drive Traffic to Your List
Beyond Onboarding: Broadcast Emails, Launch Emails, and Other Sequences
Building and Managing Your Street Team

*Chapter Sixteen*

# PURPOSE AND IMPORTANCE OF MAILING LISTS

Whenever I talk to writers who have not paid attention to building an email list, invariably I hear things like the following:

"*I don't want to spend time building an email list because it means I have to be a sales person.*"

"*I know I should have one, but I don't know what to say.*"

"*I'm already really invested in social media, so I don't need an email list.*"

"*I'm selling fine on Amazon. They can do a better job of getting to my readers than I can.*"

"*Come on, it's the 21$^{st}$ century, no one uses email anymore!*"

My goal for this overview is to address all of the above statements. If there is no reason to spend time building an email list, why does every marketer worth their salt absolutely demand their customers have strong, vital email lists? It's because they KNOW it is the best way to build customers who come back again and again to buy products.

## CONTROL YOUR REACH

Today, you're able to reach an average of 1-2% of your Facebook Fans.

Twitter feeds are like being in the middle of the biggest city in the world and trying to catch a passing strangers attention. No matter how great your Twitter presence, a very small percentage of your Twitter following sees any one specific Tweet.

No matter the platform you are on, your reach is limited. Email is not perfect either, according to studies, 22% of emails sent get lost in the junk or spam folders or are blocked by ISPs. But that still leaves you with an average of **78% messages delivered**! No social media platform can promise that.

Once that email is delivered to the recipients inbox, it is up to the recipient to decide how long it will "sit there" before being read or trashed. In other words, the recipient needs to at least acknowledge its existence. This is not the case in any social media.

This is the reason you keep getting clicks even several days after sending the campaign. The lifespan of a social media post can range between a few seconds to perhaps an hour at the most. Even beyond basic acknowledgment of your email, the recipient also has the opportunity to save it, forward it, file it, refer to it again and again. Though some of that can be done in social media, the finding-it-again part is much more difficult.

## KEEP CONTROL OVER YOUR BIGGEST MARKETING ASSET—YOUR READER DATA

An email list is critical because you can't build your marketing on rented land and be able to count on it always being there or the rules being the same. If you've ever lived in a rented apartment or house, you already know that you are at the mercy of the landlord. The landlord can decide she is returning from her two year stay in Scotland six months earlier than planned, and she wants to move back into her house. The apartment management company can decide they will charge significantly more rent because the market will bear it. News of rents going up $20-30% is not unheard of this year. Even worse the landlord can decide they are going to tear down your house to but up more homes in the same space, or remodel so they can appeal to a clientele that can afford to pay significantly more.

All the platforms you count on—social media, book distributors, and yes even the email hosting companies—are most interested in making money and increasing their own growth. This means they can change the rules at any time, sell to another company, or go out of business. Do you want to trust all of your reader data to someone else?

Don't think it happens all that often? Just look around at changes that have occurred in the past three years. Facebook is a free service. Yay! However, over the past three years, they decided to limit the reach you have with your fans. It used to be everyone on your fan page had the opportunity to see yoru status posts in their feed. Now it is about 2%. Some of that was legitimately to provide a better experience to their customers by curating their feeds to things they had already shown a continued interest in seeing. However, let's admit it also increased their advertising business. If you pay for more reach—including to your own fans—they are suddenly not at all worried about putting your post in front of their users.

When you have permission to send content to a fan by email, no one can force you to pay for that. You own that data. Only specific fans can stop you from sending them emails.

It IS important to build your audiences on Facebook, Twitter, Instagram, YouTube. However, you don't own those names or any information about those users and how they interact with you on the platform. Yes, you get all kinds of analytics but none of it is identifiable. You don't know if it was Maggie who liked your fantasy video and David who liked your romance video or if one of them liked both videos. You don't know if it was your long-time fan, Kathy who clicked on your call-to-action to purchase your latest boxset or if it was a new customer you know nothing about.

It is that kind of data that you can get from well-developed and segmented email lists that you control. Having that data does two important things: 1) It allows you to deliver content to a segmented list of users (e.g., information about your fantasy books to the people who have shown an interest in fantasy, and information about your romance books only to people who have identified they want to hear more about romance); and 2) It helps you to make decisions about your business—how fast it is growing, what types of people are most likely to follow you, and what are their expectations.

Knowing exactly who your fans are also gives you opportunities to get targeted feedback from them around what they like or don't like, who else they follow, and how happy they are with your content. No other medium can do that.

**Companies Disappear All the Time**

It may seem like the big social media platforms, or big book distributors, will be around forever; but we know from experience that is not the case. Does anyone remember My Space? How about Friendster? You may be saying: "Oh that was a long time ago and everyone was just figuring out the whole social media thing. Now companies are really big. They don't fail."

Big companies fail all the time when they misread a market, don't invest resources correctly, or management makes a decision to ignore their user base and run after the new bright shiny thing. Google is one of the biggest internet companies in the world. If anyone has a handle on how the Internet works, it is Google. Have you looked at Google Plus lately? I don't know anyone who is gaining readers on that platform or relies on it for any kind of audience growth. But if someone but all their eggs in the Google Plus basket to reach their audience, they would be seeing nearly nothing.

How does a big company make those kinds of mistakes? Because, just like authors, companies try to find a balance of servicing their core customers and getting new customers. They try to spend some time and energy being ahead of the competition by investing in new opportunities, while not loosing sight of their long-time customers who like the status quo. Managing that balance and providing the resources—financial and people—to move into new markets is not easy.

Barnes and Noble's Nook is another example of a big company making bad decisions. B&N was early into the ebook market. In fact, the Nook ereader's debut was considered significantly better than the Kindle. However, due to a combination of in-fighting and management changes, the Nook and B&N ebooks are barely breathing now. They've separated the Nook business from the core B&N business and there are rumors of trying to sell it. If an author was heavily invested in the Nook platform, she would be really hurting right now because the reality is no one is paying attention to the store.

Could the same thing happen to Amazon? Absolutely. The book part of Amazon is very small in terms of income. It would not be a hard decision at all to let that business go or to stop investing resources in it. For all the authors who only distribute through Amazon, it would be a nightmare to start all over again in another platform. It would mean no, or very limited income for months and maybe years.

## PROTECT YOUR SECOND BIGGEST ASSET—YOUR AUDIENCE DATA

As an author, your biggest asset—outside of your actual intellectual property—is your readers. Why would you allow someone else to be the only one to have all the information on your readers? Why would you allow another company—I'm looking at Amazon and B&N and Apple and Kobo—to be the only one who tells you what your reader wants and if your books are delivering that experience to them?

As much as I love my distributors, I don't actually trust that they have MY best interests at heart in terms of getting content to my readers. Their first interest is to meet their own company goals and needs. If it happens that my goals and needs intersect in exactly the way they want, then we may find a nice collaboration. However, it is also possible—even likely—that our goals and interests will diverge as the months and years go by.

**Okay I get it. But isn't Email Dead? How About Texting Instead? Maybe I should be collecting phone numbers instead of email**

Hmmm...maybe we should be collecting phone numbers. Not a bad idea, but something that is very hard to get from customers. Outside of providing my phone for two-factor account authentication security, the phone number I give to any company that requires me to fill it out online is 555-1212.

Why would I want to give permission for strangers to interrupt my peaceful day with a phone call? I'm much more willing to give out my email address because I can schedule it at a time I want to pay attention to it. I can also ignore it, delete it, or unsubscribe if I don't like the content I'm receiving.

When you first get to your desk in the morning what is one of the first things you do? I know I check my email. Invariably, all kinds of communication has been piling up while I was asleep—fans sending me questions or thanks for writing my books, my bank telling me they've just deposited my social security check, my mother letting me know what she's planning to do today, and lots of email from a variety of companies trying to tell me about their products.

How about at the end of the day? Checking email once last time before I go to bed is a habit of mine. Why? Because there are a lot of one-on-one communications I'm expecting. These range from income opportunities, ongoing coordination on projects I'm doing with my teams, requests for me to join in fun events, and of course personal communications with friends and family. I don't want to miss any of them. None of those come to me via social media.

Yes, there are some annoying emails. As I'm writing the final pages of this book I am sick and tired of all the early Christmas sales, extensions of Black Friday and Cyber Monday starting before Halloween and going through the end of the year. But that doesn't make me stop opening my email. I continue to open email from people and companies I look forward to hearing from. In fact, I count on those emails to uplift me, challenge me intellectually, and teach me something new. I don't necessarily have that expectation of social media status updates—though it is nice when they do that too.

## EMAIL IS INTIMATE WHEREAS SOCIAL MEDIA IS PRIMARILY PUBLIC

Email is still the preferred method of effective communication now and, I believe, well into the future. Email is more intimate than any social media platform because it is a one-to-one communication. Your email is more than a "status update." The inbox is the place where you receive *important* communication from people you actually know and care about.

When you send an email to a reader, no one else sees that email unless the recipient purposefully shares it. Because of that intimacy, email is the most scalable way to make sales with new customers and to build deeper relationships with steadfast customers.

*Chapter Seventeen*

## SELECTING A MAILING LIST PROVIDER

Assuming I've convinced you to invest your time and resources into building your email list, the first step is picking the right mailing list provider. Some people think they can do this on their own. After all, all it takes is sending an email. Everyone knows how to do that.

When you are sending one email at a time with unique information it is true, you must handle it on your own. However, if you are growing your email list correctly, you will soon be sending emails to thousands of readers and sending them one at a time would be a full time job.

There are programs which incorporate the ability to send mass emails from your website. That is one alternative. However, I would argue against that. Unfortunately, we live in a time when there are many bad players in the marketing arena. Spam is rampant and the last thing you want is to be marked as a spammer.

In order to be whitelisted, there are many hoops to jump through. Some you have to do on your own, but others take a huge investment in technology infrastructure that most authors cannot afford. The ability to send email quickly, to check that the email entered is legitimate, to stop robot spammers from getting to your emails, to meet all the governmental regulations around the identity of the sender, and even more regulation and checks.

It is important to have an email provider that meets all of those regulations and is a whitelisted provider. Any providers that are not whitelisted are likely to have your email end up in junk and spam folders.

You also want to be sure that the company you select provides a good amount of automation to make it easy for you to send your emails as your lists grow, and that they have good customer support when you don't know how to take the next step or something goes wrong.

## HOW TO SELECT A MAILING LIST PROVIDER

There are plenty of people who have the BEST mailing list system in the world. Just ask them. The vast majority of new authors go with whatever is the least expensive—or even free. This can work for small lists and it is a good choice for people just starting out who are planning a slow build or just want some time learning the concepts and technology without having to pay for it.

However, the bigger your list gets the more difficult it becomes. There are two types of providers: 1) The list-based provider (MailChimp, MailerLite, Sendy) and 2) The subscriber-based provider (ConvertKit, InfusionSoft, Constant Contact, AWeber). They both work but by using two very different paradigms. When you begin, a list-based provider seems fine; and they are definitely less expensive. However, the more you use your list, want to track engagement, are concerned about duplicate subscribers, and want more data on how each subscriber is interacting with you, the more you will need a subscriber-based provider.

Certainly you want to look at features you need and costs, but you also want to look at the core of the system and make an informed decision as to if you are willing to pay less now and move everything later. Or if you want to pay a little more now and spend time setting up your list with all the parameters you need from the start. Either decision is viable and it is completely up to you based on your career, your finances, and your confidence in growing quickly versus slowly.

## LIST-BASED SYSTEM PROS AND CONS

**Pros of a List-Based System**

Most are easier to get up and running quickly because they run on a simple list and it is easy to understand that concept. Want a list for your romance readers? Create one and add them. Want a list for your SF readers? Create a second one and add them.

They are always less expensive than a subscriber-based system. For example MailChimp allows up to 2,000 subscribers in their free plan. Though the free plan has limitations, that is still a good deal for people just starting up.

These systems know they are appealing to users who are starting out with mailing programs, so they go out of their way to make it easy with drag and drop templates for building your newsletter or emails. They know that users like images and they make it easy for you to add them almost anywhere you want.

List-based systems have been serving beginners for decades. They've matured to providing easy access to things people like (e.g., merge tags) so you can create emails in a similar way you would create a word document for a letter.

These systems can and do often offer the same features as subscription-based systems (e.g., tagging, segmenting). However, the implementation of those features requirers a lot more coding with less ability to protect the lists. This means when something goes wrong, it is likely to go wrong in a big way—like actually losing the list data and having to start over.

**Cons of a List-based System**

The biggest con is that most list-based systems often have one subscriber counted multiple times. This falsely inflates the number of real subscribers and, the more you have, it can push you into more expensive plans for those inflated numbers. Just as it is easy to add subscribers to different lists, it is easy to duplicate those subscribers multiple times because the lists are separate entities that don't know there are duplicates. So, if you have a reader who loves your romance books AND your fantasy books AND your YA books, that reader may be counted three times in your subscriber total because that person is "subscribed" to three different lists.

Automation sequences in list-based systems tend to be more clunky —especially if you need to appeal to people in more than one list or a segment of more than one list. You cannot easily narrow your automation by adding or removing people from a specific sequence. It can be done, but it is usually not easy or something that most non-technical users can undertake.

Options for segmenting users, based on their actions, are limited. For example, if you are looking to learn which of your readers likes stories that contain a mystery or suspense, you will have to send the question to each different genre list and create three different groups (within each list) that respond positive. Then, if you want to create a new group with all those people that is a fourth list. Counting those people again in your overall subscriber numbers.

Most list-based systems have no way to send an email to a mix and match group of subscribers on different lists. Again, it can be done but requires special coding. Some of the better list-based systems have become better at creating these queries for you in order to build that new list on the fly, and provide the data you need.

If you want to track specific users based on whether they clicked a link or took a specific action, list-based systems make that difficult and most of them are unable to provide that service for you.

## PROS AND CONS OF SUBSCRIBER-BASED SYSTEMS

### Pros of a Subscriber-Based System

One email address equals one subscriber, no matter how many groups, segments, or other tags are associated with that subscriber. In other words, a subscriber-based system has ONE master list so that no subscribers are ever duplicated (unless one person signs up under several different email addresses).

As subscribers take actions or show preferences, they are given tags based on those actions. You can take any combination of subscribers and select them for a specific campaign through these tags. You can combine subscribers into larger groups (segments) without duplication.

You can track specific subscriber actions across multiple campaigns and actions. For example, below is a screenshot of a particular subscriber in my ConvertKit database. You can see that this person has tags associated with her that relate to my romance and fantasy books. You can see which forms brought her into my mail list. Which automated sequences she received, contests she has participated in and if she opened an email and if she clicked on a call-to-action link.

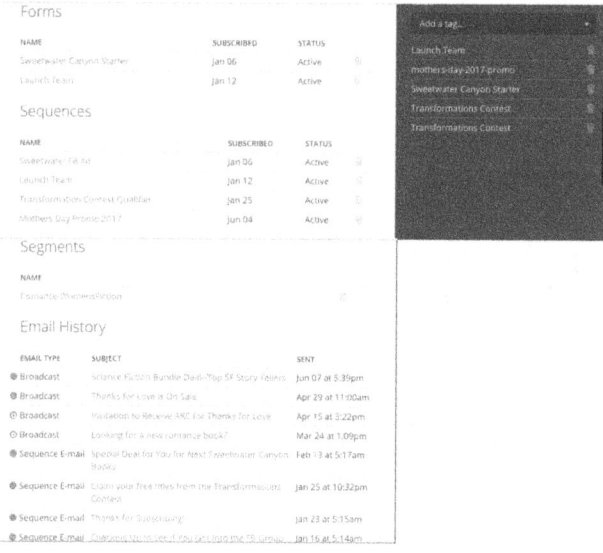

This reader first joined my email list through a Facebook Ad targeted to readers of romantic women's fiction novels. She entered a sequence attached to that ad of several emails, which ended with an invitation to join my Launch Team (some people call this a street team). She accepted that invitation as evidenced by her completed form titled Launch Team. That put her into another sequence to get invited to the closed Facebook Group for those members.

It also shows that she has opened every email I've sent her (solid blue dot next to email). She has clicked on the call to action in two emails—one to read and review an ARC for my Thanks for Love novel and another to purchase a novel in my Sweetwater Canyon series.

It is this level of detail about readers that I find invaluable and helps me to target very specific details without having to find them and send out individual emails. You can only find this detail and use it to your advantage via a subscriber-based system.

## Cons of Subscriber-Based Systems

These systems are more expensive. As with most email hosts, there is a monthly fee and it goes up based on number of subscribers. However, the base fee starts at a higher rate. For example, I have 12,000 subscribers on my list. As of this writing in August 2017, the cost for that on ConvertKit is $149 per month. If I were to use MailChimp, the cost would be $140 per month. However, for me what I save in tracking and automation ease is well worth the difference of $9 per month. Starting out with a subscriber based system and only 2,000 people on your mailing list will be significantly higher than a list-based system. Sometimes as much as 40% higher.

Subscriber-based plans are designed for serious email marketers. That means there is an assumption on the part of the software developer that an experienced technical person is setting this up for you. Therefore, the drag-and-drop graphics of list-based systems are not common and the number of common template choices are limited. Though you can create a specialized template for yourself, it will take someone who understands HTML and CSS coding.

That being said, some subscriber-based software developers are working on making this more robust and easier for their users. Also subscription-based services will often partner with or integrate with a company who specializes in software designed for building beautiful squeeze pages or landing pages. For example, ConvertKit partners with LeadPages and integrates directly so that a reader coming to your

"Landing Page" hosted on LeadPages is seamlessly added to your subscriber list with whatever tags or segments you wish to attribute to that campaign. Unfortunately, these partnerships tend to add even more monthly costs for the author because you are subscribing to two providers now.

## DO YOU NEED A FANCY SQUEEZE PAGE OR LANDING PAGE?

I do not use these third-party landing page templates, or cloud-based software from landing page providers, because it is one more monthly fee that I don't want to incur. However, authors who are constantly doing email-building campaigns (e.g., every month or multiple times a month) through giveaways, contests, and other options may find a good reason to invest in one of these companies if it is important to you to have beautiful, modern landing pages that are easy to build and wow potential readers or buyers.

Does having a beautiful, impressive landing page get more people to follow through on signing up for your mailing list? Or buying a book you are advertising? I don't have a definitive answer to that based on a good data sample across multiple authors or genres. I can say that, for me, what drives traffic to that page—Facebook Ads, Contests, Giveaways—is more important than the page itself. I've seen no difference in my own readers in clicks on an image-rich full-spread landing page vs. the basic landing pages that come with most email providers.

What IS critical is making sure that your landing page somewhat matches whatever your driver images are. For example, if you used a picture of a woman throwing magic fireballs on a Facebook Ad that sends people to your fantasy mailing list. Then that same picture should be repeated on your landing page. In that way, readers know that when they get there it relates to the ad they picked in Facebook. If it looks completely different, many people will leave thinking that they've landed in the wrong place or somehow made a mistake.

In addition to matching whatever ad or contest drove them to your sign up list, your landing page can have more than that image (e.g., a book image and brief description or reviews, or a list of reasons to sign up to your list). Just keep it brief and make it easy for someone to sign up.

I have trialed LeadPages and it is an amazing platform. I ran some tests on my own pages for about three months using the LeadPage option for a campaign and the basic ConvertKit template landing page option. I saw no significant difference in number of people signing up for my email list or purchasing a book. For my own needs, I am satisfied with the limitations and less robust landing page templates available from ConvertKit at this stage in my career. (Note: I'll talk more about Landing Pages (Squeeze Pages) in the chapter on Drip Campaigns.

## EMAIL ENGAGEMENT

Knowing you need to communicate with email regularly, you also need to make some decisions on your strategies. Those decisions will then dictate how you want to collect names and what you want to learn from your subscribers. How you want to track and analyze the information also impacts your decision on which mailing list provider will best provide that information to you.

**Decisions Needed Before Creating a Subscriber List**

**1. Are you readers a homogenous group or not?**

If you write in multiple genres, do you think you have significant cross-over readers? In Romance, for example, if you are writing contemporary romance you MAY have some crossover into Contemporary Romantic Suspense if your themes, voice, and heat level are similar. Where you might NOT have cross-over is if your contemporary romances are light and funny, but your romantic suspense is dark and challenging (some people read this as depressing). Also, if one of your genres are based an today's urban sensibility and the other is based in a paranormal world—even if the world looks like today's urban world—you may not have many cross-over readers.

If you write in a single genre, or you believe there is a strong cross-over reader group, then you will want to start with a master list and later segment it by specific elements where you can send emails only to a part of the list. However, if your genres are really diverse and the likelihood of cross-over is small, you will want to start with a way to keep these groups of readers separate.

If you are using a list-based system, like MailChimp, you will need to set up a separate list for each group and make sure that your email campaigns and automations are specific to each of those separate groups/lists. If you are using a subscriber-based system like ConvertKit then you will want to identify the "tags" to use for your various types of subscribers. For example, I write in several genres, so I've set up six different primary tags: romance, romantic suspense, science fiction, fantasy, young adult, and nonfiction. Every campaign I run is related to one of these tags. In that way every subscriber is tagged with what they are participating in.

Whether you are using a list-based system or a subscriber-based system, doing this advanced thinking will save you a lot of time and trouble as each of your genre readerships grow.

**2. Do you have one author name or multiple pseudonyms?**

When I began my email campaigns with MailChimp, I began with one list for all three of my names—mistakenly believing there would be lots of cross-over. That was NOT the case. Once the list went beyond about 500, I then had to spend time dividing my list into three separate lists in order to manage it more effectively. If your author names are related to a specific genre or type of book, then you can decide whether you want to segment by name or genre. If each name has additional genres associated with it, it may be best to not worry about the name but instead worry about segmentation by genre.

If you send an email to an entire list of mixed readers, you will experience lower open rates and higher unsubscribes. This is because you are sending them information that only a specific percentage of your readers are interested in seeing.

It is a natural tendency to think: "I have 12,000 people on my list and I know only 6,000 of them like romance. However, I don't want to ignore the other 6,000 in case there are a few cross-over readers." I believed that too. The number of unsubscribes continued to rise. Even a few of my launch team members unsubscribed. Because I use a subscriber-based system I knew exactly who unsubscribed and under which campaign or email. When I followed up, they said they didn't mean to unsubscribe from everything, but they didn't want to get information about my romance books and they thought if they unsubscribed at that email moment I would know they only didn't want those emails.

This is where running separate campaigns is critical and knowing where each subscriber best fits. If you DO have cross-over readers (about 15% of my list does cross-over to at least one other genre) they won't have a problem signing up again for a different list or responding to a question about what they read so you can tag them with the appropriate segment.

Some authors believe that sending out a "newsletter" once a month that covers everything they are doing solves the cross-over or segmentation problem. It doesn't. When there is high diversity in your subscribers there may be long periods of time when those who signed up for a specific book/genre don't get any content they really want. That then leads to one of two things: 1) They unsubscribe; or 2) They stay on the list but ignore your emails. Both responses are bad outcomes.

In addition, multiple marketing studies have indicated that any email should have only ONE call-to-action. That means only ONE thing the reader is asked to do. If your newsletter provides multiple links (e.g., link to my new book release, link to a contest I'm participating in, link to a multi-author bookset I'm in, link to an offer on a different discounted book) then it is most likely that the reader will click NONE of them. It causes decision paralysis or overwhelm.

**REMEMBER:** Readers want to hear from you regularly. However, they want to receive valuable content relating to THEIR interests every time.

## WHAT IS SEGMENTATION AND HOW DO YOU USE IT?

Segmenting a list means identifying attributes about your readers that are important to you. Of course, in order to do this you need to be collecting data on them. For example, how do you know which book a specific reader purchased or liked if they sign up to join your list at an in-person book signing. After the signing you have their name and email address and that's it. The reality is you DON'T know unless: 1) you had them indicate the book name or genre preference on the sign in sheet; or 2) you have an amazing memory as to what you talked about that indicates their preferences. I don't know about you, but my memory of people and conversations ends about 30 seconds after I move onto the next person.

Businesses with a known physical presence and geographic demographic (e.g., a bookstore, clothing store, grocery) tend to segment their list by geographic location so they know where to target advertising. Though authors may use this tactic as well, it is unlikely to be very effective except when doing in-person events. For the most part, authors are selling everywhere at once and even around the world. The information that may be more important to you are genre preferences, series preferences, theme preferences. In other words, anything that specifically relates to your books that you can capitalize on to ensure those readers receive valuable content and the experience they are expecting.

The only way to get that information is to ask. You can ask on the sign up sheet—though the more information you ask for the less likely someone is to complete it. You can ask at in-person events and make coded marks next to the person's name. However, that is fairly conspicuous and, for me, requires to much administrative attention when I should be focusing on the individual conversations.

Something I do is regularly survey my readers. Two years ago I did a small survey of my readers. I asked four questions.

1. Mark the genres you are interested in reading (I listed about 8 possibilities)
2. How often do you want to hear from me? Their selection

options were: Every week, Every two weeks, Once a Month, Once a quarter.
3. Do you want me to share other author's books and freebies and contests in addition to my own?
4. Do you listen to audiobooks?

To encourage people to participate in the survey, each person was given a survey number (so they could remain anonymous). A number was then randomly drawn for a prize. Approximately 20% of my readers responded to the survey.

From that survey, I received new and important data that I used to provide those readers with content I'm confident they will appreciate. It allowed me to segment my subscriber list and to make sure I did not send emails to them about books or themes they didn't want to receive.

Because the majority of the responders (nearly 60%) indicated they wanted to hear from me twice a month, it allowed me to move forward with confidence on more frequent emails. I was very surprised by this. My expectation was that once a month would be the request.

I continue to do reader surveys whenever I have a question I need answered. For example, this year I started receiving emails from a few readers complaining about the number of contests I was doing. At the start of the year I had participated in approximately 7 contests in a period of three months to build my list. Those few emails made me wonder how many people on my list were upset about my frequent contest opportunities.

I decided that I would offer them an opportunity to opt out of any more emails on any contests. I sent an email to my list and explained that I had received some complaints from readers about so many contest emails. I told them if they did not want to receive any more emails about contest offers, to click on a specific button that said NO CONTESTS. Anyone, who clicked on that button was automatically tagged with a "no contest" tag and thereafter any time I sent out an email about a contest, that group was excluded from the email.

It only ended up to be 68 people who chose to be excluded.

However, I have now retained 68 people who may have decided to unsubscribe on the next contest email I sent.

**Don't be afraid to survey your readers**. They signed up to your list for a reason. For the most part, they want to provide feedback. Asking their opinion shows you care about them as an individual, that you are not just using them as a recipient of sales pushes.

## Chapter Eighteen
# SETUP AND QUALIFY NAMES

There are hundreds of ways to get names on your mailing list. However, what you want to end up with are names of people who are likely to read your book and therefore buy future books. I call this a Mailing List of True Fans. Good quality mailing lists have better open rates and better engagement rates in terms of clicking on links, responding to your calls to action.

## WAYS TO GET PEOPLE ON YOUR MAILING LIST

There are a myriad of ways to get people to sign up to your email list. The more ways you provide the better. However, don't feel you need to implement every one of these right now. There are several I haven't implemented yet. The key is to have more than one way to reach your audience and get them on your email list.

*Have signup sheets at EVERY event you attend.* If you give a talk at your local writer's group, provide a chance for people to sign up for your email list. If you go to a conference, bring your email list sign up sheets. If you are doing a signing, be sure to have your email list sign up available. If you are attending a fair, showing your books at a library reading, always, always, always have your email list sign up sheet with you. A lot of people will sign up who don't buy that day. Some times you'll only get a couple of people and other times you may get twenty. The number doesn't matter. Without a sign up sheet, I can guarantee you will get a big zero.

**Put a call to action in the back of every book (ebook and print).** After the last page of the story and before any other back matter (e.g., author bio, other books) you want to ASK your readers to sign up to your email list. This is the best chance to get them, while they are still in love with your book and with you as a writer. In your ebook, provide a direct link to your signup form online, so it is easy to just click and do it. In your print book, type out the link. Below is my call to action, feel free to steal it, modify it, and make it your own.

*Keep up with new releases in this series, as well as my other books by joining my mailing list. You will receive news of what I'm doing and get special offers on new books, as well as opportunities for free books that no one else gets. I never spam you, I don't share your information, and you can unsubscribe at any time.*

Because I write in multiple genres, the link to join my mailing list is different for each genre. That helps me segment people immediately.

**Make sure your website has a way for someone to sign up for your email list.** Don't make it hard for readers to find the place to sign up for your email list. Have it easily accessed. Either by appearing on every page or through the menu or your Contact page. You can see how I set it up on my website. I give away a free book to get people to sign up, but you don't have to do that, you can just detail the value of signing up.

**Add a link to your sign up page everywhere you are on the Internet.** On your blog, on your FB page, on your Twitter page, on Pinterest, etc. You don't want anyone to miss the opportunity to sign up. You can do this with posts that are kept at the top of your feed (pinned to top) or with actual buttons within the page. See my FB page and the Signup button in the header, or my Twitter page where I've pinned the tweet to the top of the page about signing up for my newsletter.

**Add a signup link to your email signature.** This can be as simple as "*Sign up for my newsletter*" or a little more complex by giving good reasons to sign up like: get new release info, learn about giveaways, get discounts only for newsletter subscribers, etc.

**Have a simple call-to-action at the end of your newsletter.** Here is an example: "*Did you enjoy this newsletter? Maybe your friends would too! They can sign up here.*"

**Use a website squeeze page.** A squeeze page is a page that consumers go to that has only one thing on it—a call to action. This is also sometimes called a "Landing Page." In this case it is a call to sign up for your email list. In order to do this you need to offer something valuable (e.g., something for free). If you have a lot of books, give away the first book in a series. If you have only a few books, consider giving away a novella or a couple of short stories packaged very nicely with a cover and in ebook form. This is particularly helpful whenever you are running an electronic campaign via your newsletter or other social media to get more signups. Here are two examples of good squeeze pages.

Mark Dawson, a thriller writer from the UK

Joanna Penn, also a thriller writer from the UK

**Use Autoresponders once someone signs up.** These are automatic emails that are sent at specific times after signup with no additional effort from you. You can create what they say within Mailchimp. Some ideas for fiction writers is to immediately send a thank you email and take a little time to explain why you write and talk about what readers can expect from you. You might even have an email about what books you like to read. The key is to let your readers know you are human, you are likeable, and that they just might have something in common with you.

***Provide incentives for people to recommend their friends.*** For example, I am running a campaign in November to get more people on my list. I am offering a free book through a special landing page for that, but I don't want my regular email list people to miss out. So, I'm going to offer them a free book too whenever they refer someone. It doesn't have to be a book, it can be a short story, the first three chapters of your work-in-progress, or anything else you can think of that would entice them to sign up or help get others signed up.

***With every email you send, remember the three Fs*** – Fun, Fearless, and Free. Always have something that matches one of those Fs as a click for your subscribers, and be sure to encourage them to share it with their friends.

**Fun** might be a link to a comic, a fun image, or a virtual event.

**Fearless** might be a challenge to do something and then share it back to you via FB or Twitter e.g., Send me a pic of the craziest shoes you'd love to try on. Tell me about your most embarrassing moment. What is the most heroic thing you've ever witnessed?

**Free** can be something you are giving away or something someone else is giving away that you can share.

## WHAT TO CHOOSE? SINGLE VS. DOUBLE OPT-IN

The main difference between single and double opt-in is how many times a user must confirm that they want to be added to an email list. **Single Opt-In** requires a reader to only submit their email address to a signup form one time. There is no need to confirm their sign up. No need to check their email and click on a link. As soon as the user signs up, he or she is immediately added to the email list.

**Double Opt-In** has been the standard for years, but there is now some questions as to if it is the choice most authors want to make. Double Opt-In requires the reader to go through at least two steps and sometimes more depending on the mail provider you are using and the process for beginning an email drip campaign. In essence, when a reader first encounters your form, she provides an email. However, she is not yet on your list. Next she is sent a ***confirmation email*** where she must click a button or a link that confirms her desire to be added to your email list. Only after this confirmation is the user officially added to email list.

Some authors and marketers believes that this double opt-in process gives you a cleaner list. In fact, until October 2017, the default for MailChimp was double opt-in. They have now changed that default to single opt-in.

Let's look at some pros and cons of each method.

### Pros of using Single Opt-In:

- New visitors are added to your list immediately after providing their email address.
- You can instantly start them into your drip campaign and begin engaging. If you offered an incentive (e.g. a book or short story for free), they get that immediately too which means they can start reading and get to know you within minutes of showing interest by giving you their email.
- You tend to get a lot more people on your list with single opt-in than with double. Some of the reason for that is because people don't check email as often as they used to and so never confirm a link. OR your confirmation email ends up in their junk folder and they don't see it in time to confirm.

### Cons of using Single Opt-In:

- You *will* get fake emails. If you are offering content immediately upon signup, a user could give a fake email address, so they can get your content, and then never receive another email from you because the email is fake. One of the ways to avoid this is to have the content delivered with the first drip email (a delay of perhaps a minute instead of instantaneousy), instead of allowing an instant download once they complete the form. In that way, if the email IS fake, they won't get the content because the download link was sent to their fake email. If they gave you a non-existent email, your first email with the content will bounce. If they gave you a junk email address (e.g., maggie-freebie-books@gmail.com), there is a high liklihood they will never see it because they don't check that email. They use it only to get whatever freebie you are offering instantly.
- You will also get incorrect email addresses due to typos. A user may sign up for your list in good faith but accidentally mistype their email address, thereby giving your email list

something that will bounce. Again the fix is like that discussed above.

When I began my email building efforts, I chose double opt-in because I heard lots of talk from authors about freebie seekers who don't give real emails. However, I never offered instant access to my free book (e.g., as soon as the email is entered they are sent to Book Funnel or Instafreebie). I always sent the Book Funnel link in the first drip email. Consequently, when my first drip email went out (within a minute of getting the email on the form), I was shocked to find that the opens were a dreadful 23%. I could not understand why people would sign up for a free book but then not open the email to download it.

Then, I checked how many people in the list had confirmed. Only, 36%! I took the same list and marked the entire list as confirmed. (Note: This may not be available in some email programs). Then I resent the email to all who had not opened. My opens went from 23% to 82%.

If you are following this, it is likely you would now be saying: "Sure, but then how many unsubscribes did you get *after* they got the freebie?" The answer is 2%, very few. Of course, not everyone stayed around through my 2-3 month email campaign, but my opens remained above 50% consistently and still do even for people who have been with me for a year or more.

Of course, my experience may not be yours. So, let's look at the pros and cons of using double opt-in.

### *Pros of using Double Opt-In:*

- Increased Engagement is common because you know that the user *really* wants to sign up for your email list as they have both signed up on your form and then confirmed their signup after receiving the email.
- The double opt-in process does protect your list from spam addresses that would bounce. If a bot or fake email address

is entered in the opt-in form, then it will not be added to your list until that email addresses is confirmed. This means a healthier email list that gives you more accurate statistics immediately.

## *Cons of using Double Opt-In:*

- You are creating more steps for users to take to get your content, thereby risking that the visitor may not complete the signup process. Perhaps they truly wanted to be on your email list but forgot to confirm their email, or your confirmation email went into their SPAM folder.
- The confirmation email has a risk of seeming spammy to begin with. Depending on your email provider, it may come from a place not recognized by your reader (e.g., emailprovidername@provider.com) Sometimes, authors try to get around this by having a message that shows after the form is completed alerting the user to add the email provider to their list of acceptable receivers. Not surprisingly, most users have no idea how to do this and that will stop them from receiving that confirmation email.
- If you send a confirmation email, followed by a welcome email, and then the product delivery email for the user, then they can have three emails from you in quick succession which can scare a reader into thinking you are spamming them.

For me, the biggest con of double opt-in is that you will miss out on possible customers. I would rather end up giving away a few books to freebie seekers who will never become truly engaged with me, than to miss out on hundreds of possible customers who are interested but for some reason did not confirm that email.

The double opt-in versus single opt-in decision is dependent on what risks you want to take. There are risks either way.

*Do you want to risk having people on your list with no intention of ever buying anything?* Double opt-in doesn't guarantee sales. However, it does tend to guarantee that those readers went the extra step to be on your list. The up side is you aren't delivering content to people who only want free stuff. The down side is that your list grows significantly slower. My experience is about 75% slower.

*Do you want to risk missing hundreds or maybe thousands of potential customers?* Single opt-in will let a lot more people through, a certain percentage of which will be freebie seekers. One way to mitigate the risk is to monitor your list regularly and to build your drip campaign to not be giving something away with the majority of your emails.

If you see people who have not opened anything beyond that first email with a free incentive, then remove them from your list. I do this once per year. I send an email letting them know I am unsubscribing them because it appears they are not responding to my emails and I don't want to be a spammer. Within that email, I give them an opportunity to click a button to say "Please keep me on the list." If they do nothing within 14 days, they are automatically unsubscribed.

*Chapter Nineteen*

## DRIP CAMPAIGNS

### What is a Drip Campaign or an Automated Email Sequence?

Drip email marketing campaigns get their name from an agricultural method where water is gradually released on crops to nurture them—feeding them regularly—and producing the best possible yield. In drip email campaigns, a series of emails is sent to subscribers automatically. Just like the drip watering, each email in the sequence is triggered by a designated time interval *or* the email subscribers' actions.

Drip email campaigns are also called "autoresponders," "lifecycle emails," "nurture campaigns," and plenty of other names. The beauty of this kind of email campaign is that through automation you can set any number of sequences, for any number of potential events, in advance and have them trigger in the background. In other words, you don't have to manually track it every day or manually create an email for each individual circumstance.

### Drip Campaigns Provide A Sales Funnel

A sales funnel moves something from point A to point B. In the perfect scenario, a sales funnel gets you prospects where you want them to be—among a list of readers who already like your genre. Contrary to popular belief, a sales funnel does not refer to pouring marketing material into a reader's inbox. I know when I see that from anyone—even authors I like—I immediately unsubscribe.

Far too frequently, I subscribe to a mailing list based on something I'm interested in (e.g., a free book or tip sheet or a video) and then I get something almost daily trying to upsale me to something costly. I haven't even had a chance to evaluate the free thing. What happens? I unsubscribe. Maybe what that person had to offer really is something I might be interested in later. But I'm so miffed at being sold to right away, when I haven't even had a chance to look at the original offer, that I see it as a bother and I see the person being too focused on sales instead of me as a customer.

The reality is there is plenty of competition in books. Even if I'm really interested in your book and it's content, if I'm not ready to buy and you bombard me with marketing materials I'll disappear. I'll wait until I'm thinking about that kind of content and ready to read it. Then I'll go looking for examples. I may not find your example again. If I do, because of my previous experience with too much marketing, I won't try it again. That's because I'm confident there are other people who have the same content but the purchase experience will be nicer.

A good sales funnel leads your prospect through a set of emails that help them get to know you, get to know your product, and then offers them opportunities to try it without too much downside (free/discounted). This is called generating a "warm lead." If the reader likes the first bits of content, believes you want to get to know her, book she will CHOOSE to try another and another even though she has to pay for them.

In the perfect scenario, between the time someone hears about you and your book(s) and the point where they click the "buy now" button, your new customer will have been convinced about the utter brilliance of your offering. The sales funnel works as both a marketing tool and a filter. As a marketing tool it is bridging the communication gap between you and a potential reader by giving them time to get to know you and what you write without worrying about being bombarded with sales materials. It also works as a filter by qualifying your potential readers before moving them to the next stage.

It is okay if the majority of your prospects fall out during the qualification stage. It does you no good to have 10,000 people on your email list if only 100 of them are really interested in what you have to offer. Just like my friend who had over 30K Twitter followers. It sounds like a heady number and something to point to with pride. However, if they aren't engaging with the content then chances are they aren't getting the content or willever going to act on offers. Keeping dead weight (customers who are unlikely to ever buy) on your mailing list does you no good and, in the end, actually costs you money to maintain them.

## 5 STEPS TO DEVELOPING YOUR DRIP CAMPAIGN

### *1. Qualify Your Subscribers*

Not all subscribers are created equal. As I've said in previous sections, some join because you gave away something for free. A number of authors join because they want to see how you are doing something, but don't intend to read your book. Some join because they were in the mood when they first encountered your campaign, but are not necessarily interested enough to continue. Some join because they were at a party or participated in a contest. Some join because they were face-to-face with you at a signing and couldn't say "No" to sign up on your list.

You need to make some rules for yourself as to who is a QUALIFIED reader and who are lookie-loos with no intention of ever reading your books—free or paid. The sooner you stop treating all signups the same, the sooner you'll get more of them reading your emails and responding to your call-to-action.

Your subscribers probably have some characteristics in common. But there are important differences that distinguish certain "types" of list members from others.

- ***Sign up timing.*** Someone who joined three months ago has different needs than someone who joined yesterday.
- ***Genre Interests***. Particularly if you write in more than one genre, one person may have signed up because she's interested in your romance. Someone else may have signed up because he's interested in your non-fiction. IF your follow up emails are in the genre the person isn't interested in, they will not engage.
- ***Interaction Type.*** Readers DO have preferences about how they interact with you. Though email marketing IS the #1 way to control reader interaction, you have to also recognize that some people prefer sharing information with you via social media. Messenger, for example, is a way I've seen more and more readers interact with me. It has the one-on-one feeling of emails but they don't have to ever leave Facebook.
- ***Quickness to Engage.*** Some readers respond immediately to any request you make. Others may take a week or months. Knowing which ones need immediate engagement is important to keeping them happy AND eventually making them into your superfans or part of your street team.

You won't know any of these differences until you start sending emails. However, if you create your emails in such a way as to gather this information it will provide excellent feedback to you for further emails.

A good example of drip marketing would be an automated email sent a day after a visitor signs up for your email to thank them, then invite them to also LIKE you on FB or Engage on Twitter. This will give you immediate information as to those who might want to engage on social media. In another email, several days or a couple weeks later, you can share your range of genre interests (always first talk about yourself as a reader) and then ask them to share their favorite genres and why (call-to-action without any request to buy). This now provides information for qualifying the type of readers you have.

Setting up automated email marketing drip campaigns can move the potential customer along the sales cycle and constantly nudge them to engage more with you and your content. The more engagement, the more likely they are to buy when the time comes. These automated campaigns free up your valuable time and resources that may be wasted trying to chase readers who will probably never buy a book from you. Automated campaigns help you to weed out the people who: only download free books; aren't interested in your genre; only buy books that are bestsellers; only buy books that are recommended by their newspaper; and many other reasons.

Getting as granular as possible makes every member of your list feel appreciated, feel that you are listening and providing for their needs from you and your books.

## 2. Pick One Goal per Campaign

Someone who signed up to your email list yesterday probably isn't ready to hear about your new $15 boxed set of your series. In fact, they probably aren't ready to have you ask them to buy anything yet. The #1 cause for people unsubscribing shortly after getting on your email list is if they are immediately asked to buy something the next time they hear from you. To many readers that behavior is considered spam and that is why people are reluctant to give emails and why they often give a "fake" email or an email that they rarely look at when signing up for a list.

Someone who's been on your list for several months and has engaged with you around things other than buying your book is more likely to respond favorably when you do a campaign that asks them to BUY MY BOOK.

You may already know that you set up a website where each page has only ONE goal to convert a customer. In the same way, it's smart to limit each drip email campaign to also have only ONE goal—one Call-to-Action.

A lot of authors (myself included in the past) try to craft emails that reach Everyone (with a capital 'E'). They think that the more they share of different opportunities, the more likely someone will choose something they like. However, this rarely works for two reasons: 1) When confronted with two many choices, the majority of people decide NOT to choose anything. Remember, people are busy. They are scanning emails. They don't have time or want to take time to make a choice. 2) The two most important parts of your email are the subject/headline to draw them in and the ONE GOAL BIG BUTTON they can push to engage. People who scan emails love this. If they like the headline, "What is your favorite book?" and want to answer, they will immediately look for a way to respond (big button) and often skip the middle if they are in a hurry.

By defining a single goal for each campaign, you significantly increase the odds of your subscriber engagement.

Here are a few examples of single goal campaigns:

- Welcome new subscribers to your list and build engagement
- Get current subscribers to engage in a simple way (LIKE FB, say "yes" or "no" to a single ask, or reply with a one line response)
- Reengage subscribers who haven't opened emails for a while
- Confirm purchases or downloads
- Recommend a book based on subscriber engagement (yours or another author's book)
- Deliver valuable information about your characters or other educational content

Drip email campaigns are the perfect place to be creative and let your personality shine through as a brand. The only limits to how you can use them are your imagination and delivering content through email.

### 3. Create Valuable Content for Your Drip Email Campaign

Now you have a list segment you're targeting and a specific goal in mind. The next step is to fill your drip email campaign with valuable content.

The biggest difference between regular broadcast emails (like newsletters or release announcements) and drip emails is that your emails are now more personal instead of newsy. Your emails are designed to fit a specific subset of subscribers. Broadcast newsletters are trying the *something for everyone* approach, they aren't at all personal. Drip emails build on each other and move subscribers closer to your specific goal (buy a book). Drip emails are shorter. Usually no more than three to four short paragraphs. Think about how you might write to a friend or an acquaintance of a friend who is just finding out about you as an author.

Author's run into trouble when their drip emails sound like they're automated. You might use email software like MailChimp or ConertKit to execute your campaigns, but the content needs to FEEL personal. You want to talk about yourself in first person (I). You want to invite the reader to do things just like you would a friend. You want to be more informal than formal. You are using an approach that says: "I want to know you as an individual person, and I want you to know me in that way too." Using emojis in your email is not only acceptable, but certain demographics think it makes it even more personal. THIS personalized type of experience is what gets readers to engage, to click, and ultimately to buy.

## 4. Identify the Frequency of Emails

Once you have your drip emails loaded up and ready to go, you need to choose how often to send them. There aren't any hard and fast rules for this. Dan Zarrella from HubSpot (a company who conducts campaigns for businesses selling products regularly) found that if you plan to email at least four to five times monthly, you might as well email much more often because there's only a *slight* decrease in click-through rates.

For me, as an author, I think that's too much. I know that when I get emails every week from a company—not only books but any online retailer—I tend to ignore them and eventually I unsubscribe. However, don't rely ONLY on your personal reactions. Think like a reader, not an author. As an author I don't have the time or the will to read extraneous emails and once a month would be plenty. However, I also forget about things when they only come once a month. Particularly, new things that haven't become a habit for me to check.

When I polled my reader list, I asked them how often they'd like to hear from me. The choices were: once per week, every two weeks, once per month, or once per quarter (which had been my default newsletter timing). I was surprised that **the majority chose every two weeks**.

When I set up my automated sequence, I thought about what I might like to get if I were reader and just trying out an author for the first time. I've signed up for a lot of people's books or educational classes or newsletters. A lot of them use an automated sequence. I learned that I appreciated getting an email that confirmed my signup. I also didn't mind getting an email that checked that I was able to download whatever they sent me (book, tip sheet, essay, etc.). What I did NOT appreciate were the emails that started coming every week or two trying to upsale me to an entire book series or to their $500 super special course that would change my life.

My automated sequence uses what I liked and not what I didn't like about those others campaigns. I also used logic. If I was going to ask my readers to leave a review, I wanted to be sure it was a good two to three months after they downloaded a book. I wanted to give them time to read it and plenty of emails in between to just get to know me before I asked anything specific. Even if I had a great book coming out in a week, I would NOT send the information on that book with a buy action if the person just joined in the past few weeks. There would be plenty of time for them to buy it later.

I've illustrated a couple of automation sequences at the end of this chapter so you can see what my choices were.

The reality is that everyone is different. Some people can get away with being more aggressive with emails, while other people can't. It's a combination of your personality and the value of your content. For example, there is an email list I subscribe to for marketing content. In my opinion, the person who runs this list sends FAR too many emails and too many of them try to upsale me on a regular basis. However, I don't unsubscribe because all the other content is REALLY VALUABLE to me. In other words, it's worth the spammy emails to get to the stuff I want to know.

On the other hand, there is an author whose books I really like so I subscribed to her email list. However, she sends emails way too often for me—at least once a week and sometimes two or three times per week. And the content she sends me doesn't interest me—what costume she bought for a convention, the meals she had while on vacation, cute pictures of her dogs in a variety of poses, and about every third email talks about a book to buy or the next one up for pre-order. She is prolific and tends to have a new book or novella out every month. But the emails are just too much for me. I finally unsubscribed. Will I still buy her novel length books when they come out? Maybe...if I notice. But I may not notice because I'm no longer on her list.

## 5. Test, Track, and Tweak

In the beginning of this description I said the great thing about automated emails is that once they are set up, you can rest easy and let them work in the background for you. They save you time and you don't have to think about it or do a lot of manual follow up. However, it is NOT a complete set-it-and forget-it-for-a-year solution.

The only way to know for sure if it's working as expected is to test, track, and tweak. In the first couple months, be sure to check your data and see that it is meeting your expectations. Here are the three things I check.

1. ***Check the open rate after three days*** (it will go up with time as not everyone opens it the day you send it out). Anything above 35% is considered good. I shoot for 50%, and can sometimes get that if I do a resend, about three days later, to those who didn't open.
2. ***Check to see how many people are clicking on the call-to-action***. Anything above 15% is considered good. Track to

see where they go after they open the email. Did they go to my website? To one of my social media platforms? Did they leave a comment on my blog? All of those are good. It means they are engaging with me.

3. **Check to see any sales increases**. Even if the purpose of the email was not to sell a book, when people are engaged they may still go buy one if the content you provided reminded them they'd been meaning to buy. Note: When the purpose of the email IS to announce a new release and get them to buy a book, a 15% click on the buy link is good. However, don't expect that all those clicks will actually by. Approximately 50% of clicks to a buy page don't follow through. So, in the end anything above 7% is a good result. If your non-follow through are higher than that, there may be a problem with your book page.

## HOW TO KNOW WHAT TO TWEAK

Setting up drip email campaigns and filling them with valuable content is hard work. For places where customers are not following through, look first at your headline/subject line. Could it be tweaked to be more interesting? Maybe people see it and it's not interesting enough to open.

If you are seeing opens but not enough clicks on your call-to-action, that means the reader isn't interested in participating. Why is that? Maybe the call-to-action is too hard to implement. For example, asking someone to send you an email with feedback is more time consuming than filling out a short survey form where they click answers. Or just ask for a single YES or NO opinion with two big buttons. Or in a cover reveal with three options to choose a cover, ask the reader to just click on the one they like. Simplify, simplify, simplify the call-to-action.

Once you are getting the numbers you want (at least what is considered "good" by the industry) let it sit for a while and generate you some signups or some sales. Check it again in 6 months and see if it's still performing. Sometimes, campaigns run a course—particularly when your targeted readership is tapped out or needs to be made a little larger.

## Two Examples of An Automated Sequence

### *Example 1: Subscriber Joins My General Email List*

You have linked to your general email list everywhere—on your website, on your FB page, your Twitter account, the back of your books. When I began doing email list subscription, in the FREE Mail-Chimp account, I simply sent a Thank You letter and provided some information. Then the subscriber waited until I put out a newsletter (it was quarterly back then). Today, you need to "nurture" that new sign up. Consider this three-step sequence.

**Immediately after someone joins my list, I thank them.** I talk, briefly, about how much you appreciate their support. I share a little about why I write in the genres I do. A typical call-to action in this first email is: "I'd love to hear who your two favorite authors are. Email me your answer at Maggie@maggielynch.com

**Two weeks later, send an email with some piece of valuable content.** It might be an excerpt from a book. It could be some FREE information that is NOT available to the public and hadn't been announced even in a previous email (e.g., a Christmas short story for the holidays). Remember, your fans are special. My call-to-action is asking them to join me on my FB fan page or Twitter page. When they do join my page, I ALWAYS THANK THEM AND ACKNOWL-EDGE THEIR JOINING.

**One month later send an email inviting them to join an event with me.** (**Note**: *I don't use this anymore because I've stopped doing special events, but it was a good growth tool*) This could be a special FB group you've created for fans. It might be a monthly event you do on FB or Twitter. It could be a live web conference or radio call- in or any other way you regularly connect with fans.

**NOTE:** Remember, these are automated emails so it must be something that you do EVERY month on a schedule. For example: "Thank you for being such a great fan. I'd love to invite you to my fan's only monthly web conference where we talk about everything romance. I always invite at least one other author to be there with me, so it's not just me talking. We meet the second Wednesday of every month from 7-8pm Pacific Time (10-11pm Eastern Time)." Give them the link. "I hope to see you there so we can chat in person!"

**Example 2: Free Book Incentive Drip Campaign**

I have a sequence that works for several free book giveaway options. One is for a first in series book, **Undertones**. Though the vast majority of my readers get the book on retailer sites where I don't have control of their names (Amazon, Kobo, Apple, etc.), I also offer it on my home page, through FB and Twitter, and in some events where a free book giveaway is required. All of these event triggers send the reader to a Landing Page to sign up to email list and then to get the free book. https://app.convertkit.com/landing_pages/157087

I also include the offer of the first book free in the other books in the series. That link also goes to the same landing page above. **Note:** This gives me the opportunity to capture their name when they buy one of the other books at a retailer. All of these events go to my UNDERTONES FREE list and triggers a four-email sequence.

*Immediately upon requesting free book on my Landing Page, they get an email with an immediate download of the book.* The email thanks them and tells them I hope they enjoy it. I do NOT do any additional call-to-action or selling at this point. The call-to-action is to download the book. **NOTE:** Though I do have their email, they are going to my *UNDERTONES FREE* list. They are not a part of any TRUE fan list at this point.

*Three days later they get an email asking if they were able to download the book* and giving them contact info for me if they had a problem. Again, no call-to-action except to contact me with a problem. This shows that I care that they were able to get the free book and I don't expect anything else of them. **NOTE:** I have not had a single person tell me they were unable to download the book. However, I always get people who said they never received the download link. This is how I catch people who ignored the first email (particularly after a big promo when several authors may be emailing) or the first email went to junk or was lost.

*Three weeks after the second email, I tell them a little about me and what to expect in terms of how often they will receive emails.* The call to action is for them to join me on one of my social media sites. Depending on what I'm pushing, I change this call to action every three months or so. If I'm growing my FB site, I'll ask them to join me there. If I'm looking to get YouTube subscribers, I'll ask them to join me there and provide a link to a particular YouTube video.

*One month later I ask them if they enjoyed the first free book and did they see the offer in the book to get the second book in the series, Healing Notes, for free.* Some people ask me if, by giving away the second book free, I'm still carrying the freeloaders. Sure there will be a couple, but not many. The freeloaders usually have not even opened the first free book at the three-week mark. People who download free books tend to download more than they can read in a year and sometimes in many years. Those people will never see the option in the book for the free download because they haven't read the book. Those same people will have used their "fake" email or the one they never check to get the first free book and have not opened my automated email #2 or #3.

For a reader to get the second free book, they have done one of two things. The best scenario is that they actually opened the book and read it. Saw the free download for the second book and went to that landing page. There is a different sequence they enter once they go to the second book's landing page. The second scenario is that as a part of my automated sequence, they have now opened THREE emails I've sent and in the third one they clicked on the free download button (call-to-action) and agreed to be on my mailing list again. I'll trade a second book for that kind of email loyalty any day.

## HOW LONG SHOULD A SEQUENCE BE?

You can build your sequences to be as long as you want. At the moment, the above is my four-step sequence. After the third engagement, the subscriber becomes a part of my "regular" email list for the group who likes contemporary romance or women's fiction. If they do download the second book, they enter into another four-email sequence that ends in an offer for them to join my Launch Team (street team).

Here are the next five steps in the sequence whether they download the second book or not. The call-to-actions are in bold to make it clear.

**Two weeks after the qualifying emails,** I will share some information about me as an author and how much my fans mean to me. I'll talk about some of the emails I've received from fans that were especially meaningful about specific books in the genre. I'll let them know that I personally answer every email. (This is true by the way. My VA does NOT answer my personal emails.) I'll share a book I've read in the genre that was meaningful to me. CTA: **I'll ask them to share with me, by email, a book they've read by any author that really made a difference to them.**

**Two weeks after the one above**, I will share some special inside info about the characters in the Sweetwater Canyon series and how they were developed. Each one has a story as to how I gave them their problems and why I chose to write THAT story. CTA: **I'll ask them if there is a particular type of character, or character problem, they'd love to see in a book.**

**Two weeks after the previous one**, I will talk about the next book the third book in the series, *Heart Strings*, and where they can find it. Again, I'll focus on the character(s) and why I'm writing about them. I'll share how it relates to me as a person. CTA: **Because the story has the heroine caring for her dying father, I'll ask them to share any time they or a close friend/family member had a health issue and what they learned from that experience.**

**Two weeks later I'll do my "importance of reviews letter."** I have a standard letter that thanks my fans for doing reviews, and explain how important they are for an author. CTA: **I'll ask them to do an honest review for at least one of my books they've read.** And if they send me the link to the review I'll send them something for free (a short story or novella) **NOTE:** Even if the person does a one star review they will still get the free thing. However, this has never happened to me.

**For anyone who completes Step 4, I'll invite him or her to join my Launch Team.** I'll outline the benefits (ARCS and other insider info) and expectations (sharing info on social media, reviewing when they can). This is the beginning of creating my super fans. They need to go to a page on my website and agree to the conditions to become a part of the Launch Team. CTA: **Click on Link to Launch Team Agreement page**.

As you can see, there is a lot you can do with automation. The MORE you automate the less time you have to spend in thinking up things to send. Because people come through the process at different times, if you did this yourself you would need to be processing people every day and tracking what they did manually.

Of course, the setup does take time and eventually the automation ends and you need to determine what kinds of emails everyone gets once they get to that end. You also need to determine what amount of time you want to be engaging with your fans on a daily or weekly basis. This is TRUE engagement with TRUE fans, not the usual social media general engagement.

## HOW TO KEEP YOUR SUBSCRIBERS

One of the easiest ways to grow your email list is by making a very clear value exchange with your subscribers. An example would be: "Sign up to my email newsletter and get this free something. (e.g., ebook, novella, MP3 audiobook, PDF, discount for something, video advice, etc.) You can do this within your email autoresponder by providing a download link with your thank-you page or thank-you email.

That being said, trading an email address for a digital download isn't going to get you anywhere if your newly subscribed fan hits the

'Unsubscribe' button as soon as he or she gets your next email. That's why it's important to offer more than just a "free download" when someone subscribes to your list. What you really want is to create a mutually beneficial relationship. You provide your subscribers with cool stuff (weekly, monthly, quarterly) and they spend the time to read your emails and occasionally buy what you're selling. A big part of that "cool stuff" is valuable content that they want. However, there is also an expectation of special treatment.

In order for this relationship to work, you've got to give something to your audience in every email. That's right. Every email you send is also another opportunity for your subscribers to "unsubscribe." To keep your subscribers, you need to always add value.

One of the mistakes new authors often make with their email subscribers is to send out lots of broadcast notices of what they are doing (like they might on Facebook or Twitter). These notices include events in a specific geographic area where many subscribers don't live, or talking about their kids or vacation or progress on the book. These are all things that can engage some readers but NOT in your email. Those things are better left for Social Media posts.

If you do want to let people know about events by email, then make sure to segment your email list by geographic location. This means you have to ask them something about where they live. Do NOT ask for their address, it is one way to make sure no one subscribes to your list. People don't like giving out their physical addresses. Also, remember to add value even to simple event reminders. How about a purchase discount for your subscribers who come to your event or simply include a funny video or joke you've seen or heard lately.

REMEMBER: Before you click send, ask yourself, "Does this email contain a good value to my subscribers?" If it doesn't, take the time to include something special. Remember it can be anything:

- discount on a book (yours or someone else) or an announcement of a free book
- download that has information they will value
- a funny comic

- YouTube video
- link to a blog article on a topic they will appreciate
- a contest only they know about
- request for feedback via a survey or a single question
- ask them to help you choose something (cover model, colors, character name, which cover for next book is best? Etc.)

Your subscribers will reward you by staying subscribers whenever you provide value.

## HOW TO WRITE SUBJECTS THAT GET READERS TO OPEN THE EMAIL

The subject line to your email is the most important part. Boring subject lines are the leading cause of deleted or ignored email. Try to create a bit of mystery or tension in your headline so that your audience can't help but open your email to see what's inside. Also, remember that a lot of people read email on their phone. So make sure the exciting bits of your subject line come in the beginning of the sentence and are not cut-off.

Try new things. If you always write your subject line in a certain format: "Fall 2017 Newsletter: New book release" people will lose interest. Instead, try something like, "Have you tried this?" or "Did you ever wonder why xxxx?" A little bit of intrigue goes a long way in subject lines.

Consider this subject line from a mystery/suspense writer: "You Are Not Alone." Provocative right? Not all subjects need to be as fear inducing, but do consider what the hook is going to be.

One way I learn to practice writing subject lines (also known as headlines) is by looking at newspapers or online news organizations. One is Upworthy. Business Insider reported that they ask staffers to create about 25 headlines for every news article before they choose the best one. I don't go to that much trouble, but I do often write five to ten before settling on the best one.

Here's Upworthy's secret formula for clickable headlines:
Outrage + Uplift + Mystery = Clicks

Whether you see Upworthy's headlines as manipulative parlor tricks or clever journalism is up to you, but writing engaging subject lines, headlines and social posts is incredibly useful to anyone trying to promote themselves online. Why not use Upworthy's headline formula to better engage your readers? We want our fans to like and share our newsletters, our social media posts, open our emails and click on our links. How can we use this magic formula to increase our fan engagement?

**Announcement of an upcoming book**. Normally, I might use a headline like "Don't forget: Subscribers get this book for 99 cents first week." It's not a horrible headline. It's honest and direct, right? But wouldn't it be better if I could write something that would undoubtedly get more engagement, increase email opens, and ultimately increase my concert attendance? I guess I'd need to add some outrage, uplift, and/or mystery.

Below are three examples using the Upworthy techniques. All of these relate to my release, ***Heart Strings***, the third book in my Sweetwater Canyon series of contemporary romances. Each one does a headline first (H) – 60 characters or less. Then first paragraph of email. 50 words or less.

### *For my book release*

#### H: Heart Strings, only 99 cents for one week

Sarah must face her lurid past. (Mystery) It may mean giving up Sweetwater Canyon forever. (Outrage) Unless the man who betrayed her trust has changed. (Uplift)

### *For a link to a music video relating to the story*

#### H: Listen to the song that saved this story

Writing Sarah's story was difficult after my father died (Outrage). This song is what saved me. (Uplift). You'll see why when you listen. (Mystery)

*For an informational link relating to one of the themes in the story*

**H: Don't let alcoholism ruin a life**

Alcoholism devastates families (Outrage). When Sarah goes to care for her dying father she is thrust back into her frightening childhood. (Mystery). If you know anyone living with an alcoholic please share this article with them. (Uplift).

**Why Does the Formula Work?**

It works because it relies on the most basic elements of storytelling. Stories are firmly rooted in conflict and resolution. The more outrageous the conflict and resolution are, the more curious we become. The 'story' is what happens in between the conflict and resolution. Upworthy's techniques draw us into the mystery. If the outrage and uplift push our buttons, we will click to read the content. There are no real details on how to connect the Outrage and the Uplift. But when well written, we must find out! It's a diabolical formula.

Remember: Your content must be good for this formula to work. Getting clicks is not the end goal–getting fans is. If you trick people into clicking on links that lead to boring content, then you're going to get disgruntled followers. I would save this technique for your best content. Use it sparingly and you will be rewarded. Overuse it and it will become a cliché.

## CONTENT MUST BE VALUABLE (TARGETED) TO YOUR READERS

Because readers have trusted you to send content they want, sending one email to all subscribers in a diverse list of readers is not good practice. Ideally, you would send content based on the reader's interests AND where they are in the buying cycle.

If you know, for example, that a reader has already bought your first book in the series, you don't want to continue sending them emails to buy it. On the other hand, if you have set a book free or discounted

AND you know which of your readers clicked to download or purchase it, then you want to be sure to send them targeted emails about getting the next book in the series. In general, the more targeted the emails with valuable content, the higher the response and engagement rates.

## MANAGING AND ENGAGING SUBSCRIBERS

You need to send regular, valuable content. At least once per month. Every bit of content needs to have a call to action. The action is NOT necessarily "buy my book." It is often simply asking a question like: Which cover do you like best? What do you think I should name this character? Name two of your favorite authors. You are simply trying to engage and to track that engagement. Ideally, each call-to-action will also lead to generating the VALUE for the book before it is released.

Most email systems have some way to tell you which of your subscribers are following-through on the call to action. If it is clicking a link, the system should certainly be able to track that. If you are asking a question, then you know directly who has answered when they send you an email.

No author has 100% open rates or very high engagement rates from emails. It is considered VERY good if your open rates are above 50% and your engagement is above 10%. More typical open rates are closer to 35% and engagement rates are around 2%. Set your expectations accordingly.

If people are not engaging with any of your emails—not opening over a period of time—then you MUST remove them from your list. I know this is hard, especially when your list is already small. If you do not remove them from your list, it will continue to decrease your open rate and your engagement rates and that can also hurt your deliverability scores. Email providers do not like to see continuously low open rates because they know it is more likely to end up with higher unsubscribes.

Mailing list providers are consistently monitored and rated based on high or low unsubscribes and open rates. Those email providers with higher unsubscribe rates tend to have personal email accounts (e.g., gmail, Comcast mail, AOL mail) marking all emails from that provider as spam, which then leads to even lower open rates because readers don't ever see your email. This then leads your email provider to throttle delivery of your emails and sometimes to stop them all together and indicate that you are in violation of the terms of service.

My rule of thumb is to check at least once a month to see what my engagement rates are. If you are doing a lot of emails every month, you may want to check more frequently. As I average two emails per month, that means I have sent 6 emails during that quarter. If a subscriber has gone without opening an email during that time, then I put them into a special sequence letting them know they will be removed from my list. I give them two more chances to engage by letting them know I've noticed they haven't been opening my emails and I do not want to send content they don't find interesting. If, however, they have just been busy but still want to stay on my list they can click the big button that says "Yes, I still want to stay on the email list." When I do tell them this, about 50% of the time I get a response telling me they want to remain on the list. The other 50% I delete after one more send.

## IF YOU ARE NOT GETTING ENGAGEMENT, TRY SOMETHING DIFFERENT

Unlike FB or Twitter or places where you advertise, email is a marketing tool where YOU have complete control. You can test to see what kinds of content your readers want. You can even ASK them. Don't be afraid to try something new. In fact be open about what you are doing. Tell your readers you are trying something new and really want their feedback. In that way, if the feedback is they don't like it you can thank them and not do that any more. The good news is THEY ENGAGED! Better yet, when you do experiment you might find a tactic that really works and makes a big impact not only on engagement but future sales.

### Eight Differentiators for Email Marketers

These six items are ones that many authors, and even small businesses don't pay enough attention to in their email marketing campaigns. We've discussed all of them in this chapter, but it doesn't hurt to review them and pay attention one more time.

### 1. Mobile Displays are Key

If your email and landing pages don't display well on mobile devices—particularly phones, you're losing engagement and likely sales. Though more than 70% of business people read on their phone, do business on their phone, visit websites on their phone, and read email on their phone, only 21% of them have integrated mobile into their email program. (2017 Mobile Usage Report from Smart Insights) That means they've given little thought to how their emails display on mobile and what interactions their users are having with them. Mobile email users are headed toward 4x growth over the next two years. Fortunately, most major providers—both list-based and subscriber-based makes it easy for you to make sure your emails look good on a phone.

However, looking good is not enough. Always check your email campaign on a phone. How much must the person read before they get to the call to action? How many scrolls or swipes? How long is a reader likely to stay engaged. If you are doing a monthly newsletter that looks like one scroll on the big screen attached to your computer, you may find it is 10 scrolls on a phone. Most users will not go past three scrolls, and where is your most important information?

Be aware that many readers turn off images on their phone. This is because they take up a lot of space and cause more scrolling. Be sure that any links or CTAs you have are not just embedded in images or they may never be seen. For example, when I have the free book download in my incentive email, I have the URL embedded in the image so the user can just click the book cover and go directly to Book Funnel. However, I also provide the linked URL below it just in case images are turned off.

### 2. Lists and Segmentation

A MailChimp study found that segmenting email lists increases open rates and click through rates. This makes sense, of course, because you are sending only to those readers who will want your content.

There are several ways to segment your list. You can do it by:

- Geography
- Purchase history
- Behavioral data
- Demographics

This is particularly important for those who write in multiple genres or write in both fiction and non-fiction. If someone loved your sweet, Christian romance they may not want to also hear about your next paranormal erotica. Combining those lists may get you some unsubscribes. Whereas segmenting the list allows you to send information on your sweet books to the right group and information on your erotica to a different group. It also retains the ability for you to send something to everyone that is appropriate as well (e.g., Happy Thanksgiving Holiday)

### *3. Format and Length*

Many information marketers still find the simple, almost plain-text style of email performs best. Why? Because the email looks more personal to the recipient. It's like getting an email from a friend, compared with getting an email from an advertiser.

Of course, readers do have some expectation of something more than plain-text when it comes to your books (e.g., a book cover). The occasional picture or other fun item is okay, but don't get caught up in a rich visual experience with animated gifs, pictures on every line, background graphics, etc. It makes it more difficult to download, to read, and more scrolling on mobile devices.

It's not just the format and style, though. It's also the length of your email. If you are sending informational emails (e.g., "You might be interested in my latest blog post on X) then short is the rule. Just a couple lines and a link. If you are sending something more substantial

—a personal story, an excerpt, a reflection on an event, then longer is okay—think no more than 300 words.

### 4. *Images*

We now live in an image driven world. Most people make decisions based on images more quickly than they do based on written content. It is critical that you find images that fit the content and are attractive to your readers—particularly at the top of your email. Certainly, if your newsletters or emails contain your branded header it is a cue to your readers that this is really you (just like a company logo is a cue that it is an "official" email. Beyond that make sure that any image you include is critical to understanding the email and that they are similar to your brand. For example, if your brand is rich, photo-like images for book covers and discussions, then any image in your email should follow that same look and feel. On the other hand if your books feature cartoons or line drawn graphics or simplified colors, then images in your emails should follow that branding.

Again, when it comes to images, less is more.

### 5. *Personality*

Email is one of the most personal mediums we have. What other medium allows you to reach people almost anywhere they are (even places where they shouldn't take their phones) at any time of the day?

Few people will read your emails if they find them boring. Yet many people write their emails, or their newsletter like a corporate brochure.

Let the engaging, intriguing, unique person that you are—your voice—shine in your emails. Readers love believing they know you personally. Whether you are projecting your "real" self or your author persona, what matters is that you let your writing reflect that personality. If your books are casual and humorous, readers expect you to be the same. If you write historical books in a time period where things were very proper, then writing your emails in that same voice may be welcome.

## 6. Subject Lines

Out of all the elements in email marketing that are tested, the subject line is analyzed the most. There are good reasons for this. First, it is easy to test because people open an email based on the subject line in the email. Second, it's been shown that certain words are considered "spammy words" while others invite the reader to open and read the email.

There are all kinds of studies that point to whether a shorter or longer subject line is better and whether or not to capitalize, add symbols, use numbers, and so on. The reality is what worked for others won't necessarily work for you and it changes from year-to-year based on unscrupulous emailers who try to game the system. Make sure your subject lines are true and clear to the content.

Most of the spam trigger words used by email marketers are not used by authors. However, without realizing it, here are some that will get your email sent to spam folders OR not opened because they have been over-used. Remember, these words can appear in the body of your email and be fine. But don't include these words in the subject line.

FREE (anything—free gift, free book, free offer, free preview)
Act Now
Buy Direct
Drastically Reduced
Fantastic Deal
Guaranteed
Income
Incredible Deal
Join (hundreds, thousands, millions) of others
Limited Time Offer
No Cost, No Fees, No Obligation
Opportunity
Opt In
Order Now
Promise You
Risk Free

Save $

Sign Up Now

Urgent

In other words, anything that has words sounding too good to be true should not be used in the email subject line. You want to grab the consumer's interest but not have them thinking you are out to fleece them.

The good news is that many email systems will let you check your subject line against known problems and provide you feedback on that. It will not force you to change the subject line, but you should consider what impact it will have on open rates.

## 7. Focus Content with ONE Call-to-Action

Most of us have been taught to do newsletters with our readers. When I started out, I thought my newsletters had to be filled with lots of interesting stuff and multiple opportunities for something free, or to attend a signing, or to know about my new release, or to give my teaching schedule for the next three months. Consequently, I would include ALL of those in every newsletter.

After talking to some marketing experts, and trying their advice myself, I came to realize that those super newsy and multiple-choice newsletters were, in fact, hurting me. First, most people scan emails. This means if you give them multiple choices, they are likely to ignore all of them because it requires a decision on which one to take and that takes too much time. Second, in that scanning process, most people don't read beyond the first three to four lines unless it really gets their attention (see section on writing good headlines earlier in the chapter).

To address this, it is best to use short (not too fancy—one primary image) emails that are engaging and have one goal—one call to action that you want your readers to take. It also increases the chance someone will click on that action if there is a nice big button to click. Even if the button is to send you an email, or go look at your blog. People scanning the email are used to clicking buttons. So give them the opportunity to do so.

## 8. Avoid ALL CAPS and Lots of Exclamation Points !!!

The use of all-caps in any email correspondence is still seen as screaming. And because many spammers use this to draw attention to their message, readers see the use of all caps as spam too. The same goes for exclamation points, particularly in the email subject line. However, using exclamation points (ONE at the end of a line) within your email to emphasize a point can work well if used sparingly.

*Chapter Twenty*

## DRIVE TRAFFIC TO YOUR LIST

**Organic versus Paid Email Growth**

Organically growing your email list can take a long time. It is a way to ensure that the majority of your signups are, in fact, people who want to hear from you. They didn't sign up just for the freebie you were offering, or the contest you were running. This is the way I grew my list from 20 of my family and friends to 400. But it took me four years to get that far.

If you want to grow your list faster, you will need to find a way to target YOUR type of readers and then drive them to your email signup page. This usually involves spending some money. Whether that is to get your book out via discount book lists or setting up a contest with some prize you've paid for. This book is focused on driving traffic paying less than $100. Most new authors don't want to—and should not—spend more than that.

Once you have three books or more, you may want to invest substantially more in your email growth and you would do that through paid advertising on Facebook, through Amazon Marketing Service (AMS) ads, or through BookBub ads. That kind of advertising is an entire book itself. Consequently, it will be covered in the next book on Marketing, ***Advanced Author Marketing Through Paid Advertising*** due out in mid 2018.

Because building a good sized mailing list (minimum of 5,000) is critical to authors, the one place you should spend marketing money is in driving traffic traffic to your list.

**NOTE:** This is NOT buying signups! It is targeting readers through advertising, newsletter placement, or simply budgeting for whatever you are giving away. NEVER pay someone for names to add to your email list. You have absolutely no guarantees that those names are your readers.

If you are unknown or you have reached the limit of the pool of people you've found organically, then you must find a way to interest new readers to sign up to your list. Most authors entice people to sign up by offering something for free or at a great discount (free generates a lot more signups). Free does NOT have to be a book (though that works really well). Here are some non-book items I've used as incentives for sign ups.

***A unique item like an inexpensive bracelet or necklace that relates to the story/books.*** My fantasy series uses certain Celtic mythical creatures as talismans for my characters. I found a store that creates many of these as a charm or necklace for $15 each in a nice quality silver. They look really cool and fantasy fans go crazy for them. When I run a contest to win one, and drive people to sign up for my mailing list, I can get hundreds of entries in no time. All for a cost of only $15 and mailing the prize to the recepient.

***A short story relating to your series.*** For those who don't have a big backlist of novels where they can giveaway the first book in the series, offering a free short story that's never been published can be a good item. Do take the time to format it nicely and give to an attractive cover. Longer shot stories (novelettes of 8,500-10,000) words are a nice size. This becomes a premium item because it is not available anywhere else.

***For nonfiction authors, offering a two to four page handout or tip sheet is often a great way to get readers.*** Because I write technical books, I can do a two page tip sheet that summarizes a specific step-by-step process and get lots of people signing up to be on my mail list. Alternatively, an extracted chapter from a book also works.

***Offer someone else's book that relates to YOUR genre.*** This is especially valuable in a contest where you are trying to get readers, interested in your book. You offer a famous author's book for free AND your book for free. Of course, if you do this, you better be darn sure your free book is up to par and doesn't pale in comparison.

***Engage in a "list swap."*** A "list swap" is when you and another author—or a group of authors all agree to feature one author's book to their newsletter at a particular time. It is called a swap because that author's readers are exposed to your work. Those who are interested may choose to give you their email in exchange for your free book. It is a wonderful way to piggy back on another author's list without them actually giving you any names on their list.

The best time to use this is if you have another book in the series releasing. You give the first book away for free, while at the same time featuring the new releasing book. The promise of the list swap is that you will do the same for the partnering author when she is ready to release a new book and makes her first in series free.

Those who can build a network of authors in their genre, can double or triple this opportunity by a group of three or more authors agreeing to do this for each other. There are several keys to enticing a group to do this. 1) Your book is perceived of equal quality to the other author's book(s); 2) The size of your list is close to the size of the other author's list. If your list is 400 people and the author is at 5,000 she may not perceive that sending to your list is worthwhile. But it never hurts to try; and 3) You will push the other author's books as hard as you do your own—not only in an email to your list, but also on your social media, in a blog post and anywhere else you engage with your fans.

All of these giveaways cost some amount of money. Money for the item itself and shipping (if it's not an ebook).

Having an email list of TRUE fans is not about bragging rights as to who has the highest number of people on their list. It is about who has the most loyal fans; who has a list of people who will go out and buy the next release; who has a list of people who will share your news with their own network; who has a list of people who will share that you are a really cool person to get to know. If you have even 100 TRUE Fans, you will have a better list than someone with 5,000 fans who don't engage, don't spread your news, and are just waiting for the next free thing.

## GOOD LANDING PAGES DRIVE TRAFFIC TO YOUR LIST

The purpose of a landing page is to attract leads (potential readers) and to start building a relationship with them by SHARING something of value—your books, articles, knowledge, training program or whatever you have to offer. The landing page provides a focused environment that articulates the value of joining your list and an easy method for doing so. An effective landing page has very little text, one arresting graphic, and a field for input of the email address. Some authors also collect the first name or both first and last name. Once the selected fields are completed, the potential reader clicks on a button to sign up. If you are offering something free (e.g., a book, short story, prize) that button click will also trigger an event for the person to receive that incentive item.

There are many ways to create a great landing page and lots of software that will help you do it.The easiest and most direct way is to create a landing page by using your email list provider's forms to do the work for you. By using their form it will make sure that the emails you collect will go directly to the appropriate subscriber list and receive any additional tags you want assigned to it. By using the provider's forms and templates, your gathered emails will not have to pass through a third party platform, or be downloaded and sent separately via a CSV file, or be converted to the right format to fit within their list structure.

The term "squeeze page" is often used by marketers to describe the role of these landing pages. It means you are trying to "squeeze" the focus of the buyer to a single message and get them to take action. In order to create that focus you don't want any other distractions on that page. You don't want that person to be able to go anywhere else before clicking on buy button product or signing up to the email list.

For me this "squeeze" metaphor embodies all the things I hate about sales. My mind pictures a smarmy person who has backed me into a corner and won't let me leave until I sign on the dotted line. This is NOT what I am recommending for getting people on your list. It is true that being completely annoying will get you a lot of sign ups. However, the question is if those sign ups will be loyal customers.

There are parts of the "squeeze page" mentality I think authors can borrow to make the liklihood of a potential reader acting as we want. However, I am not an advocate of making it exceedingly difficult for a person to leave a page until they complete the requested sign up. This is also why I do not use the popup mailing list window that does not allow me to see more content on a page until I provide my email. I will simply leave the page and never return.

## WHAT DOES A "HIGH CONVERTING" LANDING PAGE MEAN?

"Conversions" are measured by the number of people who actually provide their email and click the button. If you have some type of analytics associated with your page (e.g., Google Analytics) you can see how many people get to your landing page. You can then track, by the number of new emails you receive on your list, how many of those actually clicked and completed the form. For example, if Google tells you that 1,000 people went to your landing page in the month of August, but the number of new emails you received from that page was 50 that month. You then know that your "conversion rate" is 50 divided by 1,000 or 5%. The higher the percentage the higher your conversions.

Most large businesses work hard to get a 10% conversion rate. Assuming you are targeting the right audience, authors should shoot for at least a 25% conversion rate. I have often achieved a 50-60% conversion rate once I have settled on the appropriate campaign.

The Landing Page is not the only thing that guarantees success in a campaign. There needs to be good targeting to get the right people to the landing page. I talk more about that at the end of this chapter.

**Landing Page Optimization** (also known as a Squeeze Page)

Every marketer you talk to will talk about the importance of "squeeze pages." These are landing pages separate from your main website (or popups on your website) that have one purpose only—that is to get people on your email list. Marketing statistics indicate that using these squeeze pages generate email signups more than 1000 times faster than any other method.

The typical author squeeze page offers something for free (one or more books). In order to get the free item to the person, that person must supply information (e.g., email address). Most of these pages don't ask for anything else EXCEPT an email. I like to ask for a first name so I can personalize future emails. Landing pages tend to have a good graphic and one or two sentences summarizing an offer, and an assurance of no spam.

The key to the squeeze page is that it has no distractions from the call to action. The key to getting people to the squeeze page is sharing it everywhere—Twitter, FB, blogs etc. This means, if you are running the squeeze page (landing page) on your website, you want to make sure the reader cannot see your navigational menu or any other objects that might distract them from completing the email sign up form or getting the incentive. Most good landing pages have the author's name and then the informational copy and a good image of the incentive. That's it. AFTER the email is provided, you can send the reader to your website home page or anywhere else you like.

I use ConvertKit forms for my landing pages, so that is where I am most comfortable. However, I will provide examples for both MailChimp and ConvertKit as I know many authors use MailChimp.

First, let's look at few examples of Landing Pages I believe are effective to get people to sign up.

Here are two examples of author Squeeze Pages giving a free book as an incentive. In Mark Dawson's options, he sends the books over three emails to keep you engaged. Then he sends additional emails later to remind you of other books you can buy. In Joanna Penn's example, after you download the free book, she automatically takes you to a page talking about another deal (a boxed set of a different series).

Because you get free books in both of these cases, you might try them out and see where it takes you, what the thank you pages look like and what other emails you receive over a couple of weeks. It really is a great study in how to build your list and extend your reader engagement. Even if you aren't ready to build your own landing pages right now, these are good examples. You may also try one of mine as well. I have three incentive books: a contemporary romance / women's fiction first in series; a fantasy first in series; and an author guide first in the Career Author series.

Mark Dawson http://www.markjdawson.com/

J.F. Penn http://www.jfpenn.com/free-thriller/

My Landing Pages are served not on my website, but from ConvertKit's website. There are pros and cons to this approach. The pro is that ConvertKit has fast servers and I don't have to maintain them on my site. Though I do have links to them on my home page. The con is that there are a certain percentage of readers who may be turned off by going to a place called "ConvertKit." It sounds like I am doing something a little shady.

So far, no one has mentioned this problem to me so it may be all in my head. The solution would be to move the landing pages to my website, or at least make it appear they are there by the link including my domain name maggielynch.com

Maggie Lynch Women's Fiction https://app.convertkit.com/landing_pages/157087

Maggie Lynch Fantasy https://app.convertkit.com/landing_pages/214400

Maggie Lynch Author Guide https://app.convertkit.com/landing_pages/93200

**Create a Landing Page with MailChimp Subscribe Form**

MailChimp now supplies a type of drag and drop form for getting email signups. They have a basic template and then a couple of design options. The form setup is limited in terms of placement of images, text, and the button. However, it can still be an attractive option depending on what you choose. The Landing Page pictured below is one I did two years ago. It is likely there are now more options to make it even more attractive.

The ones created in ConvertKit also used a template form, though they provide a few more template options than MailChimp and more options for changing font sizes, image sizes, and button sizes. In both cases, the end result is still viable and gets the job done.

## TARGETING

Conversions are NOT only dependent on the landing page. They are also dependent on how people come to that page and how well you identified your audience and provided a direct route to your page. The "targeted" part of marketing is reaching the people who are most likely to be your readers based on information you know about them.

Casting a wide net to all breathing females between the ages of 18 and 80 is not targeting. There will be a lot of people in that group who prefer to watch movies instead of read. Or who prefer mysteries insetead of romances, or many other things. The key is casting as narrow a net as possible yet still have sufficient numbers to grow your list.

A narrow target for me is women between the ages of 45 and 65 who read women's fiction, enjoy movies from Hallmark and Lifetime, and use hashtags like #amreading, #romancelover, and #familystories. Will there be as many women who fit that category as do the wide list? No. However, there are still sufficient numbers (in the millions) for me to work with. To further narrow the target I might look for people who read a particular series that is similar to what I write. For example, I often target readers of Barbara Freethy, Inglath Cooper, and Susan Mallery books because there book themes are similar to mine.

This means when I'm looking at using a brief boosted post to get traffic to my email list (say $5 per day for a week, a total of $35) I'll put those author names in my targeting along with the gender and age demographics to narrow the list to people who read my kind of books.

## Chapter Twenty-One
# BEYOND ONBOARDING: BROADCAST EMAILS, LAUNCH EMAILS AND OTHER SEQUENCES

**Writing the Actual Email**

Here are examples of emails or other "nice to do" marketing things you can use to build fan loyalty. Of course, you can set these up in advance and then execute them on certain dates (e.g., for a general holiday email) or you can send them as a "broadcast" email. This is something that goes out to everyone on your list, or everyone in a segment of your list.

When I have a contest, a giveaway, or some other free opportunity that is coming up, I don't want any of my fans to miss out. I would send an email to all fans in the genre of the giveaway.

A new book cover is always a great time to send an email. Or, if I'm deciding between two or three cover designs, I can ask for fan feedback. Once the cover is finalized I can do a cover reveal and gush about how much I love it.

When I'm feeling particularly sunny and friendly and have something awesome to share about my daily life, it can generate an email. It may have nothing to do with my book. It could be something as easy as a few photographs of beauty (e.g., scenery around me, people doing amazing things, a heartfelt video). This goes to my overall brand regarding caring, helpful, everyday heroes that crosses all my genres.

The key with this is that it can't be overtly religious (unless you write religious fiction exclusively) or political. I may personally see a lot of things that appeal to my personal religious beliefs or politics. However, sharing those things with my fans is most likely to get half of them to unsubscribe.

Happy Holidays emails are always appreciated by fans. I like to send a "card" to my fans for Thanksgiving, the Winter Holidays (I don't do Christmas, but rather a generic Winter Holiday that relates to the season of giving, enjoying family and home, and making a difference in the world). I also do something for New Years. In regards to other holidays, it just depends on my focus during those times of year.

No matter what you decide, be consistent. You want your fans to expect you in their inbox.

## LOOK AND FEEL OF EMAILS

Unlike your newsletter, which has all kinds of fancy things—pictures, sidebars, graphics, etc. The emails you send between that should be pretty plain. You want it to look like a regular email to a friend, because that should be what you're writing.

If you want you can use a graphic at the end, as part of your signature line, that's okay. Just remember, this isn't selling. It's sharing. It's being "friends."

## SUBJECT LINES

We talked about the importance of subject lines earlier in the book. They are equally important for these friendly emails to the majority of your list. It doesn't have to be salesy but it does include your call-for-action in the subject. Here are a couple of examples.

SUBJECT: NEW Holiday Short Story Inside (I'm eager to hear your thoughts!)
SUBJECT: Cover Reveal for TWO VOICES (I'm in love with it, how about you?)

SUBJECT: Start Your Day with an Affirmation (Here's my top three, what are yours?"

Note that each of the above includes the call to action in parentheses. You don't have to do it this way, but it does make it seem like a friendly gosh-I'm-excited-would-love-to-hear-from-you kind of subject.

## YOUR EMAIL'S OPENING LINE

Many email providers (Gmail, Apple Mail, Hotmail, etc.) show the first sentence of an email in the inbox itself, so it's important to sound personal and non-spammy. Some options:

- Use first name whenever possible. Mailchimp, by default uses their first name in the email. Other email providers have a tag you can choose to insert as to if you want to use their name or not. You can modify that with a beginning like Hi <first name>, instead of just their name alone. Of course, if you didn't ask for their name then you are out of luck. Using something like "Hi Maggie" sounds pretty friendly to me.
- Use a typical opening you'd use in an email to a friend. "Happy [Day of Week]!" or "I'm loving this [type of weather], it makes me feel [mention something positive.]

Whatever you choose, think of it like you would write a friend. Of course, you want it to be in the personality/voice that your readers know for you AND that your comfortable with using.

## THE BODY OF YOUR EMAIL

Write the body of your email like you are writing to one person. Even though your list may be in the thousands, remember that each person getting this email believes it is addressed to him/her personally.

- Write like you speak, NOT like you're writing your novel. It's okay — no one will be grading your grammar!
- Use short paragraphs to break up your email. Long walls of text overwhelm readers who read online.
- Keep the entire email to 3-4 paragraphs tops.
- Read your email out loud and see if it sounds natural, friendly.
- Stick with ONE topic. This is not a time to talk about five other things going on.

## INSERTING YOUR CALL TO ACTION

- **Add your call to action in at least two spots.** Since most readers skim emails, it's important to repeat yourself. I usually put it toward the top and then again toward the end.
- **The link or action should be a linked piece of text that is part of the natural conversation in the email.** For example see where I put the link within the lines below.

"<u>Check out my short story</u> and let me know what you think." OR "I'd love to hear from you by <u>commenting on this question in my blog</u>."

Then don't forget that big yellow or orange button to click to make it easy to engage.

Like your opening, your closing line is up to your personal taste, but consider how familiar you wish to be. I personally like signing off with either "Thanks," or "Cheers." Some people prefer to be a little more formal like "Best Regards," or "Warmest Regards."

Whatever you use don't get too familiar by using "Love," or "Much love.' For my taste things like: "Sincerely," OR "Yours Truly," never sound sincere to me. Probably because I've seen them used in business so much. But that may just be me. If those are your favorite closings, go for it!

## PS: DON'T FORGET THE POST SCRIPT

I have to admit I've never used P.S. on my emails to fans and rarely even use them to friends and family, unless it's someone I know really well and I'm trying to be funny. (I'm emphasizing the "trying" here).

However, I read a marketing research article that said that the "fun asides commonly found at the end of letters and emails are actually the second most read part of the message." So, I'm going to try it when I'm in the mood on future emails. The one thing would be NOT to do it with every single one. Doing that would dilute its effectiveness.

Another option for the P.S. is to restate your call to action. I like this idea.

## ONLY WRITE WHAT YOU WOULD WANT TO READ

The #1 rule of writing emails that are personalized to your fans is they should be interesting and something YOU would want to get from an author you like. If it sounds boring to you, don't send it. If it sounds spammy, don't send it. If it sounds like you're trying too hard to be "friends," don't send it. If YOU believe it's valuable information and YOU would like to get an email like this, then you should feel good about sending it.

No matter how awesome your emails are, some folks WILL unsubscribe. Don't take it personally. People unsubscribe for all kinds of reasons.

- They only wanted the free book, and never wanted your emails anyway.
- Their life is really busy and they decided to unsubscribe from all lists for a while. (This happens a lot around the holidays)
- Something happened in their life that made them decide to limit emails. For example, after someone is truly spammed (not by you of course) they often over react by dropping off all email lists.

- They really don't want emails from authors at all or they only want to hear from you when you have a new book.

Don't worry. The reality is you don't want people on your list who don't want to be there or aren't really fans. Your real fans will stick with you and those names are golden.

## WHAT IF I DO SOMETHING REALLY STUPID?

I have personal experience with this at least twice! The key is to apologize and beg forgiveness. Interestingly, when you apologize most people take pity on you and it actually makes them feel closer. It makes you human. The two times I've done something really stupid I received more emails from fans about that than anything else I've sent.

The most recent time was when I was working on a way that people could sign up to receive my regular blog posts by email, instead of having to remember to go to my blog. Most email providers have a way to connect a signup form to your blogs RSS feed. Because I was learning how to do this in ConvertKit for the first time, I was VERY careful and double-checked they I had this set up correctly. I did a test to myself before hitting publish.

Because I actually have two blogs—one for my fiction fans and one for my author fans—I was very careful to only include the right segment for each blog. I double-checked that I'd selected that segment correctly and associated it with each form. Then I published and said "Go!"

Three days later I went to check how many people had signed up for each blog, and I was flabbergasted to see that close to 300 people had unsubscribed from my list! Panicked I wondered what I had done. I hadn't sent an email in almost a month. The number of people who had subscribed to my blogs over that period of time was less than 50.

After much angst and research I realized I had FAILED to remove the default audience selection in the broadcast email. The default audience is ALL subscribers. Even though I had carefully added each segment and maid sure they were correctly connected to the right form, I failed to remove the ALL subscribers that appears by default. That means that 12K plus people were receiving both my fiction readers blog posts and my author blog post feeds (about one every day from each blog, so two on some days)! I'm sure my fans thought I had taken a special class in how spam increases sales, and they started unsubscribing. Actually, I'm surprised more people didn't unsubscribe. Thank goodness I caught it in only three days instead of ignoring it for a month.

I immediately crafted an email. This time I made sure it did go to ALL subscribers on purpose. This was my headline: **My Deepest Apologies…Color Me Embarrassed**

I went on to apologize, admit to a giant brain fart, and explained what had happened in a combination of embarrassment with a little humor. In the process, I told them about the blogs and how they could subscribe if they wanted. I ended with a promise to not do this again.

It worked. I haven't received any further unsubscribes. As I said above I received more emails from fans empathizing with my dilemma and specifically stating their forgiveness than I had on any broadcast email I've sent in the past year. It is my highest engagement broadcast email. Several people wrote to say they were considering unsubscribing so were happy to get my email this time.

The best part? In spite of my stupidity, I received a number of sign ups from people who WANTED to get the blog feed all the time anyway.

The point is you **can** recover from stupid mistakes. You are human and most fans understand this. Just admit it, apologize, and move on. Some fans will love you even more for owning up to your mistake.

Will I ever get those 300 unsubscribes back? I don't know. They made a quick decision over a three-day period. I suspect some of them would have unsubscribed anyway. Obviously, I hadn't built a good enough relationship with them yet for them to think twice that maybe it was a blip. Some of them may have been fans but not my steadfast fans.

Once I discovered my error, I did everything I could do. Once people unsubscribe you do not have an option to write them and apologize. No email provider will let you do that. All I can hope is that maybe they are part of my social network, and maybe they will give me another chance sometime. If not, then they are not my readers. And that's okay.

## *Chapter Twenty-Two*
# BUILDING AND MANAGING YOUR STREET TEAM

As a newbie writer for short stories back in the late 1970's and early 1980's I remember believing that once I was published, all of these strangers would read my stories, fall in love with them and then tell absolutely everyone they knew about the story. Before I knew it I would be famous.

I never thought I would get rich after writing short stories, and I didn't. Fast forward thirty or so years and I started writing novels. I'd matured. Obviously short stories are a small market, but certainly now that I was writing novels I could expect that to happen. After all, I saw hundreds of people waiting in line to have just five minutes with their favorite author at a book signing. I remember the Harry Potter phenomenon when tweens would camp out for days at their local bookstore to be the first group to get the new book. Certainly, that would happen to me too. And that was before viral social media.

Um...hasn't happened to me. How about you?

In some ways, the concept of a street team is purportedly one way you can get a little of the virality started. Originally, street teams were people who literally "hit the street" to talk up a product—to show how fun, exciting, trendy it was to buy something, wear something, get something first. The record industry used to have street teams who would spread the word of a new record to all their friends, go into record stores and make sure their band's new album was easy to find and in the front of the bins.

I remember a time when certain authors would ask their street teams to go to their local bookstores, find the authors book and turn it face out on the shelf so it would be easier to notice among the other five hundred books in that genre section. Some of them would be so bold as to hang out in the aisle near the book reading the book and if someone would walk by the street team member would ask: "Have you seen this book? It's amazing. I can barely put it down." In other words they were informal salespeople for the author. They were unpaid superfans who did this simply because they loved the authors books and loved being part of an "in group" of fans who received special recognition.

## WHAT IS THE PURPOSE OF A STREET TEAM IN TODAY'S WORLD?

I haven't seen anyone in a bookstore in a long time, but the primary purpose is still the same though the tools may be different. That is to get word-of-mouth going—buzz—about an author and their books. This can take many forms. Talking it up to their friends. Posting about the new book in social media. Reading ARCs and providing reviews at launch time. Sometimes even coordinating or hosting parties should the author come to the member's town or nearby.

In reality, a street team can be all these things but most are not. People are just busy and overwhelmed. Not to mention most readers—like many authors—are introverts and don't feel comfortable being too out there with their praise. Most authors rely primarily on their street team to do reviews. Reviews have become the primary social proof that a book is worthwhile. And seems to be like pulling teeth to get people to do them regularly.

If you put a lot of effort into nurturing your street team you may be able to work up to the other expectations of helping your books go viral. There are ways to help them get there, but it does take vigilance and consistent work like everything else in this book.

Honestly, I'm struggling with this myself as are most authors I've talked to about their own street teams. Because so many people are building a team, it can seem like it becomes who is giving away the best stuff to get the best team members. I'm not willing to compete at that level. I've met a lot of authors who had teams of 100 or more and are now down to 25 or so because those are the ones they count on to follow through. I can empathize with that approach. The question I have is 25 enough for the time investment, or is it better not to have a team at all.

My team currently hovers between 150 and 200 depending on the latest campaign. I do have expectations and they are laid at clearly on a private web page every street team member sees and agrees to the premises when they sign up. Here is a copy of what it says.

---

As you probably know I wouldn't be anywhere without my readers. Though there are aspects of publishing I really enjoy, there are many that are just time consuming drudgery. The reality is that the reason I write is YOU, the reader. When I get a note from you or a comment on Facebook or Twitter about how you loved my book, or how it helped you in some way, it makes my heart sing. I mean REALLY sing.

I've also learned over the past six years that readers want to get to know me as much as I want to get to know them. So, I figured, why not include you in my publishing journey? After all, it's all thanks to you that I get to write in the first place – shouldn't you get to feel part of that somehow?

That's why I started Maggie Lynch's Launch Team. I know it's not a particularly creative name like some author's and their teams have but it says the purpose right in the title. The purpose is to launch new books to as many of my fans as possible and to bring in new fans that you think would like my books as well.

**Here's the deal:**
**In return for your help in launching new books, you'll get:**

- Free advance copies of EVERYTHING I release –

including books and audiobooks (and any other cool formats that come along in the future.
- A personal acknowledgement, thanking you by name, inside every book release that you agree to review Your name will be in the back of both my ebooks and paper books.
- I love to give out thank you's to my team members. I won't tell you about all of them because then they wouldn't be a surprise. I also run raffles on a regular basis just for my launch team members. This mean you'll only be competing with a few hundred instead of tens of thousands of people.

Being a member of my launch team is completely different than being part of my mailing list. Think of it as a V.I.P. list. You'll be part of a select group of super-awesome readers. And, in addition to getting free copies of EVERYTHING I release before anyone else, you get to see exactly what impact your support has on the success of my work.

**Okay, so what's the catch? There is always a catch, right?**

Being part of the Launch Team means you'll be asked to leave a review of the Advance Reader Copies (ARCs) within a certain time period after receiving your copy (usually 2-3 weeks). As far as catches go, I'm hoping that's not too bad! *So, if you'd like to be part of the team, just click the big yellow button below and sign up!*

> YES, I WANT TO BE A LAUNCH TEAM MEMBER

---

Because only people who have been through at least two email drip campaigns even have the opportunity to see this page, I don't know how it would go if I opened it to the public readership. My experience has been that only 10-12% of email members who receive this offer follow through and ask to become a member of my Launch Team. I assume that is because they take it seriously. My hope, of course, is that they aren't joining because they want the ARCs—yet another freebie. I don't think so.

However, in spite of the people accepting the responsibility and choosing to be on the team, out of the 150+ currently there, in my private Facebook group, about 30% remain actively engaged. About 30% to request ARCs when I have a new release. Of those who do request particular ARC, I have a 90% follow through to actually leaving a review in the required time frame.

This means that somewhere between 60 and 70% of the people currently on my team are not active and do not request ARCs. I haven't decided what to do about that yet. Some authors cull their list regularly based on lack of participation. Others keep it open, figuring that people are just busy and when they have the time they will come around. It all has to do with how much time do you want to spend nurturing and managing and what is the payoff.

I can definitively say that since I've build this street team, my releases have gone significantly better than before. I tend to get 25-30 reviews within a couple weeks of launch, whereas before I felt lucky to have five reviews. The people who are active in the Facebook Group not only support me but support each other, and that is rewarding to see.

Given the numbers who are active and the percentages who participate in ARC reviews, in order to have a real significant impact, I would need a team of approximately 500 members.

In other words I don't have all the answers. However, I will share what I do to manage and nurture my current team and what some of my joys and concerns are. I have not yet found a great book to detail these things, so have no definitive resources to share outside of my own experience and that of other authors I've asked to share their experiences.

## HOW DO YOU FIND PEOPLE TO BE ON YOUR STREET TEAM?

In the previous chapters I talked about how you can start to build your street team through your email drip campaigns, selecting those fans who have become steadfast in engaging with your emails. You can also look for fans on social media, or put out a general call for members.

I prefer to use my email list as the best way to build my street team because I want people on my team who have actually read my books and already like them. They are my superfans and we've already formed some type of bond over the 8+ emails they've received and engaged in. Because they are so valuable I expend a good amount of energy, and some money, making sure these superfans are well cared for. After all, these are the people who are most likely to share my books with friends, give me reviews, and cheer with me when I succeed, or offer a sympathetic shoulder when everything doesn't go quite as planned. In other words, they have become my book family and some of them will become actual friends.

Other ways authors have used to find members are:

**Putting out a general call to their current email list.** I know a couple of authors where this has been very successful, getting them upwards of 500 people. For me, 500 sounds scary to manage, and it makes me wonder if I can provide enough value to keep them.

**Talked about the opportunity on social media** and ask people to sign up who are interested. I haven't seen quite as any people feel this worked well for them. Social media tends to be a more transitory place for most readers, and that makes it harder to pin them down and expect a larger investment of time.

**Created a one time teams for a specific launch and then reform when a new launch is needed.** There is some good in this approach, in that the time commitment is very limited. Again, the question for me is what's in it for the team member and am I willing to give that to them?

An important decision to make is how you want to be in contact with your team once they've joined. I manage them within a private Facebook group. Some authors prefer to be in contact only by email. I like the private group because it is a place I can visit almost every day and check-in, see what is motivating them, and give them special insight into what I'm doing.

## WHAT MAKES A GOOD STREET TEAM

I think the most important aspect of a good street team member is that it is someone who already likes you and your book and truly wants to be a part of your career. This is usually manifested in the following ways they want to engage. Members enjoy:

- Having opportunities to discuss the details of a new book with the author and with other people on the team. They like to be the first ones to read the book, ahead of other friends.
- Giving feedback about cover art, character names, and asking questions of the author about future books in the series.
- Floating ideas about future blog posts and themes
- Special opportunities for giveaways where the odds of winning are better than large contests
- Getting free past books if they want to leave reviews
- Being recognized as important to the author's writing career

There are some special things I do for my members. One is to recognize their birthday, sending a public card within the group. This seems to be a favorite thing because other members jump onboard and comment also wishing the person a Happy Birthday. I've learned that for many of my members (my demographics are women age 45 and up), this is the most celebration of their birthday they get. It really makes them happy!

For their birthday, I let them request a book of their choice. Surprisingly, even though they can get my ebooks for free by simply leaving an honest review, about half of them request a signed paper book book as their birthday present. This really makes me happy because it reinforces they are part of the team because they actually enjoy my books.

I do run an occasional contest where they can win a prize (prizes are always books—mine or other authors who write in my genre). The contest entries are associated with specific tasks. For example, I was looking for quotes from my books so I could create image cards with them for a campaign I'm trying for a year on my Title Taste Thursday posts. An entry into the contest was provided for each quote. A few of the members provided 8 or 9 quotes, while most of the active people (again about 30%) provided one or two.

I'll be looking for more ways to provide specific tasks for them. I have found that when I started my team I had a false belief that they already know what to do to help me spread the word of my books. The reality is they need to be asked to do very specific things or nothing would happen.

Here are some things other authors have shared with me that they do with their teams.

- Schedule regular live video chats with their team. Some people do this month, while others do it less frequently—two to three times a year.
- Provide a physical welcome pack. Depending on the author some of the things included in that packet are bookmarks, a pen with author name, signed bookplates, a press kit, a surprise free book or set of books, a signed author headshot.
- Give advance notice of author appearances in their area where the author plans a special tea or catered meal to hangout with street team members in that area.
- Access to exclusive content such as character charts, images of the characters world—may include locations, cities, homes, etc.

## HOW STREET TEAMS CAN GO WRONG

Sometimes, in spite of the author's best efforts to make the street team experience positive, it can go wrong—either for the members or for the author. From discussions I've had with authors who have given up on having a street team, it seemed that he expectations were either not clear or not enforced or ignored by members. They cited the following problems.

It's easy to quickly fall into the trap of: "I only do work for you in exchange for gifts." Authors who gave up on their street teams seemed to feel their members were primarily freebie seekers. This can happen because of the free ARC or book given to get reviews. I think it also happens because authors here about other teams where gifts seem to abound and they feel a need to compete.

It's important to know what your boundaries are stick by them. I often have my members telling me that don't "need" gifts. They are happy to be of help. I think gifts should not be constant or it does build that "freebie" mentality among some members.

Sometimes members can become too helpful. Some authors complained about members inviting all of their friends and family to also join the street time because they wanted to share the perks with them. This is a management problem. It is important to make it clear how people get invited to the team and to manage the technical aspects of member approval—particularly on Facebook where the differences between private groups and secret groups make it difficult to add people (secret groups) or too easy to be open (private groups) which then allows members to invite people.

Social stuff is complex: readers could feel too much pressure; cliques could form within a street team, and one could feel like a wallflower in especially popular street teams.

It is time consuming to properly manage a community like this consistently over time. Some authors see their team as really important when they are releasing a book, but would rather forget them or leave them be while they are writing the next book. This can make team members feel used and then non-compliant when it comes to getting ARCS and leaving reviews. It is important to understand the real motivations of most street team members. That is they want to be your "friend." They want to know you and feel special because of their relationship with you. If this is not something you wish to nurture, then having a street team is probably not the right choice for you.

It does seem that people who join street teams are also in other author street teams. This makes it more difficult to keep members' attention and authors feel they have to compete with others to be the "best" team.

Some authors reported being very disappointed that the people who signed up were not nearly as passionate about the work as they expected. I think this is because authors have an expectation that they have magically tapped into a willing group of people who will conduct themselves as professional marketers, when in fact they are volunteers and most know very little about marketing. They are willing to help with the time they have available, but they need to be taught and given specific tasks.

## SUMMARY

Street teams can be very effective, but they DO take time and energy. If you are the type of person who isn't really interested in hearing the minutia of your fan's lives, then running a street team is not for you. The thing about superfans is that for some of them YOU are the most interesting thing that happens that day.

Authors who think of their street team members as family tend to have more tolerance for the ups and downs of different personality types. If you still want a team but can't stomach managing it, then hire someone who is good at that. Someone with a bubbly and/or caring personality. Alternatively, some authors have managed to get one or more of the team members to be the coordinators and manage most things. Those member-coordinators are usually compensated with extra attention and gifts for their work

If the author's expectation is professionalism and marketing know how, they will be disappointed. Instead, it is wise to hire a marketing person or team to do the types of things you want your street team to undertake.

Having worked with volunteers at nonprofits for nearly 30 years, I can say that volunteers come to the work with both the passion of helping someone they believe in, but also the commitment (or lack thereof) of a person who is not being paid and has a life beyond being on the street team. In other words, just because you need to have a big marketing push on your book Valentine's week; it doesn't mean your street team members are willing toggle up their planned vacations, night on the town, children's classroom needs that week, or any other thing related to their family or personal lives. These types of "other things" crop up ALL the time.

For me, I think street teams can make the difference in many areas for an author's career. However, they are not THE answer to getting ahead. I have a street team primarily because I truly enjoy getting to know my fans. Knowing they are there and supporting me is sometimes exactly what I need to keep writing in the tough times of life or the hard times in the middle of a book.

I am grateful for anything they do for me because I know they do it primarily out of love. There are times I am disappointed when certain tasks don't get done. However, most of the time, I know it's because I didn't ask far enough in advance or I failed to outline the task very well. Managing my writing time, my marketing time, business time, AND the street team can sometimes seem overwhelming. Learning to forgive myself for being human and not always keeping up with them needs to be equal to me forgiving them when they don't meet my expectations.

Can a street team help you? Only you can judge if it is something worthwhile investing your time, energy, and money into.

# YOUR MARKETING PLAN

Calendaring PR and Marketing All Year
Launch Checklist
Backlist Rejuvenation

*Chapter Twenty-Three*

# CALENDARING PR AND MARKETING ALL YEAR

Anyone responsible for marketing and PR runs into the problem of how to keep it all coordinated and moving smoothly. Most professionals do this with what is called an "editorial calendar." An editorial calendar sources and tracks all of the pieces of content you need to have ready and when it will be used during the year.

If you are a spreadsheet person, or a project manager, this is probably second nature to you. However, if you are primarily a creative—go with the flow—personality you may cringe at having to use a spreadsheet. You may even cringe at the thought of "planning." For those who love spreadsheets, you are very fortunate, there are already plenty of free templates available on the web. Here is one link with several free downloads you may find useful. Smartsheets https://www.smartsheet.com/9-free-marketing-calendar-templates-excel

This chapter is going to address the needs of those authors who are not natural spreadsheet developers and perhaps even have an allergic reaction to writing too many things down. (I am raising my hand here too).

Most authors tell me they are writers not marketers, and they enter into the entire marketing enterprise like they might enter into the job of shoveling out manure in a horse barn or pig sty. That attitude makes it even harder to set aside time to plan a schedule when you don't want to do it in the first place. My way of dealing with this is to try to find a balance between being forced to have an annual PR and marketing plan and putting it into a a framework that isn't overly time consuming or feels like turning in a doctoral dissertation on marketing.

**One thing is certain: if you don't do some planning and calendaring, the content doesn't get done and the marketing never happens**. This tends to be the default for a lot of authors. They say: "I'll get to that when I have a little more time." But the time never happens.

Whether you decide to approach your annual marketing calendar with a spreadsheet, by writing several lists and tacking them to a bulletin board, or by putting it into a Word document, it doesn't matter, **as long as you have committed to get it done**.

To be effective, the reality is you will need to put out some kind of PR or marketing content nearly every day of the year. In order to make this a reality it means planning ahead by weeks or months,. If you do that, you can take advantage of scheduling tools and do it in chunks instead of coming up with the content each day. I do my posts and blogs in one day for an entire month of content. Sometimes, I create and preschedule two months at once when I know something is coming up that will take my attention (e.g., a major holiday where I'll be with family, a time of year where I want to be outside more instead of at my computer, a planned medical event where I know I'll be out of commission for a while). Doing it in advance and scheduling means while I'm busy doing other things, my posts will still be going out every day without me having to create them during that time.

## IDENTIFY THE TYPES OF MARKETING YOU WILL DO

The first step is to make a list of the types of marketing you are willing to do in the next year. Then associate content with that marketing type. Finally, set dates or how many a times a week or month you will engage in that marketing. The primary types of marketing we've discussed in this book are:

**Contacting and Partnering with Influencers** –This is the network of people who have influence over opinions of books, may do reviews or know where to get reviews, have the ability to increase discovery and buzz. These may be celebrities, bloggers, or even author authors who already have a very successful career.

Marketing to influencers can be very effective IF you can get their attention. Sometimes influencers only pay attention to those who already have some good success, because it makes influencers are judged by who they hang with. You may want to only schedule one day a month to be spending time trying to find and partner with influencers.

**Email**—Email campaigns are a type of marketing that is cultivating your core supporters and providing them information both for themselves and to share. I would suggest you want to plan a minimum of two emails a month, and in times where you are doing book launches there may be three or four contacts in a month.

**Social Media**—Identify which platforms you are going to target in the coming year. If your growth is already pretty good on Twitter, you might target more content toward Facebook or Instagram. If you view video as being a critical target for you, then planning and finding appropriate video will be a major time undertaking. For those platforms that are heavily targeted, let the content be designed specifically for them. You can then determine what of that specific content can also be pushed to other platforms with ease.

Another possibility is to do a round-robin type of marketing on social media. One day is Facebook, the next day is Twitter, the third day is Instagram, etc. However, given that tools allow you to target all platforms with one post, I would suggest using a plan of all platforms with the occasional judicial exclusion of a particular platform when the post or visual doesn't seem to be the best use of that platforms growth.

**Blogging and Guest Blogging**—If you have a blog how can your topics compliment other marketing you are doing? For example, when I began using book quotes and images, I tied it to longer form blogging on that quote. What other ways can you combine simpler content marketing (e.g., an image, a video, a link to a puzzle) with longer form marketing.

If you don't have a blog yourself, consider seeking out guest blog opportunities to keep your name on the Internet and being exposed to different audiences than you have already cultivated.

**Paid Distribution**—how much do you want to budget for paid ads, distribution of your marketing to paid newsletter customers (e.g., BookBub, ENT, Kindle Nation, etc.) Another paid distribution plan would be if you decide to outsource asset development. Some authors are comfortable with creating their own images, while others feel very challenged by that. If you are in the latter category you will want to spend some time identifying quality freelancers at budget costs you can afford.

Sometimes your cover designer will offer to do marketing images for a very reasonable price—particular when they involve use of your cover in some way. Otherwise spend time determining who the media assets will be created our sourced for your posts.

## BEGIN PLANNING CONTENT BASED ON THEMES

The easiest way to begin planning your content is to choose themes that you will follow throughout the year. One way is to do something on a weekly basis that will be consistent throughout the year. This would be like assigning a name and theme to each day of the week, as I discussed earlier in the book. This gives a framework for each daily post. Knowing what your daily themes are also lends itself to some basic organization. You can set up folders for collecting the images, videos, or other assets to fill those daily themes. In that way, while you are watching other posts or noticing things you like on the web, you can drop the information into one of those folders. If you use stock photos (remember Pixabay has free creative commons images), you can spend one day a month searching for enough images to fill up your folders for the entire month.

A second approach is to find three core themes you want to focus on for the entire year, and about nine supplemental themes. Combined that makes a nice tidy 12 months of themes. Your core themes are the kinds of things that might be found on your homepage or even in the title attribute of your home page (e.g., About, Products/Books, and

Building Buzz for Coming Soon products). The supplemental themes might correspond to seasons, holidays, or focusing on one of the types of marketing identified above. Whatever you select, this helps to set up your marketing for each month. Be sure to mix and match so that you don't do the same thing two months in a row.

For each theme, brainstorm content you could create for that topic. Don't limit yourself at first: When you think of an idea, write it down quickly and move to the next. Then start creating or sourcing the content that you've identified.

**Choose a keyword for every piece of content you publish**

By choosing keywords and phrases that embody your brand and books, you will have them ready to go and can associate the best keywords for each type of content in advance instead of trying to determine the hashtag or keyword at the moment you are ready to send out the content. Making a simple list of keywords that correspond to your brand will help to speed this process

## NOW CALENDAR

You've assembled the pieces and the metadata to associate with them. The final step is to actually put it on your PR and Marketing calendar. You want to record at least one piece of content for each day. Include the following information for each piece of content.

- **The date** the piece of content will be published
- **The topic or headline** of the content piece
- **The channels** where your content will be published: This can include only your owned channels (such as your blog, Facebook Page, website, YouTube page, email newsletters, etc.), or you can expand your tracking to include paid channels as well.
- **Content formats:** Is it a blog post? A video? A podcast? An infographic? An original image? To get more mileage from the content you create, you might want to consider

repurposing it into other formats at some point. So it's handy to keep tabs on the types of assets you have on hand right from the start.

- **Visuals:** Don't overlook the appeal that visuals—images and videos—lend to your content, both in terms of social sharing potential and overall brand recognition. Tracking the visual elements you include in your content efforts – such as cover images, logos, illustrations, will make it easier to ensure that your work has a signature look and cohesive brand identity. Also marking when a particular visual was used will make sure you don't double up by accident.
- **Topic categories:** This helps make your calendars more searchable when you are looking to see for which target topics you already created a lot of content, as well as which targeted topics haven't been covered often enough.
- **Keywords** and other meta-data, such as meta-descriptions and SEO titles (if they differ from your headlines), which will help you keep your SEO efforts aligned with your content creation.
- **URLs:** This info can be archived as an easy way to keep your online content audits updated, or to link to older pieces of content in the new content you create. The ability to link both backward and forward helps to keep content relevant from year to year and to add to your SEO efforts.
- **Calls to action:** This helps you ensure that every piece of content you create is aligning with your company's marketing goals.

How you to decide to calendar all of this is up to you. This is where a spreadsheet can be helpful. However, you may wish to also get a large deskpad calendar where each date has plenty of room to write, and simply write exactly what the content and related items will be for that date.

The end result for a single day might look something like this.

---

August 26 – Headline: What's Up With the Sweetwater Canyon Gang?
Content Types: Blog post, Facebook, Twitter, Instagram, LinkedIn
Image: Cabin in Mt. Hood with music overlay playing instrumental piece—*Aspirations*.
Category: Sweetwater Canyon
Keywords: contemporary romance, women's fiction, musician life
URL link: https://maggielynch.com/sweetwater-canyon-series/
Call to Action: Buy Boxset at a 25% discount from purchasing the books individually

---

Good Luck and Happy Calendaring!

## Chapter Twenty-Four
# LAUNCH CHECKLIST

The first thing to realize about a launch checklist is that 90% of what needs to be done for a book launch is actually done BEFORE the launch date. Many of the PR and marketing things we've already discussed are the same tactics you use when launching a book. The difference is that you are focused on the launch week and month in order to get your book off on the right foot.

However, do NOT obsess about this. I've seen many authors who put all of their time and money into launching their book only to see it fall down in rankings and sales within two weeks. This is the old publishing paradigm. Big traditional publishers do focus on the book launch because they need to move their marketing teams onto the next book. Consequently, once the book is out about a month, everyone leaves the book to do whatever it can do on its own—no more pushes, no more PR, no more thinking about that book. Start writing the next one and hope it gets a big launch too.

The reality of book marketing today is that you have to count on the long-tail. That means you need to focus beyond the initial book launch. In fact, many authors do what is known as a "soft launch". That is the book is up but very few people know about it. That is used to get reviews and sales—usually at a lower price—prior to the official book launch.

Furthermore, most ranking and sales algorithms (Amazon is the prime example) favor a book that is getting consistent, ongoing sales over a book that gets a bunch of sales in one day and then nothing the rest of the week. If you plan well, you will have a build up to the launch and a post launch campaign. Those two pieces will be more important than the actual launch date itself.

A book that runs a promo and gets 500 sales in one day, but then the next day gets 10 and the next day 5 will drop quickly in the rankings. Whereas a book that consistently gets 20-30 sales every day for 10 days will do much better and be given more exposure. This is because vendors would rather see consistent sales over a longer period of time rather than one time sales that quickly become nothing.

It's also worth noting that reviews and the price of your book do not affect the sales rank algorithms. However, sometimes pricing can get early sales and therefore more reviews. Reviews DO provide credibility for a book and will aid in getting more buyers over a longer period of time.

Particularly in the digital marketing arena, books remain available AND VISIBLE for years. You can take advantage of that. Some of the ideas I'll discuss below do, in fact, leverage backlist books in order to help your new book launch be more successful. In addition, the final chapter in this book talks about continuous backlist rejuvenation.

So, let's get started on that launch checklist. I'm going to mention all the things that might go into the "perfect" launch. I'll admit that I don't do all of these things myself, and chances are you won't either. The key is to pick those things that work with the marketing and PR plan you've already calendared for the year. These pieces of a launch (approximately 5 months of content) should be slipped into your ongoing marketing. In other words, don't give up on your ongoing marketing plan and focus ONLY on your launch book for five months out of the year. Instead, add additional pieces (or substitute focus on one book instead of 3 or 4 in a month.

## PRE-LAUNCH

**Set up a pre-order.** This is best done if the book is finished, edited, and ready to go. Do NOT set up a pre-order if you aren't sure you will make the deadline. I know it is difficult to hold off on launching a book when it's already done, but if you can—even just one month—and set up a pre-order period it will give you time to build your marketing campaign and yet have an actual buy site where people can go.

Pre-orders are particularly powerful if you are writing in series. You want to have the next book available to order the moment the reader finishes the previous book, loves it, and wants to be sure the next book comes as quickly as possible. Most vendors allow you to set up a pre-order 90 days in advance of the book launch.

**Set up an incentive to collect email addresses.** Though I hope you are doing this continuously, it is important to do this in advance of your book being available—particularly if this is your first book. As you don't have a book to give away, think of other incentives that may be valuable to your reader. Here are some quick ideas that relate specifically to your launch book:

1. Give away the first chapter with a promise to deliver a chapter every two weeks until launch. If you are doing this 90 days in advance, that will giveaway for the first six chapters. Be sure that sixth chapter ends in a way that the reader is dying to know what happens next. This primes them to buy the book when it becomes available.
2. Offer another author's book that is similar to yours. I don't mean that the plot and characters match up well. What I mean is that it is in the same genre, has the same tone (light, dark, humorous, issue-based, sweet, sexy, etc.) and so would attract the same audience. It helps if the book is from a successful and well-known author. This helps your reader to think of your upcoming book in the same quality category as the book you are giving away.

3. Offer a short story or prequel you've written specifically for the launch.

If this is a second or third, or later, book in the series then this is a great time to make your first in series free in exchange for an email address. Do a special push for this one month in advance so that when new readers finish that first book they will be primed to purchase the next book. This works particularly well if the launch book is available on pre-order.

**Set Up An Author Central page on Amazon** https://authorcentral.amazon.com If you already have an Author Central Page, be sure to update it with your new book.

Also, set up author pages on other vendors where you are distributing your book (B&N, Apple, Kobo, Google) or places that invite authors to set up a page for free. Some of those are:

BookBub https://www.bookbub.com/partners/author-profile
GoodReads https://www.goodreads.com/author/program
Library Thing https://www.librarything.com/
Shelfari – Note, Shelfari is now part of Goodreads
LibLib https://www.libib.com/
BookLikes https://booklikes.com

**Create a sales page for your book.** I always create my book sales page on my website the moment I have the cover from my designer. This page gets tagged as "Coming Soon" and also appears in a section on my website for books coming soon. By having a sales page, it provides a place to link when doing promotion prior to the launch. Of course, if your book is on pre-order anywhere, this same sales page will provide direct links to those vendor sites. Here is a sales page for a book I have coming out in 2018. https://maggielynch.com/book/vanished/

Note that it has all the same features as the sales page for any book that has already been released. The only thing it doesn't have is a buy button. When the book goes on pre-order or goes live, the button will be changed to a buy button at that time.

**Create a Pinterest Board for Your Book.** It should contain your book cover, ideas or images you used while writing the book with quotes or inspiration that relates to the book. As content is available from fans, bloggers, or review posts you now have a board where you can track and pin all that content.

**Change Social Media Cover Images** to include your book. If your cover image is static, as mine is, this is not something you need to do. However, many authors have a cover image that is changed regularly to feature their most recent release. At a minimum you might want to pin a post/tweet to the top of your social media page that features your new book.

**Change Your Bio** in various social media to include that you are the author of the new book. If you only have a few books, it is common for your bio to list them. However, once you go past five books or so, it is unlikely your bio will include each book title.

**Identify and Begin Using a Book Hashtag** associated with your launch book. It's best to have something that matches your book's title and is easy to remember. If your title is short, it is easy to create e.g., #thanksforlove. However, if your title is longer create a hashtag that uses the most important parts of the title. For example for this book instead of #secretsforeffectiveauthormarketing which is far too long, I use #authormarketingsecrets

**Recruit or Revive Launch Team Members**. If you have been building a launch team or street team, now is the time to let them know your new book is almost ready for launch. Consider start talking about your new book 60 days in advance to get the buzz going on your team, and then begin assigning promo tasks 30 days in advance.

If you don't have a launch team yet, now is the time to recruit them. A quick way is to put out the call to everyone in your network. Let them know the book is launching and you are looking for ARC readers who would be willing to post an honest review within the first two weeks of your book going live. Put up a sign up form for those who are interested in participating. This can be done via your email provider (recommended). Or you can do it via a Google Form or some other form builder that is easy to get up quickly.

**Create Media** that will be used for your social media posts. As I am writing my next book, I tend to keep an eye for images that relate to my story and save them for pre- and post-launch. I also have a file of links to videos, personality quizzes, genre-related memes, and other content around the web that might be candidates for posting. In that way, as the launch date nears, I have a lot of choices and I'm not scrambling for content.

Remember, you will be posting content about your book at least once a week in the run up to launch and for at least two months after launch. This means you will need 5 months (20 weeks) of material that can be linked to your launch book.

**Make Plans for Giveaways**. Something that creates buzz are giveaways that relate to your launch book. The most effective giveaways are other books in the series if you have them. However, you can use other items that might relate to the book, like the necklace I discussed in the driving traffic to your mailing list chapter.

In addition to determining what to giveaway, you need to line up participation in other giveaways with authors. This can come in many forms,

- Participate in a multi-author boxset in your genre, where one of your earlier books in the series is available. Best to do this one to two months before launch of the new book.
- List Swap with another author, as discussed in the previous chapter for driving traffic to your email list.
- Participate in a contest that features your book as the giveaway item. Again, it is best to do this with other authors in order to gain more traction from not only your own books but theirs as well.

**Send out a Press Release** about your book to local media. The press release should feature a book "one sheet"—the cover, the blurb, release date, and price. But to give it the best chance at actually being used in the local paper you need to localize the pitch so that the editor can see why their readers would be interested. For example, *if* the story takes place in your hometown, that is important to feature. If you are going to be doing any local promo (book signing, meet the author event, part of a panel of authors at the local library) be sure to include these in the press release as well. If the book was inspired by a local personality or hero, mention that. In other words, think about what you would like to read about a local author.

**Schedule and Write Book Pitch Copy** for blog posts, guest posts, podcasts, social media, in person engagements

**Plan for Facebook Live or Instagram Stories** during your launch week.

**Place your book image with a buy link in your email signature line**.

## ON LAUNCH DAY

- Remind your launch team to submit reviews of your book.
- Kick off all promotional tours during the first week—guest blogs, your own blog, podcasts, social media promo etc.
- Send out a special email sharing your excitement about the book launch. If you are doing a "soft launch" with a discount price prior to the official launch, send this email out then. Then send it again, once the price ahs gone up. Thank everyone for buying during the discount. Remind them to share their love the book to their network.

## POST LAUNCH

Continue to talk about the book for the next month or two. Share good reviews. Talk about things that have happened that make you happy, excited, thankful.

Take time to thank your Launch Team or any other fans who were part of making this happen. Make sure they understand it was THEIR enthusiasm that made all the difference.

Take at least a day to celebrate your accomplishment—whether that is a quiet toast at home, or a full celebratory dinner out, or a weekend getaway, make sure you schedule time to celebrate. It is hard work, and a lot of angst, to get a book written, published, and launched.

Even if your book doesn't do as well as you hoped during that first week, still celebrate your accomplishment! You need to recognize that you just did something 99% of people don't do—write and publish a book.

Let the dust settle for at least a month before doing any kind of post-launch analysis. It takes that long for you to get any significant data back from vendors, social media tracking, or google analytics. Trying to do any analysis before that will only drive you crazy as you watch the day-to-day gyrations of sales.

A month out will give you some perspective and provide a lot more data. Two months out is even better. Try to look at the data as an outsider and determine what you would tell a client who asked for what went right and wrong. Make a list of both the triumphs and challenges and attempt to determine why they happened. Then sit down with a revised marketing and launch plan for the next book.

No one does this exactly right the first time, and most people still continue to learn and make changes after EVERY launch. The market changes, your availability and time changes, and you need to adapt to that.

Try not to do any negative self-talk about how you procrastinated, didn't pay attention, got lazy, were too busy, forgot to schedule things, etc. The past is now gone. You can't go back and change it. All you can do is move forward. Decide what you will do differently next time and put into place steps to make that happen.

Now back to work!

## Chapter Twenty-Five
# BACKLIST REJUVENATION

One of the biggest mistakes authors make is putting all their energy, time, and money to the launch of their new books—forgetting that they have a treasure trove of old books that could be bringing in a steady income while they are writing the next book. I believe that AT LEAST equal attention needs to be given to the backlist as to the newest book. There are always more readers available who missed the book at launch and can discover you for the first time. You want to be sure that you have provided good opportunities for that to happen.

Here are some common things you can do to ensure your backlist is continuing to be relevant, generating good income, and working to support your next new book launch.

### CHANGE YOUR COVERS

Traditional publishers do this fairly frequently. Cover design trends change almost as much as art styles. For example, in one decade most the trend may be to feature the major character or a scene on the front cover—this is particularly true in romance, mystery, and children's books. However, in the next decade the trend is to feature a more abstract rendering of the theme. Think of Twilight and the large red apple vs a picture of a vampire.

It pays to keep an eye on what the most successful authors in your genre are doing with their covers. Those trends become reader expectations. If you want to be categorized, in reader's minds, as the same quality or type of story as those bestselling authors then your covers need to have that same look and feel. This doesn't mean they need to be exactly the same, but close enough that it is recognizable.

Another reason to change your covers is to reinforce your brand, or reinforce how a set of books are part of a series. Often when a writer puts her first book or two, she may not even know she's writing a series. The first book is conceived alone. Then two or three years later she realizes she has written a series, but the three books all have very different covers. That is a great time to go back and recover them with author and series branding, so it is instantly recognizable that these books go together.

## CREATE A SERIES WHERE YOU HAD ONLY STAND-ALONE TITLES

If you have not been consciously writing in series, consider how the books you do have can be marketed as a series. It doesn't have to be the same characters or locations. You may be able to market the series based on a theme (e.g., the coming-of-age series for YA books). Writers can often increase backlist sales by simply putting similar themed books together as a series and then creating a series look and feel with covers.

I know an author recently who had seven stand alone romance novels. She could find nothing that tied them together except they were all about falling in love and all took place in a particular state, Oregon. She is now rebranding those books as the Oregon Lovers series. This also opened up ideas for her because she was thinking of her next book being in her home state of Michigan. That could be the Michigan Lovers series. By redoing covers in a similar style, she doesn't have to change her stories, only her branding.

## REVIEW AND UPDATE YOUR METADATA

Just as with covers, what works for SEO changes. It always pays to go regularly review your book blurbs, how titles and subtitles are presented, the categories you chose for your book.

You can also take the time to add additional metadata that perhaps you didn't have when the book launched. For example, reviews that were received from booksellers, newspapers, bloggers, that aren't included in the vendor reviews. These can be added in the "editorial reviews" section of the page.

You might also consider adding an "Interview with the author." This is a great technique for getting more keywords and themes added to metadata without doing bad things like putting a string of words at the bottom of the page or attempting to fit in keywords in titles and subtitles when they don't really belong there.

Remember, everything on the page below the blurb is still scanned and indexed as metadata. An interview, written in a Q&A format gives an opportunity to include important information.

## LOOK AT STRATEGIC PRICE PROMOTIONS

Many authors use rotating price discounting to increase book rankings. I know one author who has at least one novella associated with each of her series. She continuously rotates those novellas through 99 cent price promotions each month. With 6 novellas, that gives her plenty of opportunities to provie something affordable to new readers while still tying it into an ongoing series at regular prices.

Timing a price promotion a month in advance of a new book launch is also a great tactic for getting new eyes on a book and getting readers into a series. You might consider price promotions related to special seasons or holidays as well (e.g., Valentine's Day, Christmas, Your birthday).

When scheduling price promotions also consider that it is NOT only for first in series books. That can get tired and seen too often with diminishing results. If you have a longer series, consider discounting the third book instead of the first. You get two interesting results from doing that.

- The reader suddenly realizes there is at least three books in this series. Many avid readers won't start reading until the series is completed or at least well along. They don't want to become invested in the characters or world you've built only to have the series dropped or have to wait for a year or more for the next book.
- When the first book in series is used constantly as a leader, it becomes old or too saturated as a realistic offering. Using other books seem more fresh and new to potential new readers.

## BUNDLE, BUNDLE, BUNDLE

The beauty of having a good backlist is the multitude of ways you can feature them. Whenever your book is in a bundle it is an entirely new product. The first way to think of bundling is within your series. Once you have three books, but them together as a bundle. This is a new product and it can be slightly discounted from the cost to purchase each book separately.

Some authors fear that bundling will take away sales from their individual books and result in a lower income. My experience has been quite the opposite. There are certain types of readers who will ONLY buy when they believe they are getting a deal. Bundling offers that deal without having to give anything away for free or rotating discounts. AND you get the benefit discussed above where potential readers see it as a complete set and that gives them more comfort in starting to read the series now that it is "finished."

When you do finish a series, you have options for multiple bundles depending on how many books you have. For example, an author with a 9 book mystery series might do four bundles—three with three books, and then a big bundle that contains all the books.

Bundling isn't only for your own books. There are many opportunities to participate in bundles with other authors where you can all capitalize on bringing in fans from each others networks. Usually, these bundles are highly discounted (e.g., 12 books for $9.99 instead of the usual $60 or so). Again, don't worry about whether you are stealing income from the single sale of the book. Think of it as building new fans, growing your influencer network with other authors, and learning what additional types of marketing may be effective to move your books toward higher discoverability.

## ROTATE SOCIAL MEDIA POSTS

A tool I use is in Readerlinks https://readerlinks.com/ Readerlinks is a multi-faceted resource for lots of things in your writer life—from tracking ARCs to tracking your sales and ads, as well as specific book campaigns. One of my favorite parts of Readerinks is the Random Twitter Scheduler for every book in my backlist. I load one to three different tweets for each book with a cover. The Twitter tool allows to select how often I want it to tweet one of these for me. I set it for every 6 hours. It begins at the top of the list and randomly selects one of the three tweets related to that book. Six hours later it selects one of the tweets related to the next book, and so on until it gets through all my books. Then it starts at the top again.

It's wonderful because I set it and forget it. Whenever I have a new book out, I add it into the list and then quickly review all the tweets I had and see if any need tweaking or a different image. Then I forget it again.

You can use the same concept in other social media. Just add this to your schedule in Buffer or whatever tool you use to hit the majority of your accounts. In many ways, this is what my Title Taste Thursday does. It allows me to once a week feature a backlist book—particularly when I don't have a launch coming up or just finishing.

## SUMMARY

The key to backlist rejuvenation is remembering you have a backlist. I know that sounds obvious, but authors tend to get caught up in the next book and the next and suddenly nine months has gone by and they haven't done anything to promote their backlist.

Even with a handful of books, your backlist needs to be working hard for you. With regular marketing it can bring in a tidy sum every month. I'm sure there are many more creative ideas than I've placed here, but this will get you started.

# AFTERWORD

There is a lot to learn and it can feel overwhelming. Whether you are at the beginning of your publishing career, or twenty books in, there is always more to learn. The key is to take it one step at a time and don't try to do everything at once. It also helps to network with other authors and to help each other as much as possible.

One of the first ways to find a network is to join a writer's organization. One I highly recommend is ALLi (The Alliance of Independent Authors). They are a nonprofit dedicated to advocating for indie authors around the world. They offer numerous free workshops, run online and local conferences, blog regularly, and have members who share deep knowledge. It is well worth the annual membership price. Find them here: https://www.allianceindependentauthors.org/ to join

There are also numerous Facebook private groups available. I suggest doing searches based on your criteria and determine which ones are a good fit for you.

## HELPFUL BLOGS AND PODCASTS

**My DIY Publishing Blog**. In addition to the books I write to help indie authors become successful, I also have a regular DIY Publishing

Blog. https://maggielynch.com/category/diy-publishing/ You can sign up to have it delivered to your email inbox or simply visit it on a regular basis. I talk about a variety of topics from staying motivated to business challenges and, of course, technology.

**Ask ALLi Self-Publishing Advice Podcast** is a monthly podcast hosted by ALLi members Debbie Young and David Penny. Each month they take a question sent to the podcast and answer it in depth. Depending on the question, they have a roster of guest members and those outside of ALLi who may be selected to be on the podcast.

**Mark Dawson's Self-Publishing Formula Podcast** https://selfpublishingformula.com/category/podcast/ This is a weekly podcast/webcast that features a variety of topics and knowledgeable authors. Mark also provides several free introductory instructional videos.

**The Creative Penn**, run by multi-genre, successful author Joanna Penn (J.F. Penn). She also does a regular podcast and provides a lot of free resources. https://www.thecreativepenn.com/

There are hundreds of others available as well, but these are three that are very well regarded and have a diversity of topics from beginning to advanced that I believe most authors will find useful.

## SIGN UP TO BE ON MY AUTHOR MAILING LIST

My author mailing list is the venue I use for sharing business and technology news I believe authors would be interested. This includes things I'm trying out myself or changes in the publishing landscape. Of course, it also includes any new releases I have in my Career Author Secrets series and events I'm attending where we could possibly meet in person.

Sign up here and get my first Career Author Secrets book, *Secrets Every Author Should Know* for free: https://app.convertkit.com/landing_pages/93200

Already have the book but still want to be on the list? Send me an email at maggie@maggielynch.com and I'll make sure you are added.

## VIDEO COURSES CAN PROVIDE ANOTHER WAY TO LEARN

For those who would value more hand-holding, instructional videos, and time to ask me questions about your specific situation, I am offering a selection of video courses through **AWW On The Go**. http://awwonthego.com/

Along with the courses, you will be admitted to a private Facebook group I run for helping indie authors manage the business side of their careers.

If you are looking for an in-depth, highly advanced course on running paid ads in a variety of venues, I highly recommend Mark Dawson's Ad for Author's Course. https://selfpublishingformula.com/courses/ I took this course and it made a huge difference in my life. He opens it about three times per year.

## OTHER BOOKS IN THE CAREER AUTHOR SECRETS SERIES

This is the third book in the Career Author Secrets Series. If you are just starting off in your publishing career, you may wish to go back and get the first two. Each book focuses on a specific aspect of publishing. Learn more on my website. https://maggielynch.com/career-author-secrets-series/

My fourth book on *Advanced Marketing Through Paid Ads* is scheduled to be out in late summer. Get on my mailing list or my blog to keep abreast of that release.

# ABOUT THE AUTHOR

Maggie Lynch is the author of 20+ published books, as well as numerous short stories and non-fiction articles. Her fiction tells stories of men and women making heroic choices one messy moment at a time. Her nonfiction focuses on helping indie authors be successful in their careers. Maggie is also the founder of Windtree Press, an independent publishing cooperative with over 200 titles among 20 authors.

Maggie and her musician husband live in the beautiful Pacific Northwest, and are the slaves of two demanding cats. In 2013, after careers in counseling, the software industry, academia, and worldwide educational consulting, Maggie chose to devote her time to her career as a full time author. Her fiction spans romance, suspense, fantasy and science fiction titles. Her non-fiction focuses on guiding authors to success in planning, distributing, and marketing their completed work.

https://maggielynch.com
maggie@maggielynch.com

facebook.com/maggiewrites

twitter.com/maggieauthor

instagram.com/mcvaylynch

bookbub.com/authors/maggie-mcvay-lynch

www.ingramcontent.com/pod-product-compliance
Lightning Source LLC
Chambersburg PA
CBHW051524020426
42333CB00016B/1765